Echoes of Mercy — Whispers of Love

Diaries of John Hemphill Simpson

Transcribed by Mary Law McCormick

1861, 1862, 1863 and 1865
War Between the States

Edited by: J. Michael Miller

Copyright © 2001 by
Associate Reformed Presbyterian Foundation, Inc.
One Cleveland Street
Greenville, SC 29601
(803) 232-8297

ISBN 0-914927-32-9

Printed in the United States of America

TABLE OF CONTENTS

DEDICATED TO

Nancy Jane McConnell

April 5, 1951 - July 18, 1985

whose faithful service exceeded her
shortened lifespan.

FOREWORD

The Simpson Family

The ancestry of John Hemphill Simpson can be traced to County Antrim, Ireland, where John Simpson was born on March 9, 1770. He left the Emerald Isle with brothers William and Walter, and came to Charleston, South Carolina in 1790. The Simpson family was established in the South Carolina by three brothers, John, William, and Walter. John Simpson was a mechanic by trade, and was prosperous enough to have married twice before marrying Sarah (Sallie) Stone, his third and final wife.

To this union was born six children, one whom was John Simpson, Jr., who was born February 9, 1803. As John Jr. came of age, he remained in Chester County, and took as his wife Sarah Wylie. Sarah bore John nine children, the sixth of which was John Hemphill Simpson. He was born on August 3, 1834 in Fishing Creek Community Chester, South Carolina.

John Hemphill Simpson began his higher education at the age of seventeen, when he entered Erskine College in Due West, South Carolina. In five years of intensive study, John never missed a recitation or rollcall. Following graduation in 1856, John continued the study of theology, which proved to be the main course of his life. After three years of work in the Erskine Seminary, he was licensed by the First Presbytery on September 6, 1859. The twenty-four year old fledgling minister spent the next eighteen months of his life filling vacancies in Virginia and what was later to become West Virginia, spreading the word of God to many hard to reach congregations locked away in the Blue Ridge mountains.

In 1861, the clouds of war were apparent even in the foothills of Western Virginia. John was against the death and destruction of war, writing in his diary on April 24th, "God save us from such evil," and on June 1, 1861, he wrote, "May God stay the War that is about to commence! We are in his hand." However, when war did come, he sided with his family, friends, and home state of South Carolina. John remained in constant contact with his friends and family by letter until he could stand it no longer, and left Virginia to serve his home state of South Carolina and the new Confederate States of America.

ACKNOWLEDGEMENTS

At different times our friends and relatives have urged us to have our Grandfather's diaries published. After all, he did live through that uncivil war and cared for the sick and dying for almost four long years.

One such time I remember was when we were having Thanksgiving dinner with our cousin Dr. Harvey McConnell and his wife, Nita, in Lancaster, South Carolina. Harvey decided to invite Dr. Lesesne, then president of Erskine College, to drop by his house to discuss the possibility of publishing the Simpson diaries.

Much time has passed between those initial plans and the fruition of this story that Grandfather has recorded here for us.

This story connects me with my Grandfather Simpson who died in 1914, seven years before I was born.

The following people have, over the years, shown interest in the Simpson diaries. Their encouragement and support have been invaluable.

Dr. Harvey McConnell, Moffatt Millen Ramsey, Sarah Elizabeth McCormick, Rev. Zeb Williams, retired pastor from Lexington, Va., Debbie A. Miller, wife of editor J. Michael Miller, Mrs. Ann Marion, Chester, SC, Mrs. Josephine Harper, State/Wisconsin Historical Society, Dr. J.M. Lesesne, former president of Erskine College, Dr. Bruce Ezell, former president, Erskine College, Dr. Lowry Ware, historian from DueWest, SC, Dr. Wm. Kuykendall, editor ARP Sunday School Quarterly, Dr. Robert J. Stamps, former pastor, Clarendon United Methodist Church, Board of Directors, Associate Reformed Presbyterian Foundation, Inc.

- Mary Law McCormick

Rev. John Hemphill Simpson

Chapter 1

"SPREADING THE WORD OF THE LORD"

The year 1861 promised to be a momentous one for John Hemphill Simpson. After graduating from Erskine College in 1856, he studied theology and became a licensed minister of The Associate Reformed Presbyterian Church on September 6, 1859. He was then appointed by the Synod of the Associate Reformed Presbyterian Church of the South to labor "in the bounds of the Virginia Presbytery.[1]" On November 4, 1860, Simpson left his home state to pursue a life in the service of God and the three delights of his life, "theology, Hebrew, and the violin." Writing in 1910, Simpson recalled that the three "have been my delight and constant companions on the plains and on the mountains, on the land and on the sea.[2]"

John Simpson began his labor filling vacancies in the churches located in the rolling hills and valleys around Lexington, Virginia. The three primary churches under his care were New Lebanon along Second Creek in Monroe County, Broad Creek in Rockbridge County, and Bedford. He came under the tutelage of the Reverend McElwee, a minister of the Presbyterian Church in Lexington. The primary mission assigned to Simpson was to visit the small communities surrounding Lexington and preach to them the word of the Lord.

The duties assigned to John Simpson were arduous in the extreme. He traveled through the mountain communities in the dead of winter, by train, stagecoach, horseback, or even on foot to reach the far flung mountain communities. He then recovered himself to preach at least one and sometimes two sermons to the people of small towns with names such as Broad Creek, Ebenezer and Bedford. However, Simpson would rest himself at times with comfortable games of checkers or by playing his violin and guitar.

Despite the demands of his work, Simpson's thoughts returned again and again to his family and friends at home in South

1

Carolina. The news of the impending clash between the Northern and Southern sections of the United States also weighed on his mind. He deplored the thought of civil war, praying instead for a peaceful solution to the problems of the country. As the days of 1860 passed, there seemed less and less chance for a peaceful solution.

On December 20, 1860, South Carolina seceded from the Union, followed into the month of January by six other southern states.

Tuesday, January 1, 1861
Second Creek, Va.[3]   *White Sulphur and Goshen, Va.*

Another year has commenced. O may life be preserved and may I spend my life in promoting God's glory. I read Bible and packed up my valise for Lexington; played violin and guitar. The Stage (Coach) failed to come and I had to carry my valise on horse to White Sulphur. Mr. Joe Dickson and Mr. Vance went with me and carried guitar and car' sack for me. Snow on the ground. Very cold, ice formed on whiskers. Rode till 10.

Wednesday, January 2, 1861

In the midst of deserved wrath, I am preserved. God's mercy never fails. I wish for more grace to serve him. Left Springs at 5 o'clock A.M. Very cold but I am thankful for good clothing; reached depot[4] at 3, took Cars for Goshen[5], arrived at 5 in safety. Talked until 9, retired. Thankful for life and health.

Thursday, January 3, 1861

Slept soundly last night, rose in good health – read a Psalm- took a walk. Whiled away a day at Goshen. I did not spend the day as I should, played a few games of checkers, played guitar a little. Took Stage at 4 P.M., reached Lexington at 11. Went out to Rev. McElwee. He was not at home. Mrs. McElwee was somewhat surprised at me.

Friday, January 4, 1861
                                        Lexington, Virginia

Slept late this morning, somewhat fatigued by my trip over the mountains. Held worship. Read Bible, eat breakfast although it was the fast day appointed of the President, I had eaten no supper. But I eat no dinner. Went to a Union prayer meeting in Presb.

Rev. McElwee House, Lexington, Virginia.

Church. Mr. McElwee returned from his churches. I was introduced to Misses Campbell and Miss More.

Saturday, January 5, 1861

Just two months today since I left my home, the dearest spot on earth to me. Played guitar for the ladies and then set out for Broad Creek to make appointment for preaching. Went to Mr. James Miller's, there met with some young men making up a singing school for Root; they told the people of preaching. Studied sermon.

Sunday, January 6, 1861

The Holy Sabbath has dawned again. Oh, that I could spend its sacred hours in a proper manner. I had to spend the morning in preparing for the pulpit. Went to church, found a respectable audience. Preached from 2 Cor. 5: 10. Returned to Mr. Miller's, Misses Leech and Lackey also.

Monday, January 7, 1861   *Lexington, Virginia*

Rained this morning, unpleasant for traveling. Yet Mr. John Lackey and I set out for Lexington; the rain ceased and we did not get wet. I was anxious to hear from S.C. Talked about the deplorable state of our land. We are threatened with Civil War, may God interpose. I wrote letter to Moffatt Grier; commenced one to Joe Lowry.

Tuesday, January 8, 1861

Rose late with a slight cold. I am thankful it is no worse. My general health is good. I have had a long string of mercies, I pray that it may continue unbroken. I conducted worship, read Bible, finished letter to Joe Lowry, played violin and guitar and sung some church music, retired.

Wednesday, January 9, 1861[6]

Time is ever moving and my days are passing away; may I be prepared to render up my account before God. Read Bible, conversed with Mr. McElwee and family on political items of the day. Great excitement. May God save us from ruin.

Thursday, January 10, 1861[7]   Lexington, Virginia

My life and health are still continued to me. I should be very grateful to a kind Providence, but alas! I am a sinful and rebellious creature. Oh for more grace and wisdom. Read Bible. Studied sermon but with little success. Rode out to Col. McCamey's, carried my blackboard on horse. Spent night with him.

Friday, January 11, 1861[8]

Rose early, conducted worship for Colonel McCamey and set out for Kerr's Creek to begin a Singing School at an old Presbyterian Church above Bethel. The weather was quite cold but few came out. I anticipate a good singing. Went to Mr. And. Lackey's. Spent night, played violin and sang songs.

Saturday, January 12, 1861

The light of day is pleasant after a night's rest and sweet repose. I held worship for Mr. Lackey and then went with his daughter to the Singing School. Had a good school, some very good looking ladies. Returned home and studied sermon until 10 o'clock.

Sunday, January 13, 1861

I love the Sabbath dawn, it brings rest and peace to man, and fore-tells a heavenly rest, a land where Sabbaths have no end. I rose this morning in good health, held worship and set out on horse for Broad Creek; preached with some ease and earnestness from Mat. 6.33. Spent night with Mr. Nair.

Monday, January 14, 1861

God is the great ruler of all things. The eyes of all look to him for food &c. He is good to me and what a poor return I make for his goodness. I rose early, held worship. The morning was very cold; snow and sleet fell last night. I returned home at 12. Wrote letter to Josiah Moffatt. Played violin.

Tuesday, January 15, 1861

I am daily and hourly receiving blessings from God my Creator and gracious benefactor. I should spend my time in advancing his glory but I am an ungrateful Creature. Read Bible but my heart is too much set on earthly things. Wrote letter to Mr. Baird; played violin with Mr. McClure.

Wednesday, January 16, 1861   Lexington, Virginia

Half the month is gone, how fast it is passing away. Read the Scrip-tures, conducted worship. Began to read 'The Life and Epistles of Paul'. Read 30 pages before dinner, then read *Telescope* and political papers. Saw some signs of peace. Went to town, bought a comfort and this diary, price 50 and 65 cents. Played guitar and violin with McClure.

Thursday, January 17, 1861   — clear and warm.

I am a dependent being, I owe everything to God. Like Paul, by grace I am what I am. Rose in good health, conducted worship. Read Bible, went to town, had a front tooth filled by Davidson. Studied sermon, was introduced to Miss Chapin. She played the piano, I the guitar; then I went to Colonel Brown's on way to sing-ing school. Was introduced to Miss L. Harper.

Friday, January 18, 1861

God's mercies are new every day. He loads me with his benefits. Rose early this morning, held worship for Mr. Brown. Rain prevented my going to singing. Dined with Mr. B., then went up to Calvin Harper's with his sister. Spent night with them; studied sermon.

Saturday, January 19, 1861[9]

Fair weather this morning and I am blessed with health as usual. Held worship, went to singing school at Teaford's school house, had a large school today. Very tired at night. Became acquainted with many ladies. Returned to Lexington and studied sermon until 11.

Sabbath, January 20, 1861

It is a bad habit to call the holy Sabbath 'Sunday'. I am proud of the Sabbath, it is a precious day to Christians. Rose early this morning and set out for Broad Creek; found an excellent congregation. Preached with some ease from Jno. 3.19. Went to Thos. Miller's. Spent night, retired at 9.

Monday, January 21, 1861

Rose very late this morning but I was tired lying in bed, waiting for water. Eat breakfast and set out for Lexington; reached there at 1 o'clock. Received letters from Brother Isaiah and D. L. Lockridge, dined. Had 3 more teeth filled by Davidson; $8 for 4 teeth. Talked and played guitar.

Tuesday, January 22, 1861

How excellent is thy loving kindness O God! Daily art thou loading me with thy benefits. Read Bible, commenced letter to Livie Grier. Went to P.O. Received letter from Flora Burns. Played guitar and violin. Attended Anniversary of Graham Society — not well pleased. Talked, retired at 11 1/2 o'clock.

Wednesday, January 23, 1861

Time is flying rapidly and my race will soon be ended and all will be well, trouble will have an end. Rose, blessed with health. Read

Bible, finished letter to Livie Grier. Commenced sermon on Rom. 8:28. Read papers. Played violin with Mrs. McElwee and Miss Polly More on piano. Sung some. Retired at 11.

Thursday, January 24, 1861

Oh that I could improve my time and live to the glory of God who is daily loading me with his benefits. Rose in good health this morning; read Bible, wrote sermon with some success. Played violin and guitar. Sung with Mrs. McElwee. Studied sermon for Sabbath.

Friday, January 25, 1861

Rose very early to go to singing school; eat a cold breakfast which caused me to have a headache. I deserve no good. Had a small class at the old church. Went to Mr. Teaford's. Headache ceased and I felt thankful. All the ladies went to Calvin Harper's. I studied until 11 o'clock. Received [letter] today from Sister Sarah.

Saturday, January 26, 1861[10]

My health is restored but I do not deserve such a blessing. Rose at 7 o'clock, held worship. Snow fell heavily all day. Yet many came out to Singing at School house; had a good class. Came home at dusk. Held worship. Talked about our country. Studied sermon. Read Bible and retired.

Sunday, January 27, 1861

Sabbath is the day of rest to man and beast. To man it was given as a day of spiritual improvement but I am too often thinking of worldly things. Rode to Broad Creek, preached from John 14:27 with very little animation. Oh, for more zeal. Returned home somewhat weary but blessed with health.

Monday, January 28, 1861

Rose in good health. Oh praise the Lord for He is good, his mercy endureth forever. Read Bible. Went to town, received letter from my dear father. Had an upper jaw tooth filled by Davidson. Wrote to father. Talked with the family. Played Cattle [?] door; played violin, guitar and sung.

Tuesday, January 29, 1861

I am growing older and should be growing in wisdom and understanding. Rose this morning in my usual good health, thanks to God. Went to town, received *Chester Standard*, glad to see it. Wrote sermon with but little success. Talked with Mr. Fuller on politics, played violin, guitar, wrote some more.

Wednesday, January 30, 1861

I am a fortunate individual, not in getting rich in gold and silver. I have good health, kind friends and above a kind heavenly Father. Had another upper tooth filled by Davidson. Read the *N. Y. Observer*, wrote sermon, played guitar, piano and violin. Talked, etc.

Thursday, January 31, 1861

Time is on the wing. Another month closes today; my life is drifting by. How diligent should [I] be! My health by the mercy of God is still preserved. O praise the Lord for he is good. Read Bible, studied sermon. Fixed Mrs. McElwee's lamp, played violin, guitar and piano, sung with Mr. and Mrs. McElwee.

Friday, February 1, 1861[11]

Rose early this morning in good health. Engaged in private devotion and set out for Kerr's Singing School. Unpleasant day but few attended. Spent the night with Mr. Dixon. Introduced to Ecker, a singing master, sung with him; held worship, retired at 11 in good health.

Saturday, February 2, 1861

It is my privilege to praise God every morning and declare his faithfulness every night. Held worship. Rained all last night and until 12 o'clock today. Did not go to Singing School. Set out for home, very muddy. Read *N.Y. Observer*. Studied sermon until 12 o'clock at night. Oh, for wisdom!

Sunday, February 3, 1861

How often is the Sabbath profaned by idleness, improper, unholy thoughts. May divine grace enable me to spend the day in the fear of God. Set out for Broad Creek. Had a good audience. Preached lecture on John 15:1-6. Oh for more zeal and earnestness in preaching. Went to Mr. Anderson, spent night.

Monday, February 4, 1861[12]

A day is very short, but long is eternity. To be happy or miserable forever! What a momentous reality. Let me die the death of the righteous and let my last end be like His. Held worship, set out for Lexington; called at Mrs. Lackey's, heard some music, played some. Home at 1 o'clock. Went to town, played piano etc.

Tuesday, February 5, 1861

I am a weak, frail creature, subject to decay and death. But by the mercy of God my life is still lengthened out. Read Bible this morning. Had more teeth filled in evening; played piano, violin &c. Served some for Mrs. McElwee, taught M. L. McElwee vocal music; held worship, bed at 11.

Wednesday, February 6, 1861

Rec'd letters from Maym & Sister Mag Moffatt. May I never forget my obligations to God. He gives me my life, food and raiment. Oh that I could praise Him aright. Read Greek Testament, felt dull from chloroform in my tooth, had three more filled. I am subject to decay. Called to see Misses Davidson. They called on Mrs. McElwee, also Dr. Freeman and his daughter and 2 law students, 2 cadets. We had a pleasant time and good music.

Thursday, February 7, 1861[13]

I am a weak creature prone to evil as the sparks fly upward. Yet God is good to the unthankful and the evil. Rose late this morning. Read Bible, studied sermon. Mr. McElwee set out for Bedford. Played violin, talked with Miss McElwee and Miss Polly More. Retired in good health at 10. Rec'd letter from Mr. Baird.

Friday, February 8, 1861

Rose early to go to my Singing School. Very pleasant morning. Received a letter from Moffatt Grier and the Yorkville, S.C. paper.

Had a very good school. Went to Mr. Miller's; his wife was lingering with consumption. How thankful I should be for health of body and mind. Retired at 10.

Saturday, February 9, 1861[14]

Rose early. Had a good night's rest. Permitted to behold the light of another day. This is my father's birthday. He is growing old. Had worship and went to the singing school — a very fine day, a good school. Came to Colonel McCamey's; spent the night. Studied sermon until 12.

Sunday, February 10, 1861

I love the Sabbath but never spend it as I should. Held worship, prepared to preach the gospel. Went to Ebenezer; preached for Mr. McElwee from 2 Cor. 5:10. Oh, for more zeal and earnestness in delivery. Dined at Col. McCamey's. Returned home fatigued; talked; held worship, etc.

Monday, February 11, 1861

My days are running out. Preparation for death should be constantly before my mind. I long for a blessed immortality when I die. Rose in good health. Read Bible, but I spent the day rather unprofitably. Wrote letter to Mr. Dickson [Second Creek]; played violin, etc.

Tuesday, February 12, 1861

Did not sleep very much last night from a heavy rain, but I am thankful for the mercies I enjoy, far richer and more abundant than I deserve. Read the Bible; oh for more wisdom. Went out to Timber Ridge to see Dr. Thompson. Met with a Rev. Ballagh of N.Y., a missionary to Japan. Had a conversation on his great work.

Wednesday, February 13, 1861

Rose early, had a good sleep. Thanks to God for his mercies. Talked with Dr. Thompson and his family; played the piano, violin and flute and sung with Rev. Ballagh. Dined and then returned home. Played guitar. Mr. McElwee returned from Bedford. Talked politics, &c.

Thursday, February 14, 1861

Time goes by very rapidly. I am not improving every moment as it flies. Too much time lost. Rose in good health; thanks to God for his mercies. Read Bible, talked with Rev. McElwee. Played piano and guitar. Studied sermon. Played violin with Miss Polly More on piano for last time.

Friday, February 15, 1861

The month is half gone today. Rose early, conducted worship and set out for Kerr's Creek Singing School, accompanied by Mr. McElwee as far as Richard Miller's. Had a small class. Went up to old Mr. Miller's, spent night. Read Thornwell on "The State of the Country" in N.Y. [paper]. Retired at 12 o'clock.

Saturday, February 16, 1861

I am too much disposed to forget my obligation to my Maker. He gives everything I enjoy. Held worship. Went to Singing School at school house. Had a good class. Heavy snow in evening — and cold. Went down to Alfred Miller. Spent night. Studied sermon.

Sunday, February 17, 1861

Sabbath has come again but I am not well prepared for the sacred duties that devolve upon me as a minister of the gospel. Had worship, studied for the pulpit. Preached at Bethel in lieu of Rev. McElwee. Oh, for more zeal in delivery! Dined at Mr. Dixon's, returned home, very cold. Went to town with Miss Polly More.

Monday, February 18, 1861[15]

I should be very thankful for numberless blessings I enjoy from day to day. I have been blessed with another day's life. Read Bible, the blessed Book; alas, I study it too little! Went to town to see dentist. Read newspaper. Talked with family. I am not growing much in knowledge. Played violin, etc.

Tuesday, February 19, 1861

Rose in good health of body and mind. I deserve nothing, yet I am crowned with blessings. Studied Scripture. Oh that the Spirit of wisdom would rest upon me. Began letter to Henry, Esq., of Kentucky. Played piano and guitar and sung with Miss E. More.

Wednesday, February 20, 1861

I have been preserved another day in my usual health of body and mind. Oh that I could rightly appreciate these great blessings. Read Bible, finished letter to Henry, Esq.; read *Telescope*[16] and *Despatch*. Began sermon on 1 Tim. 4.8. Not much in mood to write. Sung with Mr. McElwee, played, &c.

Thursday, February 21, 1861

My obligations to God are infinite; to him I owe everything, my life is a gift of his bounty and I deserve it not. Read Bible in morning; wrote sermon. Talked to Mr. McCamey, went to town to the dentist. Received letter from Sister Sarah, answered for father. Read *Despatch* and *N.Y. Observer*, retired at 1 o'clock.

Friday, February 22, 1861

Rose early; the firing of the cannon at the [Virginia Military] Institute woke me — Washington's birthday salute! Set out to Kerr's Creek Singing School – very good class. Went with Misses Gilmore and Harper. Spent [?] with them. Eckerd took tea with them. We sung some. He went to a night singing. I enjoyed myself with the ladies.

Saturday, February 23, 1861

Sun rose bright and spring-like but the day became very rainy in the evening. I conducted worship for Captain Gilmore. Went to Sing, had a fine class, this being the 12th day. Returned to Lexington in a heavy rain. Sung with Mr. McElwee. Talked and prepared for going to Bedford to preach.

Sunday, February 24, 1861

The last Sabbath of the month has come. Oh how rapidly time flies! Rose in good health, conducted worship and set out for

Broad Creek. Preached to a very good audience from Rom. 6.23. Oh for more zeal in preaching the gospel. Went home with James Miller. Read some of Sam Davies' sermons. Retired at 10 o'clock.

Monday, February 25, 1861

I have been permitted to see the light of a new day. Rose early and set out for Bedford; passed through Buchanan, crossed two mountains. Had a pleasant and safe ride to Mrs. Eliza Ewings, reached her house at 3 1/2. Talked with her and her little boys. Retired at 10. Thankful for life and health.

Tuesday, February 26, 1861

Death has not removed me from the land of the living. God is still dealing patiently with me. Oh that I could live for Him and not for another. Rose early, held worship, read Bible and conversed with Mr. Ewing &c. Took a walk to the mill; looked at some fine sheep. Played piano at Thos. Patterson's. Sung some with Mr. Ewing.

Wednesday, February 27, 1861

Rose early enjoying the favor of God – a fine morning. Mr. Patterson went with me to the Peaks of Otter. Reached the summit at 11 A.M. Although it was smoky, yet I had a grand sight of the works of God. How great is His wisdom and Power. Surveyed the scene for 3 hours and returned with enlarged ideas of divine power.

Thursday, February 28, 1861

God's mercy and goodness are daily exercised towards his creatures and especially towards me. I have received everything from Him. Rose early this morning, read Bible and daily paper. Went to the annual prayer meeting for colleges. I opened the meeting with prayer. Rev. Penick made some remarks. I spent night with Wm Ewing.

Friday, March 1, 1861

Another month has been numbered with the past, never to return! How swift the moments fly! My life will soon pass away. Conducted worship for Mr. Ewing then returned to Mrs. Ewing's, spent the day in studying but my mind was unfit for exercise.

Saturday, March 2, 1861   *Bedford County, Virginia*

Rose late this morning. I waste too much of my time in bed. Read the Bible, conversed a little, and rode down to Thomas Patterson's & dined; played piano, violin &c. Then set out for Singing at Rev. Penick's house, but he changed it to a road working & I declined. Called at Patterson's and returned home.

Sunday, March 3, 1861

Sabbath has returned again with all its precious blessings. Oh that I could improve the time, and preach the gospel with more power and demonstration of the Spirit. Went to the Mountain Church, preached from Jno. 3.19 to a good congregation. Dined at Mit Ewings. Returned home in evening and read Flavel.

Monday, March 4, 1861[17]

Another day of great importance. Lincoln is president of part of the United States. My life and health have been preserved by the mercy of God. Read bible, wrote letter to father; read "Children & the Flowers" and newspapers. Read the Scriptures &c and retired, thankful to God.

Tuesday, March 5, 1861   *Bedford, Virginia*

Time is rolling on rapidly. But God in his mercy is prolonging my days. Rose in good health this morning, read Bible, *Telescope* &c. Oh for more zeal and wisdom to preach the gospel everywhere daily. Went up to Mr. Mit Ewing's. Spent night. Retired at 12, thankful to God.

Wednesday, March 6, 1861

Oh that God would teach me so to number my days that I may apply my heart to wisdom. Held worship for Mr. Ewing and returned to Mrs. Ewing's, read Bible &c, then went down to Thos Patterson's, dined and spent night, played piano &c, read Lincoln's message &c.

Thursday, March 7, 1861

Rose in good health by the blessing of God. Conducted worship, rode up to Mrs. Ewings. Rev. Penick called to see Messers Patterson and Ewing; went to Mr. Allen's, dined and spent evening. I had a very happy and pleasant visit. Played and sung with the ladies. Rec'd violets and arbor vitae. Returned at dusk, well pleased.

Friday, March 8, 1861   *Bedford, Va.*

Time rolls on rapidly. My life is drawing to a close. God is still waiting to be gracious. Held worship, read the Bible and then went with S. Patterson down to Mr. Hopkins' and dined. Enjoyed ourselves very well, but not like yesterday. Returned home and studied sermon until 11:00.

Saturday, March 9, 1861

Rose in good health. Heavy rain this morning. Held worship. Studied some and then went to Rev. Penick's and dined, remained for the singing society at his house; was introduced to several ladies. Returned to Mrs. Ewing's. Studied sermon, etc.

Sunday, March 10, 1861

Sabbath is a day of sacred rest. May many souls be converted this day. Oh that I could serve my Master aright. Preached at the Peaks Church from Jno. 14.27. Dined at Wm Ewing's. Preached at Temper.[ance] Hall at 3 from Rom. 6.23. Spoke to Miss Mary Allen. Returned home, etc.

Monday, March 11, 1861

God's mercy never fails. He is faithful to his promise. Oh that I could serve him with my body and spirit which are His. Rose late this morning, held worship. Packed up my clothing. Took leave of my friends and set out for Lexington. Stopped at Mr. Harvey's overnight, held worship, etc.

Tuesday, March 12, 1861

I acknowledge my dependence upon God for all I have. Set out for Lexington with a bright sky. Called at Mr. Nair's to let the pup rest. I brought it from Bedford for Mr. McElwee. Reached Lexington at 2 1/2. Glad to get back. Rec'd letters from Sister Sarah, Joe Moffatt and Joe Lowry. Talked news &c.

Wednesday, March 13, 1861

A day is very short but eternity is very long. It is very awful to think that I must be happy or miserable forever. Rose late this morning, read Bible and wrote letter to Sister Mag Moffatt. Went to town, had my hair cut and whiskers trimmed. Heard Methodist at night.

Thursday, March 14, 1861

The month is almost half gone and I am not improving my time. I am an unprofitable servant. Rose in good health, read some, then went to dentist, paid Dr. Davidson 15 dol for work on teeth. Put in some glass for Mrs. M. Talked to law students. Went to town, bought indel. ink, bought box of Janey's Pills. Played piano, &c.

Friday, March 15, 1861

The month is half gone. O time, how swift is thy flight! Life is very short at best. Rose in good health and set out for Kerr's Creek Singing School. Had a small class. Went to Mr. Teaford's, spent night. Had a slight headache, retired at 10.

Saturdays March 16, 1861

God is unsearchable in all his [ways], his name is holy and holiness becometh all who worship Him. Blessed with good health. Went to Singing School; good class. Spent night at Calvin Harper's. Talked politics. Held worship, retired to my room. Studied sermon, etc.

Sunday, March 17, 1861   Bethel - Rockbridge, Virginia

The Sabbath is of divine appointment for the good of man and all of God's creatures. O that I could improve the time! Rose in good health. Preached for Mr. McElwee at Bethel from Jno. 14.27. Sung some new tunes; invited the congregation to attend school on Saturday. Spent night at A. Lackey's.

Monday, March 18, 1861

Had worship for Mr. A. Lackey. O! for the Spirit of Prayer and Supplication! Very cold, snow fell. Set out for Lexington. Found Mr. McElwee sick with eresypelas[sic]. Read *Observer*. Went to dentist again. Talked with law students and the family. Read Bible and retired.

Tuesday, March 19, 1861

Man is like the grass, he is soon cut down and returned to dust. Read Bible. Rev. White, D.D. called on Mr. McElwee. Talked with them. Dr. Freeman called on his patient (Mc). Walked to the Institute to see the building and wrote letter to Mr. Dickson; received one from Joe Moffatt.

Wednesday, March 20, 1861

Oh how swiftly the days pass away. My life will soon come to an end. How diligently should each moment be improved. Read the Bible and studied sermon, Oh for more grace! Went to P.O. Fixed Mrs. McElwee's lamp and book, etc. Retired after reading Bible.

Thursday, March 21, 1861

Rose in good health. Very cold all day, brisk snow and wind. God rules the storm and sends the snow. Read Bible &c. Fixed some more books and picture cases. Read news papers. I spend too much time in reading trashy papers. Oh that I loved the Bible more.

Friday, March 22, 1861

Rich blessings are still extended to me. I do not appreciate them aright; but blessings brighten as they take their flight. Read the Scriptures, studied sermon. Went in rockaway to Mr. Moore's and spent night. Studied sermon until 11 o'clock.

Saturday, March 23, 1861   *Lexington, Va.*

Rose in usual good health, held worship for Mr. Moore; sat a while, then walked over to see Mrs. And. Miller lying low with consumption. Read Ps 40 and 41 and offered prayer in her behalf. Went to Singing at Bethel and closed my school. I had a pleasant time throughout the School.

Sunday, March 24, 1861

The Sabbath has come again. Glad to see it dawn once more. Studied and prepared for the Solemn duty of preaching the gospel. Set out for Broad Creek in rockaway; preached from Mat. 5.3 assisted by Rev. Ewing (O.S.). Dined at Wm Miller's; went to Mr. Harvey's and spent night.

Monday, March 25, 1861

Beautiful morning, rose at 4 o'clock and at 5 1/2 set out with Mrs. Harvey & family for Lexington, arrived at 10. Went to Dentist to get a large nerve cavity filled. Read some. Fixed Mrs. McElwee's clock. Saw Dr. Freeman dissect a cow for Mr. McElwee. Played piano & guitar for Mrs. Harvey, bought candy for children &c.

Tuesday, March 26, 1861   *Lexington - Second Creek*

Rose early and blessed with fine health. What shall I render to God for all gifts to me? May I spend and be spent in his service. Worked on the clock again, had my tooth finished. Hired conveyance, packed up for Second Creek. Sorry indeed to leave Mr & Mrs. McElwee & family. To Goshen then by R.R. to Jackson's river.

Wednesday March 27, 1861

God has preserved me in safety to my journey's end. Travelled in stage all night. Breakfast at Dry Creek. Reached Second Creek 10 1/2 A.M. Felt lonely and alone in my room. Talked with Mr. Dickson and family. Slept four [hours] in evening, read news, wrote diary. Read Bible, retired at 11.

Thursday, March 28, 1861

God's mercy never fails, he is good to me although I sin against his holy law. Oh that I could keep his commandments! Read Bible, fixed up my book &c., wrote some. Read Eadie on Divine love. May the love of Christ constrain me to spend my time in his work.

Friday, March 29, 1861[18]

Time is carrying me on to the grace [grave]. Oh that I could so number my days as to apply my heart to wisdom. My heart is wicked, my thoughts are evil. Rose at sunrise. Read Bible, studied Greek Tes[tament]. Studied sermon, read *Telescope* &c. Played guitar after eating, for recreation. Retired in health at 11.

Saturday, March 30, 1861

Through the mercy of God my life is prolonged and health continued. May I not love the blessings more than the Giver of all good. Read Bible & studied sermon, but is evil & full of wicked thoughts that hinder my progress. Played guitar, read news &c.

Sunday, March 31, 1861

Oh that I loved the Sabbath as I should. It is a precious blessing. Oh that I could do more for my Master. My heart is too cold. Studied Scriptures and prepared for the holy work of preaching the gospel from Mat 5.3. Spent evening reading Chalmers sermons, Devotions &c.

Monday, April 1, 1861

Another month has commenced its round. How swift the months fly. So pass my days like a weaver's shuttle. God is loading me with his gifts, but am an ungrateful creature, unthankful and evil. Read Bible & wrote letter to Father. Went to Mr. M. Beamer's and spent the night, talked til 11 o'clock, good health.

Tuesday, April 2, 1861

I am a guity [guilty] creature, deserve not the least of God's mercies, I am unthankful and evil. My heart is full of all uncleanness. Studied Greek & Hebrew grammar. Wrote at a sermon from I Tim 4.8 Com[mentary] after returning from Beamer, borrowed book.

Notes

[1] "Rev. J. H. Simpson's Missionary Report," *Due West Telescope*, October 11, 1861.

[2] John H. Simpson, "Christmas in My Boyhood Days," *Associate Reformed Presbyterian*, December 21, 1910.

[3] Second Creek is an area south of Lewisburg in present day West Virginia.

[4] The western most point on the railroad was Covington, Virginia, where the line ran from Staunton, Virginia.

[5] Goshen is a town north of Lexington along the railroad running toward Staunton.

[6] On this day, South Carolina forces fire on the *Star of the West*, as the ship attempted to enter Charleston harbor to supply the Union garrison in Fort Sumter. Mississippi joins South Carolina and becomes the second state to leave the Union.

[7] Florida becomes the third state to secede, by a delegate vote of 62-7.

[8] Alabama leaves the Union and becomes the fourth state to join the rebellion.

[9] Georgia leaves the Union, becoming the fifth state of the rebellion. Virginia invites delegates from all states north and south to join in a convention in Washington D.C. to find a peaceful solution to the crisis.

[10] Louisiana becomes the sixth state to secede from the Union.

[11] Texas joins the rebellion by voting 166-8 to leave the United States.

[12] Only twenty one of the thirty four states meet in the Peace convention in Washington D.C., while the commissioners of the seven states to leave the Union meet in a convention in Montgomery, Alabama to form a new nation. At the same time, Virginia overwhelmingly defeated the state secessionists by voting to bring before the voters of the state any action by the convention.

[13] The Southern states adopt a new constitution, forming the Confederate States of America.

[14] Jefferson Davis of Mississippi is elected President of the new Southern nation.

[15] Jefferson Davis is inaugurated as President of the Confederate States of America, in Montgomery, Alabama.

[16] Local paper in Due West, South Carolina, home of Simpson's alma mater, Erskine College.

[17] Inauguration day for Abraham Lincoln in Washington D.C. The proposals of the Peace Convention and other peace proposals are rejected by the Congress.

[18] Lincoln polls his cabinet to attempt to resupply Fort Sumter. Most are in agreement the Fort must be supplied and prevented from capture by South Carolina.

Chapter Two

"*Civil War Has Come at Last*"

The fever of secession swept over the South and reached into the lives of every person in the newly formed country. Every adult man and woman had to come to a decision on which cause to support. The Reverend Simpson believed that war was inevitable and comforted himself in the study of the Bible and the daily improvement of his mind. As war fever swept over the nation now split in two, Simpson deplored the coming struggle. He was called home to South Carolina where he longed to be as his brothers went to war in Confederate service.

Although Simpson did not encourage the onset of Civil War, his sympathies were with the South. One of the last deeds he did in Virginia was to play "Dixie," on his violin. Once in South Carolina among family and friends, Simpson saw the troops off to war but hoped for a peaceful solution.

Wednesday, April 3, 1861[1]

Rose up to see and spend another day. It is a wonder that I was not consumed today. So great a sinner am I. Read and studied Scriptures, wrote sermon, played violin & read news and began to read Paley's Nat. The. [Natural Theology].

Thursday, April 4, 1861[2]

Daily am I called upon or constrained to record the loving kindness of the Lord. I owe all to Him & my obligations to love Him are infinite. Rose at sunrise, read Greek Tes. Wrote sermon with much success, played guitar and violin. Studied Hebrew gram & read Paley's Nat The; retired in good health.

Friday, April 5, 1861

Oh what a blessing it is to enjoy good health, I too often forget the Giver of every good & perfect gift. Read the Greek Tes. Jno

12.1-8. Studied Hebrew in evening. Finished writing sermon before dinner, read news, *Telescope* &c. Went up to see Mr. Beamer, sick with pains. Took him Rutherford's. Played guitar. Read Paley until 11.

Saturday, April 6, 1861[3]

Another [week] closes tonight. I have enjoyed many mercies notwithstanding my many sins. Oh that my heart was pure and right in God's sight. Studied sermon. Went to Salem [Church] in evening, commenced a singing school. Studied sermon at night.

Sunday, April 7, 1861[4]

Another holy Sabbath has been numbered with the past. And have I been faithful as a minister of Jesus Christ? Alas I am an unprofitable servant! But O God, cut me not down as a cumberer. Preached from 1 Tim 4.8. O for more zeal. Read Chalmers &c, retired at 11. Thanks to God for health.

Monday, April 8, 1861

My life and health are continued another day. Read Greek Tes in morning, read news of importance in politics. War seems inevitable. Played guitar to drive away care and trouble. But God is my only strong hold in time of trouble. Read Paley Nat. Theo, retired in good health, thanks to God.

Tuesday, April 9, 1861[5]

This day has been marked by many tokens of God's love and mercy. Although I had a slight headache, I am thankful the punishment was no greater; I deserved far greater. Took a nap, wrote Sermon. O for more wisdom in spiritual things. Played guitar, read Paley, retired, free from all pain at 10 1/2.

Wednesday, April 10, 1861

My days are wasting away yet God's mercy endures forever. He has blessed me another day. How thankful I should be! but O my ingratitude. Pardon me O lord. Read Greek Tes. Wrote sermon with some success, I lack grace. Played guitar, read Paley at night, to bed at 11.

Thursday, April 11, 1861

I should be very thankful for the many blessings bestowed on me, for I am altogether unworthy of everything I enjoy. My health is good, O that my soul healed of its maladies. Read Greek Tes. Wrote Sermon, O that my labors were more abundant and efficient. Played guitar after eating. Read Paley &c&.

Friday, April 12, 1861[6]

God is infinite in power, wisdom and goodness. He made the earth and built the lofty skies and preserves man & beast; he daily loads me with mercies. Read the Bible, finished ser. on Mat 7.7. Read Paley, read news: *N.Y. Obs.* &c, retired in good health. Oh that I was thankful.

Saturday, April 13, 1861

Time is flying rapidly, my days are but few and will soon be gone. This is a world of changes and trouble. I am thankful that I enjoy it as much as I do. God is good to me. Read my Bible. Studied sermon, went to Singing School at Lebanon. Studied sermon in evening, retired at 11 o'clock.

Sunday, April 14, 1861[7]

The Sabbath is a joyful day to the Christian world. But I often misspend its sacred hours. Read Bible, engaged in secret prayer. I spent too much of my time Sabbath morning studying sermon. I believe this is wrong. Went to Salem (OP)[8] preached with some ease & life I thought, on Mat 7.7.

Monday, April 15, 1861

The month is half gone to night. Life is very short. Redeem the time because the days are few and evil. Read Greek Tes'. Studied Hebrew grammar. Wrote to my friend Joe Moffatt. No mail today, great disappointment! Played guitar & violin for the family. Wrote diary, engaged in secret prayer.

Tuesday, April 16, 1861

I am a dependent being, my daily supplies come from the Giver of all good. How excellent is thy loving kindness O Lord, therefore I put my trust under the shadow of thy wings. Read usual amount in Greek Tes', commenced sermon on Jno 11:35, wrote 2 pages. Read Paley. Played violin &c.

Wednesday, April 17, 1861[9]

I have many pleasures in this life. All my life has been marked with mercies yet I am so unthankful & evil. My life and health have been prolonged another day. Read Greek. Wrote sermon with a little speed. O for more grace and zeal. Played violin, took a walk, finished Paley's *Natural Theology*.

Thursday, April 18, 1861

O how rapidly time rolls away. This day twelve months ago I left home for Ky and Ind'. It seems like a dream. I am thankful my life & health have been continued. Read Greek as usual, forgot Hebrew today; wrote sermon. Took a walk morning and evening. Played violin, commenced Horace Paulin.

Friday, April 19, 1861[10]

Every day of my life has been marked with untold blessings. I am a daily receiver of God's goodness. Read Bible and finished sermon on the shortest verse in the Bible. Took a walk to the oil mill, looked at the big spring. Played guitar &c. Heard of Va seceding & Fort Sumter taken with bloodshed.

Saturday, April 20, 1861[11]

Rose early. Read Bible, studied sermon. Went to Singing School at Salem — had a large school, but I was not in much of a mood for singing. Came home at 4 o'clock and read newspaper. War has commenced; O God save this people from civil war if it is thy will. Thy will be done.

Sabbath, April 21, 1861

The holy Sabbath has come again but O how unfit I am for its holy exercises. I am not in the Spirit on the Lord's day. Prepared to preach as best I could, in the exciting times. Civil war has come at last. Preached from John 11:35; much excited, received letter from Mr. Baird requesting me to come. I gave out no preaching. Wm and Elihu had left for Char[leston][12]; rec'd letter from Livy Grier.

Monday, April 22, 1861

O how I long to get home, my brothers have left for the bloody battle field. May God preserve them and comfort their families during their absence. May God put a stop to war and give us peace once more. I can but pray for divine help. Packed up my trunk for home sweet home.

Tuesday, April 23, 1861

Another day has dawned, my life and usual health are continued. I am thankful for all the mercies bestowed on me by a kind heavenly Father. Read the Bible, settled with Mr. Dickson, took a walk down creek. Dined, played "Dixie" on violin and took leave of my friends and set out for home! Sweet &c.

Wednesday, April 24, 1861

God is good to me, my life and health are continued. Slept well last (night) at White Sulphur; left on Stage at 4 o'clock. Anxious to hear from the "War". God save us from such an evil. Reached Staunton at 6 o'clock. Stopped at American Hotel.

Thursday, April 25, 1861

Man is a dependent being, all my blessings are from above. Rose early, engaged in private devotion, eat breakfast and left Staunton for Richmond. Great excitement about war on the road. Reached Richmond at 3 and passed on to Petersburg, then to Weldon; travelled all night.

Friday, April 26, 1861[13]

Reached Wilmington this morning. Had a safe journey thus far. Passed S.C. soldiers going on to Richmond. Left Wil' for Col. passed more soldiers for Richmond. Reached Columbia at 4 PM. Saw other soldiers for the war. Stopped at Janey's, exchanged some music.

Rev. John Hemphill Simpson's home, Chester, South Carolina.

Saturday, April 27, 1861

My health is good as usual, I deserve nothing but am crowned with mercies. Left Columbia, reached Chester at 1 PM. "Home Again". Found Wm absent in the army at Charleston. Glad to get home once more, dined with Mr. Baird, somewhat tired &c.

Sunday, April 28, 1861

Sabbath has come again and I am at my home. Went to Church at Union with Mr. Baird. Glad to see my friends at the Old Sacred Church of my youth. Did not preach. Mr. McDonald preached two sermons. I sung for him. Glad to see my good friend Mrs. Moffatt &c.

Monday, April 29, 1861

Another week has commenced its round. Held worship, read Bible. Wrote letter to Livie Grier. W. L. Pressly called and dined at father's today. We walked over to P.O. Saw Messrs. Hemphill, Harris and others. Played guitar. Sister Mary came up with John C. &c.

Tuesday, April 30, 1861

Time is on the wing and my days are running out; how diligent I should be. I spend most of my time reading and thinking about the war. May God deliver us from such a dreadful calamity. Read Bible, played on piano and guitar. Went to church to sing with class.

Wednesday, May 1, 1861

Lovely May has come again with all its beauties. Nature is adorning herself with rich and gay colours. All things speak the Creator's praise. Read Bible; read news. Fixed Mr. Baird's pistol and shot it. Studied sermon but with little success. I long for the war to close and enjoy peace.

Thursday, May 2, 1861

Oh that I could spend my time in a profitable manner. Read Bible and studied sermon. My friend R. R. Hemphill called on me, the first time we have met in two years. We talked about old times in Due West &c. I went down to Elihu's and spent night. Found Lois sick.

Friday, May 3, 1861[14]

God is still prolonging my days and giving me health. Held worship, studied sermon and went to Neely's Creek. Preached for Mr. McDonald from 1 Tim 4.8 to a very small audience. Went home with Uncle Wm Wylie, looked at his land, farm &c.

Saturday, May 4, 1861

How excellent is thy loving kindness O Lord, therefore the Sons of men put their trust under the Shadow of thy Wings. Studied sermon, went to church, met with Lathan. He preached in morning & I in evening from Jno 3.15. Mr. McD ordained two elders, D. O. Roddy &c. I went home with Cousin Mary Simpson.

Sunday, May 5, 1861

Sabbath has come again, blessed day to Christians and all the world. Messers McDonald & Lathan administered the Lords

Supper. Lathan preached, I clerked. Very unfavorable day: cold and rainy. I was without my blanket. Went in rain to Sister Mary's & spent night.

Monday, May 6, 1861   (Rec'd letter from Henry)

My life and health are still continued. I deserve none of the numerous blessings I enjoy. May God not withhold them because I abuse them. Held worship. Went over to Elihu's, talked with Uncle John F., took dinner. Started for Chester. Stopped at Aunt Lindy Martin's. Met Wm Pressly and his wife, had a chat with them. Rain in evening.

Tuesday, May 7, 1861[15]

Oh how swift time passes away. Read the Scriptures. I need the Spirit of wisdom and supplication. Played piano. Wrote letters to Newton Dickson & RR agent at Staunton. Worked on Mr. Baird's pistol & shot it. Read news of the war. Went to the Pres[byterian] Church to Sing &c. Cool for May.

Wednesday, May 8, 1861

Days roll away very rapidly. Time is ever moving and man should improve every moment as it flies. Read Bible this morning, read war news, went over to see Mrs. Melton. Played piano and guitar. Went to P. O. Bought 37 yards of cloth for Negros, $4.50.

Thursday, May 9, 1861

I am an unprofitable servant. Much of my time runs to waste. Rose in good health. God's mercy never fails. Read His blessed word often with too little care. Worked on the old rock wash pan. Read Richmond Despatch. Played piano and guitar for Misses Alice McFadden, J. Alexander &c.

Friday, May 10, 1861[16]

Great changes take place in one year. This day one year ago I was in Chicago at the Convention which nominated the vile Abe Lincoln for President of the U.S.A. But thanks to God not of the South. Read Bible. Studied sermon, took tea with Mr. Baird. Read war news.

Saturday, May 11, 1861

Man's days are like the grass or the flower of the field. I should improve every moment as it flies. But it is hard for a minister of the gospel to study when the country is involved in War. Read Bible and studied sermon. Helped Isaiah to make some bee boxes, eat supper and spent night at Baird's. Shot pistol. Prepared to preach at Purity.

Sunday, May 12, 1861

The Lord's day has come again but my mind is too much on the state of the country. I should strive to fix my thoughts on the great work upon which I have entered. Preached at Purity two sermons from 1 Tim 4.8, Jno. 3.19. Good audience, Oh for more wisdom.

Monday, May 13, 1861

May is almost half gone. O may God deliver us from war and bloodshed. May he rule and defend us. Read the scriptures and engaged in private and secret prayer. Worked on some bee boxes. Wrote letter to Wm. Drove bees into new boxes. Played piano, learning Marseilles hymn.

Tuesday, May 14, 1861

O that I had wings like a dove for then would I fly away and be at rest, free from all war and strife of nation. Read Bible &c, read news, played piano; made some more bee boxes and put the bees in them. Very tired at night. Read Latin for Isaiah.

Wednesday, May 15, 1861

The world is in commotion. Every nation is in some difficulty. We hear of nothing but wars and rumors of wars. O for peace! Read Bible &c. Worked on the well, fixed a pipe to water the well house. Read news, eat supper at Baird's. Played piano.

Thursday, May 16, 1861

Weather very warm and dry and I have [been] working to have cool milk in the wellhouse. Read the Bible in the morning. Read news of the war. May God deliver us in the day of battle. Went to

Singing School. Mr & Mrs Hemphill attended. I love the Singing School &c.

Friday, May 17, 1861

The month is waning and so is life. I am nearer my end. Read the Bible. Oh for spiritual wisdom. Finished the well job. Worked with the bees. Visited Mrs. Hemphill. She is an excellent lady & friendly in her house. Miss Bell, her eldest daughter, is good looking. Saw Gaston from the War.

Saturday, May 18, 1861[17]

It is a great privilege to be a minister of the gospel. Yet I am too slothful in the performance of my sacred duties. Good is the Lord to me. Read Bible, papers, and went to P.O. Bought a hat. Bro. Wm returned from Charleston. O that the war was over. Played piano. Studied sermon.

Sunday, May 19, 1861

The Sabbath is a blessed day, the best of all the week. I am glad to [see] the light of the Sabbath. The Saints meet to pray and praise God. Studied sermon &c; went to Hopewell. Preached for Mr. Brice in evening from Jno. 3.19. O for more of the Spirit of my Master! Rain after noon. Read Dick Theo Bible &c.

Monday, May 20, 1861[18]

A day is very short and so is life. I should be up and doing, with my loins girded. Read the Scriptures &c, newspapers on the war. Little signs of peace. May God avert civil war. Went to P.O. Returned my hat. Worked with my bees. Sowed some buckwheat for them; played piano, finished Marseilles Hymn.

Tuesday, May 21, 1861

Time and tide wait for no man. This is a true saying. I scarcely know how I put in my time. I do very little indeed. O for more zeal in my Master's work. Read Bible &c. Read newspaper on the War. May God deliver us from ourselves. Played piano and guitar, violin &c. Fixed Wm's bees &c.

Wednesday, May 22, 1861

There is no excellence without great labor. May I strive to glorify my Master and secure my own salvation. Studied the Scriptures &c. Read news, not much bloodshed yet, may God prevent any more. Worked with bees. Elihu & Brown came up, talked politics & war &c; played piano.

Thursday, May 23, 1861

Rose in good health by the blessing of God. Read Bible &c. Went down to Robert Douglas to fix his sewing machine. Mrs D is a fine lady, had a nice dinner. Her garden is the best I ever saw. She gave me $1.00 for my work. Went to sing at church. They are getting up a class &c.

Friday, May 24, 1861[19]

Time is money, but I am too prodigal in its use. Spend too much in doing nothing. Rose in good health this morning. Studied Scriptures &c, prepared sermons to preach at Yorkville. Worked with bees, read newspaper. War is sounding in our ears.

Saturday, May 25, 1861

Rose early and in good health. Great is God's goodness towards me. Read the N. Tes[tament] &c. Studied sermons, dressed &c. took cars at 12, reached Yorkville 2 1/2 PM. Met Messers Elder & Lathan. Called at E's house, preached at night from Jno 3.11. Spent night at Dr. Barron's.

Sunday, May 26, 1861

The blessed Sabbath has come again. O for grace to serve God aright. Rose in good health. Took a walk, prepared to preach the gospel, O for Grace! Preached from Jno 12.27. Lathan administered the Sacrament. I preached at night from 1 Tim 4.8. Tea at Col Beatys. Spent night at Elders.

Monday, May 27, 1861

Rose rather late, held worship for Mr. Elder. Walked through the Female College. Took cars for Chester, arrived at 8 1/2 AM. Read

Bible &c, looked at my bees, played piano for Miss McFadden. Read news from the war. O may God defend us in all our battles.

Tuesday, May 28, 1861

It is hard for me to study any when my country is involved in a bloody war. Rose in good health, read Bible &c. played violin & piano. Worked with bees, feeding them. Read news papers &c. The truth is scarce these times in news papers, bought 50 cts white sugar.

Wednesday, May 29, 1861[20]

The month is drawing to a close. No bloody battles have yet been fought. May God say to the raging storm "peace be still". He is our only hope and refuge. Read Bible and played piano. Went to post office, no news. O for peace! My sins are many.

Thursday May 30, 1861

Man's days are like the grass. I should save every moment. Truth should be my aim, O for more wisdom. Read bible &c. Read newspapers &c, played piano. This is relief to me. Went to Singing School, had a good class, met R. R. Hemphill at church; glad to see him &c.

Friday, May 31, 1861

I am dependent upon God for every thing I have and for every breath I draw. He gives strength to all his creatures. Rose in good health this morning. Read bible &c. Went to P.O., read newspaper. O that God would stop the War & give us peace. Studied sermon, played piano; worked with bees. May is gone!

Saturday, June 1, 1861

Another month has begun its round. May God stay the War that is about to commence! We are in his hand. Rose in good health as usual. Studied sermon. Went to P.O., bought a Silk hat at Gill's, price $3.00; played piano, worked with my bees &c. Much of my time runs to waste.

Sunday, June 2, 1861

My mind is not fixed as it should be, on the great work of preaching the gospel. I neglect my studies too much. Spend too much of the Sabbath in studying sermons. Preached in Presbyterian Church for [Rev.] White from Jno 14.27 and Matt. 5.3. O for more wisdom & grace!

Monday, June 3, 1861[21]

The days roll round rapidly, "life is but a strife, tis a bubble, tis a dream". It becomes me to be active and diligent in business. Rose in good health by the blessing of God. Read his word &c, read news. O God stop the War! Played piano &c.

Tuesday, June 4, 1861

One month more and Lincoln's congress will meet, may God influence it to Stop the cruel civil war! Rose in good health &c &c. Saw some of my Virginia friends on the Cars, Mr. Stewart Patterson & his sisters from Due West. Was glad to see them, felt like going with them. Went to Singing School. Spent evening at Depot waiting for volunteers to go up.

Wednesday, June 5, 1861

Time does not wait for man. I am nearer my journey's end. O for peace! May God stop the cruel war. Read Bible, man's only comfort in this world. Went down to Depot to Salute the volunteers, 7th Regiment.[22] Saw many of my friends from Abb. and Due West. Gen Bradley, Ansley, Morrow &c, may God be their defense.

Thursday, June 6, 1861

Man is a dependent being. God is the author of all his mercies. He gives me many blessings although I am unthankful & evil. Read the scriptures &c. played piano; went down to depot to see the 5th Reg. of CSA Vol.[23] May God deliver us from War. Went to Singing School.

Friday, June 7, 1861

I am thankful for health of body and mind. How excellent is thy loving kindness O Lord. Read Bible &c, wrote letter to W. L. Pressly. Went to fix Mrs. Robinson's sewing machine. She gave me some good wine. Read newspapers &c. O God give us peace again.

Saturday, June 8, 1861

The weeks roll round rapidly, O that the war would soon come to an end. I am in good health, blessed be God. Read Bible &c. Had my boot fixed and set out for Dr. Boyce's, arrived at 4 P.M. Glad to see my friend Moffatt Grier. Took a walk. Talked about old times &c til 12 o'clock.

Sunday, June 9, 1861

The holy Sabbath has dawned again. O that I could spend it aright. Rose in good health. Read Bible &c. Studied sermon &c. Moffatt rode with me to church. I preached in the evening for Dr. Boyce from Jno. 3.27. Went to Robert Brice's, spent the night. Talked with Miss A.

Monday, June 10, 1861

Rose in good health this morning. I deserve not the blessings I enjoy. Held worship. Had some music from Miss Amanda. Set out for home at 9 AM. Saw R.R. Hemphill, a volunteer, at Cornwell's T.O. on his way to Virginia. Fixed Mrs. Robinson's machine, price $2.50.

Tuesday, June 11, 1861

I make a poor return of God's favors; I never had better health. Thanks to God. Read the Bible, the only guide to peace and happiness. Finished Mrs. R. machine. Went to Singing School, had a good class. The last night Isaiah sung with me. Retired at 11 PM, very tired.

Wednesday, June 12, 1861[24]

The month is rolling away and so is life. Man's days are like a shadow which quickly passes. Read Bible. Went down to Depot to see Isaiah leave for the army. May he be preserved in the day of battle. Played piano and guitar. Read papers. O that God would smile on us again & send us peace.

Thursday, June 13, 1861[25]

This is a day of fasting & humiliation & prayer throughout the Southern Confederacy. O that God would hear the prayers offered at the throne of grace. Read Bible; Mr. Baird & I went to the Episcopal Church, heard a good, yet short, sermon from Omstead. Called at Mr. Baird's and Wm's &c.

Friday, June 14, 1861

The weather is quite warm, needing rain. May God open the windows of heaven & send refreshing showers on the earth. Read the Scriptures &c. Finished Mr. Baird's well house. Went up town, looked for cloth for a fine coat. Received letter from Jim Lowry in Geo. Sung in evening.

Saturday, June 15, 1861

June is half gone. O that the war would cease and land have rest, the people blessed with peace. Read Bible but with too little love for it. O for more hungering and thirsting after righteousness. Fixed two umbrellas. Saw 12 cannons go down on train. W. L. Pressly came to preach.

Sunday, June 16, 1861

The holy Sabbath has come again. May the whole land enjoy rest. May peace soon be restored to our troubled country. Read Bible and engaged in secret prayer. Went to church. Pressly preached from Heb. 2.3 at 11 AM and from Rev. 3.20 in even. He spent night at Gaston's Esq. I eat supper at Baird's. Father was sick, unable to go to church.

Monday, June 17, 1861

Good is the Lord to all his creatures. Rose in good health this morning. Read Bible &c. Played piano and guitar for Pressly and Nealy, went to depot & up town, read paper, took a walk with McDaniel. Took Mrs. Robinson's needles to her, she introduced me to Mrs. Devaga.

Tuesday, June 18, 1861

Man's days are like a weaver's shuttle that swift doth pass. Read Bible, man's only guide & comfort in this world. Went to Devaga's to fix sewing machine. Fixed pistol, made a ladle for bulletts. Went to Singing School in evening. Boys are very rude and noisy.

Wednesday, June 19, 1861

Man loves peace in preference to war and strife. Oh that God would return in mercy and visit the land with peace once more. Rose in good health this morning. Read bible. Went to the funeral of Fowler, S.C.V. Called on Misses V. Melton and M. Alexander. Went to Sing at 5 P.M.

Thursday, June 20, 1861

Another day has dawned. Blessed be God for his goodness to me, many are called from time to eternity yet I am permitted to live. Read God's word and engaged in Secret prayer. Worked all day on Mrs. Devaga's sewing machine. Called on Misses V. Melton & M. Alexander at night.

Friday, June 21, 1861

God is worthy of Supreme love and adoration. But my affections are fixed too much on the world and too often do I worship the creature more than the Creator. Rose in health. Worked on sewing machine and went to Sing at night. Another S.C.V., one Wixes, died and was buried today.

Saturday, June 22, 1861

The days are very long but eternity how long! Time will soon end, but eternity will never end. To be happy in eternity we must spend our time according to the will of God. Rose early and in good health. Read, Bible &c. Worked on the well house all day. Played piano &c. Very hot day.

Sunday, June 23, 1861

The holy Sabbath has come again. O that I could serve my Master. I have no place to preach on account of the war. Oh that God would still the tumult of people and cause the land to enjoy rest and peace. Went to hear Rev. White morning and evening. Received very little from his sermons.

Monday, June 24, 1861

The month is drawing to a close. I should be diligent in my Master's work. May he not turn me out of his vineyard and his

service. O God prolong my days to show forth thy Glory . . .
Worked on well house, ceiled up the rafters and put a window in
the end. Worked on sewing machine. God sent us a fine rain.
Called on V. Melton.

Tuesday, June 25, 1861

Another day has passed away and numbered with the past. Life is
drawing to a close. Rose early this morning. Worked on sewing
machine. Went down to R.R. Played guitar in depot. Went to
P.O. Had my hair shaved. Went to Sing. Wm Pressly and wife
called, dined and went on home.

Wednesday, June 26, 1861

June will soon be gone, O that the war would close with it. God
is our only hope; he holds the hearts of kings; may he influence
Lincoln to make Peace. Rose early. Read Bible. Finished sewing
machine, took it home, received 6 dols for my work. Went to
depot to see Hampton's legion pass.[26] Rain heavy.

Notes

[1] On this date, South Carolina ratified the Confederate Constitution with
a vote of 114 to 16.

[2] On this day, President Lincoln wrote a letter to the commander of Fort
Sumter informing him of the decision to authorize an expedition to relieve the Fort, thereby forcing the hand of the Confederacy.

[3] Lincoln dispatches a courier to the Governor of South Carolina informing him of the expedition to relieve Fort Sumter. Fort Pickens guarding
the harbor of Pensacola, Florida, lay in danger of falling into Confederate hands, the Naval commander on the scene refused to land new troops
for the garrison.

[4] Permission is given by Confederate Secretary of War Leroy P. Walker
to Confederate forces under Braxton Bragg blockading Pensacola,
Florida to fire on any attempt to reinforce the garrison there.

[5] Jefferson Davis and his cabinet decide to authorize an attack on Fort
Sumter before any relief expedition can arrive.

[6] The shelling of Fort Sumter begins at 4:30 am, on this day. Almost 5,000
artillery rounds are exchanged over the next 33 hours.

[7] On this day, Fort Sumter surrenders to the Confederate forces in
Charleston Harbor. This first "battle" results in no casualties on either

side, but one Union soldier killed and one mortally wounded by a premature cannon explosion after the surrender.

[8] Old School Presbyterian.

[9] Virginia secedes from the Union.

[10] President Lincoln declares a blockade of the Southern States, and a riot in Baltimore against Union forces passing through the city leaves four soldiers and nine civilians dead.

[11] Colonel Robert E. Lee resigns his commission in the army of the United States and joins the state of Virginia. In the original diary, Simpson reversed the dates of April 20-21.

[12] William Simpson was 3rd Sergeant, Pickens Guard, which was recruited in Chester County, South Carolina. Five companies were called from Chester County to Charleston on April 11, and arrived in time to witness but not participate in the attack on Fort Sumter.

[13] Most of the Confederate war effort in 1861 was centered in Virginia, and troops, supplies and equipment were rushed into the state from all over the south by the Confederate government.

[14] President Lincoln issued a call for 42,034 Infantry and 18,000 Navy volunteers to serve for three years to put an end to the War.

[15] Tennessee entered into a military alliance with the Confederate states, thereby joining the War de facto.

[16] A riot occurs in St. Louis between Southern sympathizers and Union volunteers resulting in twenty nine people killed or mortally wounded.

[17] Arkansas is admitted into the Confederacy.

[18] North Carolina secedes from the Union.

[19] Federal troops invade Virginia, taking possession of the city of Alexandria. Colonel Elmer Ellsworth of the New York Fire Zouaves is killed by a Virginia citizen after taking down a Confederate flag. The citizen, James Jackson, is killed by the New York troops.

[20] President Jefferson Davis arrives in the Confederacy's new capitol city of Richmond.

[21] Union forces occupy the town of Philippi, in present day West Virginia.

[22] The 7th South Carolina Volunteers become part of Joseph B. Kershaw's brigade of the Army of Northern Virginia.

[23] The 5th South Carolina Volunteers become part of John Bratton's Brigade of the Army of Northern Virginia.

[24] 5th South Carolina Infantry.

[25] President Davis proclaimed this day as a day of fasting to prepare the country for war.

[26] Hampton's Legion was a regiment of South Carolina volunteers who were raised by Wade Hampton, who would prove to be one of the most prominent South Carolina generals of the war. The unit was on it's way to Virginia.

Chapter 3

"ON TO VIRGINIA"

As Simpson says in his first entry of this chapter, "Time waits for no man." The lines of battle were now drawn and the time for North and South to battle one another was now only a short time away. John Simpson chose not to enlist in the army being raised by the Southern Confederacy but to assist his state in every way he could as a minister of the Lord.

He joins the army as an unofficial volunteer, serving to bring home the bodies of the dead and comfort the living friends who have committed themselves to the Southern cause. Simpson almost becomes a casualty himself when he is stricken down by the great wave of disease that sweeps over the army after the battle of First Manassas, and must return home to regain his health.

Thursday, June 27, 1861

Time waits for no man. It behooves me to improve every moment as it flies. Another day has passed away and I am in the land of the living. Rose before sunrise, read the scriptures. Worked a little, read papers, went up town. Saw troops pass Chester.[1] Spoke to Miss Mary Brawley at depot.

Friday, June 28, 1861

How excellent is thy loving kindness O Lord, therefore the children of men put their trust under the shadow of thy wings. Read Bible but with too little love & zeal for knowledge. Went to depot, bought pair of boots & 2 pairs of socks from Poag. Took some nice honey. Sent Miss Virgie Melton, Wm and Mr. Baird some honey. Had some more rain.

Saturday, June 29, 1861[2]

I am an unworthy creature, deserve not the rich blessings I enjoy. O God consult not my merits. Rose in good health. Read Bible &c. Went to P.O. O that God would restore peace to our land. Saw more soldiers pass up to Va. Miss Joe McFadden sent me some geraniums. Studied sermon.

Sunday, June 30, 1861

This is the last day of June and it is the blessed Sabbath, a day for the body to rest, while the soul gathers new strength by waiting on the Lord in the ordinances of his grace. Read Bible, engaged in prayer. Flory and I went to Union Church and Father with us. McDonald lectured in morning, I preached in evening from Jno 14.27. Called to see Mrs. Moffatt, one of my best friends.

Monday, July 1, 1861

Another month has begun its course. Many will be its changes. Who knows what will take place, O that peace would be restored to the different parts of the country & nations learn war no more. Read the Scriptures and went up to the P.O., read papers. Received letter from Bro. McElwee. Glad to hear from him. Mr. Poag & I called [on] the Ladies at Mr. Melton's.

Tuesday, July 2, 1861[3]   — *Saw a magnificent comet tonight*

Our days are like the grass, and we soon fly, hence are no more. Rose early. Read Bible &c. Took a nap, wrote letter to Bro. McElwee. Went up to P.O. Sent letter to Isaiah. Saw volunteers of Hampton's legion[4] pass up. Called on Mrs. Gaston. Went to Sing., took Mrs. Melton & Virgie. Attended lecture on China by Taylor D.D. of Col. from Dr. Wylie's.

Wednesday, July 3, 1861

I am growing old, one month more and I will be 27 years old. How have my days been spent? Too much in idleness. Rose late this morning. Read Bible &c. Wrote letter to Joe Moffatt, took it to the office. Work(ed) with spoke machine. Went to Sing. Rev. White was out for the first time.

Thursday, July 4, 1861

How excellent is thy loving kindness, O Lord, therefore the sons of men put their trust under the shadow of thy wings. Read Bible, engaged in secret prayer, O for more grace. Called at Mr. Brawley's. No one at home. Called at Mr. Hemphill's, fixed Mrs. H's sewing machine. Sung and played with Miss Mary Brawley. Went to Singing School.

Friday, July 5, 1861[5]

The time is short and so is life. O how happy are Christians when free from this troublesome world, then there will be no disappointed hopes and I will be full of joy. Read Bible &c. Fixed up and started for Due West. Got a new cloth coat from Carroll. Took train. Borrowed 5 dollars from Mr. Baird. Spent night in Col.

Saturday, July 6, 1861

Rose early, read Bible and engaged in secret prayer. Walked to Depot, bought two fine watermelons for Mr. Grier's children. Reached Donalds at 2 P.M., found Moffatt Grier with a buggy, reached Due West at 3 1/2 P.M. Glad to see my friends; my little *pets* have grown to be almost ladies. Met Sis & Pal Sharp in parlor.

Sunday, July 7, 1861

Sabbath has come again and once [more] my ears are greeted with the old familiar church bell. But my highly esteemed friend, E. E. Pressly, D.D., is no more; often have I sung for him. R. C. Grier, D.D., has taken his place and preached today. John Hemphill & W. Lindsay sung for him. The church looked very familiar. Eat melon with children.

Monday, July 8, 1861

Another day has dawned upon us again. Read Bible, engaged in communion with God. O for more of the spirit of prayer and supplication. Went down to the female college to hear the examination, was well pleased with exercises and the new building. Due West has received an additional ornament.

Tuesday, July 9, 1861

God's goodness never fails hence I am not consumed. May I not abuse the riches of God's goodness, forbearance and long suffering. Read his Word, the Gospel of Jesus &c. Went down to Examination again; well pleased. The ladies excel boys in their examination. Dined with Mrs. Kennedy, went up to church, sung with the girls. Took part in concert which was very good. I played guitar.

Wednesday, July 10, 1861[6]

Days are short to me. I should improve every moment as it flies. Read Bible &c. went down to church, met with Misses McMorris who played piano very sweetly. I played guitar for them, "Faded flowers" is a popular song. Went up [to] Dr. Archers, played it there for Miss Sallie McBryde, it made her weep. Called on Mrs. Lindsay & Misses Gallaway.

Thursday, July 11, 1861

A kind providence is favouring me at every step; my health is good, yet I often sin against my best Benefactor & friend. Visited Messers Young & Pressly, Patton and dined with Mr. Bonner. He had a dining party, many ladies were present. Visited Mr. Lee's, returned with Lucy Calvert. Went to prayer meeting.

Friday, July 12, 1861

The [time] has come for me to leave Due West again. I am always sorry to leave my dear friends. Read Bible &c. Moffatt Grier left home for the army. The family was filled with sorrow. Joe Moffatt & Moffatt Grier & I were taken to depot by Livie & J. L. H. Spent night in Columbia. Saw the Soldiers from Va march. Read Psalm aloud &c.

Saturday, July 13, 1861

Rose early in good health. Read Bible, walked to Depot, went with some of Blues &c on their way to Va via Chester. I looked for Isaiah but he did not come up. I took a notion to go with the Company. Reached home at 12. Went up town, talked to Revs. White and Ranks [or Banks] and Mr. Harris. Bought some cloth for shirts. Budded some peaches and took some honey.

Sunday, July 14, 1861

Time rolls on rapidly, another holy Sabbath has dawned upon the earth. O that the land could enjoy peace & rest from war. I never spent a Sabbath in travelling before. Moffatt Grier, Rob Hemphill went to camp. Fixed up and went down to Summerville Camp to see the Soldiers before they left for Va. Reached camp at 9 o'clock P.M.

Monday, July 15, 1861

July is half gone and my life is drawing to a close. Rose early, at the roll of the drum, something new in my life. Eat breakfast with Isaiah in camp. Took the cars for Charleston at 7 A. M. Arrived at 9 A.M. Walked to hotel, then to Music Store. Moffatt Grier & I went down to see the ocean for the first time. It filled me with wonder and love. We walk[ed] all about the Sea shore, Beautiful Sea! Murmur Sea! I love thee. Returned to Camp 6 P.M. and set out for home 9.

Tuesday, July 16, 1861[7]

Reached Columbia at 5 A.M. Bought a pair of dog skin gloves. Went to depot, eat breakfast. Set out for Chester; arrived at noon. Glad to get home. O that the war was ended and all could return home. The 6th Reg. left Camp today for Va. Felt wearied, took a sleep, much refreshed. Wrote diary.

Wednesday, July 17, 1861

Time is on the wing, the turbid dream of life is waning. Read Bible, etc. Joe Moffatt came up to take cars for Col. to meet Jno. Hemphill with his gun from Due West. Went up town, called at Mr. Brawley's, ladies not at home. Called at Mr. Hemphill's to see Mrs. Moffatt. Belle H. played for me.

Thursday, July 18, 1861[8]

Rose early this morning. Read Bible, etc. God is good and kind to me, unthankful, evil. Made arrangements to go to Va with Joe Moffatt. Fixed up my outfit for the Camp. O that God would calm the troubled waters and give us peace again. Went over to Mr. Melton's etc.

Friday, July 19, 1861

The month is rapidly passing away. Oh that peace and harmony would return to this land. God have mercy upon us. Rose early. Read Bible &c. Went up town. Called on Mr. Brawley's family and Mr. Alexander's — sorry to tell the girls farewell. Took leave of the loved ones at home. Miss Virgie Melton gave me some geranium leaves. Reached Charlotte at 3 P.M. Glad to see Miss Laura Kerr. Took cars for Raleigh at 10 P.M.

Saturday, July 20, 1861

Rode all night on the cars. Slept but little. Travelled all day, heavy rain. Reached Weldon at 1 P.M. Lay over 10 hours, very wearisome. Left Weldon at 11 P.M. with a Reg. from Fla. Two of them were killed near Wel[don]. Travelled all night. Oh for nature's sweet restorer![9] Oh that God would give us peace again.

Sunday, July 21, 1861[10]

The holy Sabbath has come again but it has not the appearance of the Sabbath. I hear no church bell. Wickedness abounds in our country. Sabbath breaking and profanity and drunkness prevail to a mournful extent. Arrived at Petersburg at 5 A.M. Left Petersburg at 5 A.M.,[?] reached Richmond at 12. Put up at American hotel. Walked to Square, lay on the grass. Tried to find preaching [service]. Held prayers in room at night.

Monday, July 22, 1861

Rose early and in good health, thanks to God for his kindness to such an unworthy creature as I am. Left hotel in heavy rain, went to Depot at 7 o'clock, waited on train for 4 hours. Went on train with an Ala. Reg. Oh that the war would close. Travelled all day and night. Slept very little. Oh for rest.

Tuesday, July 23, 1861

Reached Manassas Junction at 6 A.M. God has preserved me from all danger on the way. Saw thousands of Soldiers from all parts of the South. Met with Rev. Bryson & Joe Polhill. Saw the prisoners taken by Southern troops on last Sabbath and Sherman's battery taken from the North. Oh that the war would end. Met with Isaiah &c.

Wednesday, July 24, 1861

Man is a dependent being, he is also an undeserving being, hence, he should be a very humble being. But alas, I am proud and ungrateful. Camp life is one of privation. Oh for peace! Saw a battlefield in all its horrors. Moffatt Grier, Isaiah & I saw men lying here & there crumbling into dust. Man is made of dust and will return to dust.

Thursday, July 25, 1861

A vast amount of labor, time, and talent is lost on account of the war. Oh for deliverance from such a curse. God have mercy upon us. Thou art our only hope. Took a walk with Moffatt and Joe, my bosom friends. Camp life is a dull place. There is no place like home, sweet home.

Friday, July 26, 1861

Time is carrying us on to eternity — where shall I spend its endless cycles? There is no pleasure or peace in this world. I long for a happier state of existence where my Savior dwells. Read Bible this morning. Camp is unfit for religious duties. May God put a stop to the war.

Saturday, July 27, 1861

Man's days are like a shadow which swiftly passes. My life is very unprofitable and it is of the Lord's mercy that I have not [been] cut off as a cumberer of the ground. Moffatt & Joe and I took a walk as we often have done in Due West, a place dear to me. Tomorrow is the holy Sabbath.

Sunday, July 28, 1861

The Lord has preserved my life and permitted me to see His Holy day. Oh that I could spend the day as it should be spent. Took a walk with Joe Moffatt. The Reg. struck tents & took up a line of march for 8 miles, passed through Centreville; wet by heavy rain. Very tired. Isaiah & I spent night with Sam Barron in Jenkins' Regiment.

Monday, July 29, 1861

Life is a checkered scene, full of care and trouble but there is a better land whose shores I long to reach. May I not set my affections on earthly things. May Jesus be my darling and chief delight. Called on Rev. Bryson. Returned to 6th Reg, fixed up tent. Thankful for health. Wrote letter home; there is no place like home, the dearest spot on earth to me.

Tuesday, July 30, 1861

Time flies, life is but a strife, tis a bubble, tis a dream, and man is a little boat just paddling down the stream. I will soon reach the changeless shore, where joy forever reigns. Read Bible, had prayer at Capt. White's tent. Soldiers need the prayers of a Christian. May God preserve their bodies & souls from suffering and death. Called on W. W. East in 5th Reg; talked with Bryson.

Wednesday, July 31, 1861

This is the last day of July — farewell thou month of fruit and melons. May the God of heaven bless the land with peace before another month rolls away. May he say to the troubled waters, peace be still. Read Bible. Moffatt and Joe and I had private meeting in the woods. Oh what a delightful privilege to join my friends in prayer when far from home. Went with Bryson to Kinchelow's and spent the night.

Thursday, August 1, 1861

Another month has commenced its round, Oh may peace smile upon the land ere it comes to a close. God grant that it may be so. Read Bible and engaged in secret prayer. Played piano. O Music! thou hast power to awaken the deepest emotions of my soul; by thee fond recollections and the sweetest pleasures are brought to mind! Bryson left for Fredericksburg after dinner. I returned to camp with cornbread and ham.

Friday, August 2, 1861[11]

My days are passing away. I am growing old; my life is very unprofitable. Oh that I was more diligent in serving my Master. May he cut me down as a cumberer of the ground. God is good to me. Health is a blessing but my sins have brought sickness upon me. May his mercy return to me. Camp life is not like home, sweet home.

Saturday, August 3, 1861

My days are rolling on and I am approaching the confines of eternity. This is my birthday. God has lengthened out my life another year. I am 27 years old. May God preserve my life another year.

Read Bible; Moffatt, Joe & I had prayer in the woods. There we have our Bethel. Joe & (I) took dinner at Kinchelow's, 1 mile from camp. R. R. Hemphill came to our camp; glad to see him!

Sabbath, August 4, 1861

The holy Sabbath has come once more. Oh that I was so situated that I could spend its sacred hours in a profitable manner. Read Bible. Moffatt, Joe and I retired for prayer in the woods. We have a delightful Bethel. God is everywhere present. Went with Joe to Sloan's Reg. to hear Rev. Craig preach. I was somewhat disappointed. Joe treated me with some sweet cakes. I did spend the Sabbath, visited some tents &c.

Monday, August 5, 1861

Oh that I could let my light shine that others may see my good works and glorify God. But my days are spent in folly and sin. Lord, by thy grace I will live more in conformity to thy will. Rose in good health. Joe, Moffatt Grier & I retired to our Bethel, a place of prayer in the silent woods. Walked with Joe & R.R. Hemphill to Centreville. Robt & I bought some bread and milk. Joe & Robert left for their homes. Joe is tired of camp life. Home is better to anyone.

Tuesday, August 6, 1861

God's mercy never fails, hence I am not consumed. If I am not a soldier of Jeff Davis I hope I am a soldier of Christ and have on the whole armour of God. Moffatt & I retired to our Bethel in the woods, northwest of Camp Pettus. There we have sweet communion with God, may our prayers be answered. I went out to Kincelow's for buttermilk. Had my hair shaved very closely. Short hair is necessary in camp.

Wednesday, August 7, 1861

When this life of trouble, toil, war and commotion is ended, then by the grace of God I will be free to enjoy the peace and tranquility of a better world. Rose in good health. Moffatt and I resorted to our Bethel, read 12th chapter of Matt. and in turns engaged in prayer. Oh what a blessed privilege! Wrote letter to Rev. Wm M. McElwee. Oh that war would cease. Conducted prayer meeting in C. Blues.

Thursday, August 8, 1861

The days pass swiftly on — man's life is but a shadow. Why complain of its troubles and difficulties, they will soon be over. Rose early, camp life required it. Took a walk with L. Gaston. Listened to a funeral dirge. One soldier in Jenkins' Reg.[12] died last night. O take me home to die! Went to my Bethel and engaged in prayer. I long to be at home.

Friday, August 9, 1861

The month is rolling away like a stream. Rose early but not in very good health. Had an attack of dysentery. I deserve not the mercies God bestows on me. There is nothing new in camp life. John Hemphill came into camp this morning, glad to see him. Received letter from home [Sister Sarah]; good news from home. Took a walk with John Hemphill.

Saturday, August 10, 1861

Third Brigade went to Centreville to see Prince Napoleon.
God in mercy has prolonged my unprofitable life. I deserve nothing but God is crowning me with his mercies. What an ungrateful creature I am. Took a walk with Moffatt to our place of prayer. We have built our Ebenezer. May God hear our prayers. Wrote a letter to Livy Grier. Took a walk with J.L.H.

Sunday, August 11, 1861

The Sabbath has come again. Oh that the land could enjoy the day of rest. May peace once more return to us. Took a walk. Moffatt had to prepare for Inspection drill. Studied sermon. Heard the chaplain preach. Rain prevented me from preaching in the evening. Reg. prepared to march. The Sabbath is too much profaned in the Camp.

Monday, August 12, 1861

Rose in good health, thanks to God for his kindness and love to me. Camp is no place for religious exercises. The soldier has to commune with his God in the midst of talk and confusion. Reg. struck tents & marched 6 miles to Germantown.[13] Heavy rain, very muddy march. Had to lie on the cold wet ground. Moffatt stood on picket Guard for the first time.

Tuesday, August 13, 1861

My health is still preserved. How excellent is thy loving kindness Oh God. Our camp ground is low and muddy; lay down on leaves for a bed. Heavy rains very unpleasant and cool. May God put a stop to the war and say, peace be still. Hear my prayers, Oh God, I am poor and needy.

Wednesday, August 14, 1861

Time is on the march and I am hastening on to my final destiny.
"One thing I of the Lord desired
and will seek to obtain,
That all the days of my life I may
within God's house remain."
Rose in good health. Read Bible, heard heavy firing. Took a walk with Moffatt Grier in the morning. Walked with Isaiah and John Hemphill to see the ruins of Germantown. Oh that wars would cease.

Thursday, August 15, 1861

The month is half gone, time is on the wing and life will soon be gone, how diligent man should be! I must give an account of the deeds done in the body. Rose with a slight cold. Went after damsons. John Hemphill left for Due West, S.C. I wanted to go with him. Nothing new in camp. Oh that we all were permitted to go home. God grant us peace once more.

Friday, August 16, 1861

There is no place like home. This Camp is enough to cause one to love a home ever so homely. Rose with a pain in my head. May God give me health while far from home. Took a walk. Engaged in prayer. Felt badly. Heard from Due West through Moffatt Grier. Took walk with Charles Brice who advised me to go home. Very wet and rainy still.

Saturday, August 17, 1861

Man is a selfish creature and his heart is full of envy. The carnal mind is enmity against God, is not subject to the law of God and neither indeed can be. May the Holy Spirit influence me to follow the path of truth and safety. Not well this morning, rain and very disagreeable; took a walk & bought one-half bushel irish potatoes, $1.00. Read some, visited the sick. Oh, home sweet home.

Sunday, August 18, 1861

The Sabbath has come once more but I have no opportunity to spend the day in a proper manner. Rose in delicate health. Read Bible, called on the sick, talked with the chaplain, got some books from him. The Camp is no place to spend the Sabbath. There is no sanctuary, no family altar! O how I love the house of God.

Monday, August 19, 1861

The time is passing away, life will soon be gone like a shadow. I am an unprofitable Servant. Rose in good health, took a walk, wished for home. Oh that God would send us peace. Regiment moved to a new camp. Carried our tents &c. Read Bible. May the spirit guide me in the path of wisdom.

Tuesday, August 20, 1861   — *clear moonlight*

My heart is full of all uncleanness; the heart is deceitful above all things and desperately wicked. Rose in good health but I deserve not the mercies of God. Took a walk with Brice towards Fairfax; he advised me to go home. O that all could go home and peace was made over all the land. Walked with Moffatt & Robt. Hemphill.

Wednesday, August 21, 1861

Life is frail. Man's days are but few. Eternity is long. May my home be in heaven. Read Bible. Took a walk. Visited the sick, had prayers with the sick. Talked with Pink Crawford who was very low and died at 11 P.M. Heard newspapers read. O that our enemies would make peace with us.

Thursday, August 22, 1861

The month is waning away & thus is my life. Rose early this morning. Went to see Crawford. Prepared to take his remains to Chester, S.C. Isaiah left for Manassas to get discharged. Talked a long time with Moffatt [Grier]. Left camp near Germantown, Va., for Manassas with corpse of Crawford.

Friday, August 23, 1861

Had a lonely ride last night; reached Beauregard's headquarters at sunrise. Met Isaiah at Manassas. Received transportation papers for myself and bodies of Crawford & Robinson. Isaiah and I walked out to battleground. Very tired. Slept in a boxcar.

Saturday, August 24, 1861

Rose early and prepared to leave for Richmond. Left at 1/4 to Seven A.M. in company with Robert Pagan. Reached Richmond at 4 P.M. Stopped at American Hotel. Walked round and received transportation. Very weary. Worn out.

Sunday, August 25, 1861

The Sabbath has come again but O how I desecrate the holy day. Walked round with one Morris of N.C. to see the corpse at depot. Saw Cadets[14] drilling, eat a watermelon, went to depot; left for Petersburg at 3 o'clock P.M., Weldon 8 P.M.

Monday, August 26, 1861

Rose before sunrise. Eat breakfast. Sent dispatch to Chester and Winnsboro. Left Weldon at 11 A.M. Arrived at Raleigh at 5 P.M. Took train for Charlotte, traveled all night. O that the land enjoyed peace. May God have mercy upon us.

Tuesday, August 27, 1861

Reached Charlotte in safety at 2 this morning, left for Chester at 6 A.M. Arrived at 9 A.M. and delivered my sad charge to Robt. Crawford, Brother of the deceased. Went up home, spoke to friends &c and went with Robt. Crawford to Waxaw Church. Filled with grief to see his mother; it was mournful. Went to Nealy's with others.

Wednesday, August 28, 1861

Slept very soundly last night & was refreshed, have a slight cold caught in Camp. Had prayers with the family. Set out for Cedar Shoals, rode in carriage with Miss Ingram and Miss Barber, took a check at Rivers. Met some soldiers and friends at Stenson's. Stopped at Messrs. Crawfords, eat watermelon. Chalmers Gaston took me to his father's & spent night.

Thursday, August 29, 1861

God in his goodness is still preserving my unprofitable life. I am a monument to his patience and loving kindness. Rose late, had prayers with the family. Set out on horseback for home. Called on John Wylie, Uncle John Fennell's; eat dinner at Aunt Linda Martin's. Called at Fudge's, Mrs. Moffatt's and Poag's out of rain. Reached home at dusk.

Friday, August 30, 1861

Rose with a dullness in my head. Innumerable evils have compassed me about, mine iniquities have taken hold on me. Therefore, make haste O Lord to deliver me, forsake me not O my God. Visited Mrs. Brawley. Mrs. Gaston introduced [me] to Miss Gidson. Sat depot and store. Eat supper at Mr. Baird's.

Saturday, August 31, 1861

Oh how swiftly the month has passed away. Why mourn over the evils of this short life? The period is drawing nigh when trouble and war will never be known. O that will be joyful. Felt dull and stupid all day. May God return unto me with health and strength. Took medicine all day.

Sunday, September 1, 1861

Another month has dawned with the light of the glorious Sabbath morn. But I am unable to go to the house of God. Oh what a privilege it is to worship God at home. Read the Scriptures and engaged in secret prayer, the door to God's store house. Lay in parlor all day, felt dull, took medicine.

Monday, September 2, 1861

Still my head is heavy and dizzy. May God check the disease and restore me to health once more; may my life be preserved that I might show forth his glory. Engaged in secret prayer and walked down to depot. Heard sad news from Camp — the death of Isaac Gaston. O that the war would come to an end.

Tuesday, September 3, 1861

Our land is in mourning on account of the direful curse "war". Oh God return to our land and restore peace to our land. Influence our enemies to be at peace with us, that our friends and relations may return to their homes in life, peace and victory. Oh God say to the waters "peace be still".

Wednesday, September 4, 1861

Oh what a blessing is health! I have been unwell for several days. My sins have provoked the Lord, and He is visiting in judgment. Dr. Ready called to see if I could fix a sewing machine for Mrs. Raney. Lingered about all ..?.. O that war would come to an end!

Thursday, September 5, 1861

Time is flying away almost imperceptibly. I should improve each moment as it flies. Still unwell and taking medicine; no one appreciates health aright until he is confined to a bed of sickness then he knows what it is to enjoy health. O that war would cease.

Friday, September 6, 1861

Still unwell, troubled with pain in my head. Yet God is good to me, "All things work together for good to them that love God, to them that are the called according to His purpose." Lay on sopha & read some, played violin, and I brought to mind many happy days gone never to return!

Saturday, September 7, 1861

The week is drawing to [a] close. Man's days are like the grass, he soon passes away. Oh that I could improve my time. But I am unprofitable servant. Still unwell, with dullness in the head. John

Walker called to see if I could preach tomorrow at Purity. Oh that I was able in mind and body to preach the gospel of Christ.

Sunday, September 8, 1861

The blessed Sabbath has come once more; it is a great privilege to be permitted to spend the Holy day in quiet at home or in the house of God. It is the will of God that I should remain at home. I am still unwell. Oh that I was able to serve my master better. May He permit [me] yet to remain longer in his vineyard.

Monday, September 9, 1861

Time is rapidly passing away, the year is drawing to a close & it will be a year of great events. May I live to see the end of the present troubles. Went to bed with the typhoid fever & began to take medicine. Oh the bed is a luxury in health but it is full of tossing in sickness.

Tuesday, September 10, 1861[15]

Still confined to bed. I long to be well once more. I will endeavor not to abuse the mercies I have so long enjoyed. Took medicine all day. Mr. Baird came up and talked a while about the war. Oh that peace was made!

Wednesday, September 11, 1861

It is wearisome to be in all the day. But I am thankful that I am not troubled with severe pains. Regard my sickness as very light, it is not what I deserve. Thankful that I am at home! Want to die at home if it is God's will.

Thursday, September 12, 1861

No one knows how tiresome it is to lie in bed all day and spend sleepless night but those who have been so unfortunate as to experience it. Fever is not very high, still taking medicine. Mr. Baird called at evening. Oh that the land enjoyed peace. Rev. Brice called this morning.

Friday, September 13, 1861

The week is drawing to a close, time never stops its onward march. Still in bed but may I not murmur or complain at the dispensations of God. Fever not high & not great pain. Thankful I am no worse. May God have mercy on me. Mr. Baird called at even. R. R. Hemphill called to see me. Glad to see him.

Saturday, September 14, 1861

The last day of the week has come, how swiftly time doth pass. Not able to be out of bed. Fever not high. Father went down to Fishing Creek. Still taking medicine. O that I was well once more. Sister and Mr. Baird called. May the war soon come to an end.

Sunday, September 15, 1861

The Sabbath has come again and I am still confined to bed, but spent the day in reading Bible and religious books as much as I was able. Fever not very high, free from great pain. God is good to me in my sickness, Oh that I was more zealous in good [works]. May peace soon return to our land.

Monday, September 16, 1861

The month is half gone. O how swiftly the time passes away. The time is short and vain is all earthly things, "there is nothing true but heaven". Still confined to the bed. Long to be well again. But I should not complain, my sickness is light. God is kind to me although I am unthankful and evil.

Tuesday, September 17, 1861

Oh that men would praise the Lord for his goodness and for his wonderful works to the children of men. Still confined to bed. Sister Mary and Emaline came up and spent the night. Mr. Harris called in evening. Oh for health, and peace once more. May God grant my request.

Wednesday, September 18, 1861

The month is drawing to a close and life is passing away. There will be no sickness in that better land, and no fevers will burn our brows. Oh that will be joyful. Still confined to bed. Sister Mary left for home. Ran Poag called to see me & Mr. Baird & A. McNinch.

Thursday, September 19, 1861

Although confined to bed time passes. Read the Bible, the only book for the sick, there they can find comfort in their affliction. Still in bed but gaining strength. Wm & Mag and Mr. Baird and Sarah called to see me. Began to read McCrie's Life of Knox. I am not well read in church history.

Friday, September 20, 1861

Man should never complain, God often afflicts his people to try their faith. May I submit to all his ways. Read the Bible, O that I was of quick understanding in the fear of God. Grant me thy Holy Spirit to guide and teach me into all truth. Mr. Baird called & talked about the wars.

Saturday, September 21, 1861

It is wearisome to be confined to bed for weeks but this is God's will concerning me and I should submit and murmur not. The week has come to a close. Read Bible and Life of John Knox. Ran Poag called. Oh that peace would return to our land. God hear the prayer made to thee.

Sunday, September 22, 1861

The holy Sabbath has dawned again. It is a blessed privilege to worship the living God. This day the Saints assemble to praise God. May many sinners be converted this day and find Jesus precious unto their souls. Mr. Baird and Sarah, William & Mag called to see [me]. Father went to Methodist Church. I read Bible and Owen on the Spirit.

Monday, September 23, 1861

The Sabbath has gone and man is again engaged in his secular employments. But the heart is too much set on earthly things. Oh that I was like a weaned child. Read Bible and Life of John Knox. Mr. McDonald called and dined. James Hamilton also called to see [me]. Thus ends the day.

Tuesday, September 24, 1861

Health is returning to me again; thanks to God for his great kindness & love shown to me. Yet I am confined to the house I have not been on the ground for nearly 3 weeks. Read the Old & New Testaments in morning. Read life of John Knox. Felt rather dull today, eat too much.

Wednesday, September 25, 1861

The month will soon [be gone]. I have been confined to the house nearly one month. Hope to [be] out in a few days if I do not relapse through intemperance in eating; eat too much supper. Read Bible and Life of John Knox. Oh for more wisdom and spiritual understanding. May peace soon return to our land.

Thursday, September 26, 1861[16]

A kind Providence has preserved my unprofitable life another day and although weak, my strength is increasing. Thanks to God for his great kindness. Rose at 7 and communed with God. Read his blessed Word. Read some of the Life of John Knox. Oh for more of the Spirit of my divine Master.

Friday, September 27, 1861

Very feeble yet God in love is restoring me to health and strength. May I not abuse his goodness. But how often do I forget his mercies! Rose about 7. Read the Scriptures. May the Holy Spirit enlighten me in the truth. Read the life of Knox before noon. Went to bed at 2 P.M. with slight fever. Intemperate in diet.

Notes

[1] Infantry, artillery, and cavalry units from all over the South were passing through South Carolina to the front lines in northern Virginia.

[2] At a cabinet meeting in Washington DC, the top officials of the Lincoln government decided on an initial war strategy making the Confederate army in Virginia the main target of the Union forces. A major battle in Virginia was now only a matter of time.

[3] Federal forces under Brigadier Robert Patterson cross the Potomac River into the Shenandoah Valley to hold Confederate forces away from the main Union objective, Manassas Junction.

[4] Wade Hampton, one of the richest men in South Carolina, paid for a unit called "Hampton's Legion," composed of a regiment of infantry, a battalion of cavalry, and a battery of artillery. They would soon be heavily engaged on Henry House Hill in the First Battle of Manassas.

[5] A battle occurs at Carthage, Missouri, in which Union forces are prevented from occupying southwest Missouri.

[6] Battle of Rich Mountain in what is now West Virginia results in the first major victory of the war for the north, and pushes Confederate force back toward the Shenandoah Valley.

[7] The Union army of General Irvin McDowell, consisting of 35,000 men march from Washington to attack the Confederate army of 22,000 men under General G.T. Beauregard at Manassas Junction.

[8] Battle of Blackburns Ford, on the Bull Run creek is the first real engagement between McDowell and Beauregard. The Union forces are prevented from crossing the Run.

[9] "Tired nature's sweet restorer, balmy sleep!" from "Night Thoughts" by Edw. Young 1683-1765.

[10] The First Battle of Bull Run results in a great Confederate victory, with the Union army being routed back to Washington. Union losses total almost 3,000. Confederate losses are almost 2,000.

[11] The Federal Congress authorizes the first national income tax to pay for the rising cost of the war.

[12] Colonel Micah Jenkin's commanded the 5th South Carolina Infantry.

[13] Germantown is the intersection of the Warrenton Turnpike and the Winchester road just outside Fairfax Courthouse. The small "town" was burned in the summer of 1861.

[14] The cadets of the Virginia Military Institute were called to Richmond to drill the newly arrived citizen soldiers of the south.

[15] Battle of Carnifax Ferry in what is now West Virginia results in another defeat for the south and a loss of more territory of the state of Virginia.

[16] A day of Fasting and Prayer in the North to support the troops away at war.

Chapter 4

"STAY THE CRUEL WAR"

In the fall of 1861, John H. Simpson tried to regain his health from the disease he contracted in the camps in Virginia. He remained at home in South Carolina, paying close attention to the events of the war, preaching sermons when he could as well as instructing the children at the local academy. Just as today, the duties of a school teacher are many and varied as evidenced by the entries in his diary.

As more and more of his friends and neighbors went off to war, Simpson deplored the continuation of hostilities, particularly as the first casualty lists came home to Chester, South Carolina. He saw the men off to war on the trains, and observed the passing of other units north to the front in Virginia. What seemed at first to be a short conflict now promised to be a long and bloody struggle for Southern independence. With Union troops landing on South Carolina soil in November, the war seemed ever so close to Simpson and his home in Chester.

Saturday, September 28, 1861

Another week has passed away yet a kind Providence has preserved my unprofitable life. Still gaining strength. O the goodness of God how great. Read Bible and life of John Knox. Read *Telescope* which is a welcome visitor. May my health & life be preserved another week.

Sunday, September 29, 1861

The holy Sabbath has come, the day during which God's people assemble to worship in His Sanctuary below. But O what joy there will be when all the children of God will meet in the courts above! Read Bible. But O I lack wisdom! May the Holy Spirit teach me.

Monday, September 30, 1861

Another month closes today. How rapidly time flies away. My days are running out, life is very short. May I be more industrious and improve each moment as it flies. Read Bible and Lewis Cornaro. On ground for the first [time] in 3 weeks. Cousin Tho. Simpson dined with us. Helped to can tomatoes. Elihu came up, all went to Manardey's lectures. Sat up til 10.

Tuesday, October 1, 1861

Another month begins its round today, months begin to appear like weeks. The time is short. Rose with increased strength, thanks to God for his goodness. Read Bible; put up tomatoes and worked with muskydine wine. Wrote letter to Betts.

Wednesday, October 2, 1861

Time is on the march and I must improve every moment. Rose with renewed strength. Praise to God for his great goodness. Read Bible; I lack wisdom! Greased my shoes, walked out; heavy rain all day. Mr. McDonald dined with us. Wrote letter to James Lowry. Played violin.

Thursday, October 3, 1861

In the good providence of God my life is prolonged another day, health is returning but I abuse the mercies of God. Read the Word of God. Played the violin. Mrs. Melton sent me some apples, roasted two. Walked down to Mr. Baird's. Worked on my hat. O for more wisdom.

Friday, October 4, 1861

Rose with renewed health. God is good to his unworthy creatures. Read Bible, man's only guide & source of comfort in this world. Played piano and violin. Walked down to the Shop & Poag's Store, bought binding for hat and essence of mint. Stopped at Baird's. Great number in town to see a negro hung [Catawba]. Played violin. Went to Elimy to sew my hat. Called at Sister's; eat too much today.

Saturday, October 5, 1861

In the kind providence of an all wise Creator, I am raised up to see a new day. Read the Scriptures. Played violin and piano. Read Seneca's *Morals*. Studied philosophy. Read *Telescope*, a welcome visitor. Walked over to Mrs Melton's, talked with Mrs. M. & Miss Liza Alexander. Baird called. Sharpened father's razor.

Sunday, October 6, 1861

The Lord's Day is a sacred day, the best of all the week; but it is too often profaned by idleness and worldly thoughts. Oh that I could think of nothing but Jesus and his great love for sinners. Read Bible, but it is a sealed book without the Spirit. Read Dick's Theo[logy] &c. Father, Baird & Sister went to Hopewell. Had worship.

Monday, October 7, 1861

Rose in general health; a kind Providence is watching over me night and day. My former strength is returning. Read Bible. Rode in buggy down to Rev Brice's. Saw his new-born babe. Spent day pleasantly; looked at his new house. He gave me $100.00 for preaching. Returned home in the rain, somewhat tired.

Tuesday, October 8, 1861

A kind Providence is still my daily guide, protector and benefactor. Yet I am ungrateful, often forget to whom I owe all my good things, worshiping the creature more than the Creator. Read Bible, engaged in prayer. Walked up town. Harris gave me $100.00. Watch mended. Bought medicine for mother. Saw Mrs. Jane Crawford & Robert C. & wife & Miss Ingram. Gave father $50.00. Mrs. Melton called.

Wednesday, October 9, 1861

Man is an ungrateful being. I live at expense of a being not Providence, yet I forget the hand that bestows the blessing. Rose early, read Bible. Rode up to Dr. Ready's to fix sewing machine. Dined with Mrs. Ready, played violin and guitar. Father went up to York. Mother is unwell; waited on her.

Chester Academy, Chester, South Carolina where Rev. John Hemphill Simpson taught.

Thursday, October 10, 1861

The month is rolling away, every day brings me nearer to the grave; how important is it then to "be doing while it is called today." Rose in general health, though weak. Went up to Academy. Rode over to Dr. Ready's to finish machine. Returned my shoes to McNinch because made of old leather.

Friday, October 11, 1861

My days are like the grass; how thoughtless am I of my latter end. O Lord, pardon my abuse of mercies and privileges. Read Bible. Went up to Academy morning & evening. Waited on my dear mother who is sick. Played violin.

Saturday, October 12, 1861

Time is rolling away, this has been a short day. Rose early. Read Bible. Went down to Mr. Baird's for his textbooks. Read Homer for the time (135 lines) and read Horace's 3 Odes. Bought a winter coat from Poag, $6.00. Stopped at Sister's.

Sunday, October 13, 1861

The Holy Sabbath has come once more. O that I was zealous in my Master's work. Rose too late. Read Bible, engaged in secret prayer. Very much surprised and rejoice to meet with Bro. McElwee [of Va] who came on train. He spent the day, preached in evening from Is. 26.3 & 4 vs. Sister Mary and John came up.

Monday, October 14, 1861

Oh how rapidly the month is passing away! Rose early. Took a walk with Brother McElwee, a dear friend to me. Went to depot, bid him farewell. Went up town. Bought sugar for bees. Sister went home. I took charge of Mr. Baird's school in evening, an arduous task; may I be successful. Read Latin and Greek.

Tuesday, October 15, 1861

A kind Providence is extended to me every day. Rose early. Read Bible, prepared for school. Fed bees. Great patience is necessary in teaching the young. Went to funeral of Ben Scaife [a brave soldier]. Came home to dine, fed bees. Returned to School. Read Latin & Greek. Retired 11.

Wednesday, October 16, 1861

This life is a life of toil and trouble. Rose early, Father absent in York. Had worship, fed bees, prepared for School, a laborious work. Came home to dine. Flora came up. Returned to school room. Eat supper at Mr. Baird's. Wm Cherry and brother came up. Read Latin & Greek. Retired 11.

Thursday, October 17, 1861

Rose early. Elihu came up at daylight. Heavy rain all day. The Chester Greys [J. J. McClure's Company] . . . Mr. Baird left with the Company as orderly sergeant.[1] Sister was overcome with sorrow. Saw the train leave. Went to school. Stayed with Sister Sarah. Read Latin & Greek.

Friday, October 18, 1861

Rose in general health. Had worship. Reviewed Greek, went to school; very much fatigued. I would rather be a soldier than teach idle children. Went up home for dinner. James Lyles dined, Played violin. Returned to Sister's. Aunt Liza spent night with us. 10 1/2.

Saturday, October 19, 1861

The month will soon be gone. How fleeting is the life of man. Rose early and in general health. Went up home. Mrs. Rainey sent for me to see her sewing machine. Had a pleasant time and a nice dinner. Returned home to Sister Sarah's at dark. Talked with Isaiah & Flora. Read Latin and Greek.

Sunday, October 20, 1861

The holy Sabbath has come again. Oh that I could rightly appreciate so great a blessing. Rose too late. Went up home. Flora and Isaiah went to church, rain prevented Father and Aunt Liza from going. Felt unwell, read and studied the Scriptures, to bed 10. Heavy rain at night.

Monday, October 21, 1861

The quiet Sabbath is gone and men are busy at their worldly interests. Would they were so anxious about their spiritual welfare. Went to School room, a wearisome place to anyone. Went up town. Bought apples. Read Greek &c. Commenced letter to Joe Moffatt. 11.

Tuesday, October 22, 1861

The day is gone and night has covered earth in darkness. I seat myself to record its deeds. Rose early with severe pain in the back. Read Bible. Studied lessons, to school &c. Bought peck of apples for Sarah. Read lessons, played violin. Finished letter to Joe Moffatt. Retired at 11.

Wednesday, October 23, 1861

How rapidly time passes away. Life is very short. Rose early this morning with pain in the back. Sent 30 dol's to Joe Moffatt by mail. Went to school room. Heard of another victory at Leesburg.[2] Oh that the war would end. Studied lessons, very weak; to bed at 11.

Thursday, October 24, 1861

God is good to me although I am unthankful and evil, his mercy never fails. Rose in general health. Went to school. Happy to meet Rev. W. R. Hemphill at depot.[3] He reminded me of happy days gone forever. Took tea with Mrs. James H. Stopped in depot, played guitar with Dr. Pride and Breniker. Read Greek, to bed at 11.

Friday, October 25, 1861

Henry Breniker[?] never spoke to Mr. H. until morn. God's mercies never fail hence I am not consumed. I am an unworthy creature. Rose early. Studied lesson, went up home. Took dinner to school, dismissed at 2 P.M. Rev. W.R. Hemphill & I went down to Mrs. Moffatt's. Held worship. Had pain in back. Talked a long time in room with Mr. H. I am glad to meet with such good men.

Saturday, October 26, 1861

Rose late. Slept with M H for first time. Eat breakfast. Henry never made his appearance. Went down to Uncle John Fennell's, took him to church. Walked through the grave yard, the 'city of the dead'. Mr. H. preached from Mark 2.17. Went to Sister Mary's with Sister. Fixed buggy, talked &c.

Sunday, October 27, 1861

The holy Sabbath has come again and I am privileged to enjoy the means of grace. Oh that I could use them aright. Rose late, read Bible &c, prepared for church. Mr. Hemphill preached from ... Stopped at Mrs. Moffatt's with father. Set out for home. Shaft broke, late getting home. Read *Telescope*, to bed at 9.

Monday, October 28, 1861

Time is rolling on, the month is waning. Rose late. Slept but little on account of pain in back. Prepared for school. Came home for dinner. Came by depot. James Hamilton spent night with us.

We went down to depot to play guitar with Brenicker on violin. Fixed my pen. 11.

Tuesday, October 29, 1861

Rose at 6 o'clock, a merciful God has kept me through the night. May I spend my life in devotedness to his service. Held worship, fixed my pen. No school today being Court Day. Went to Shop & then to Court H, heard Brooks tried for kill[ing] Gaston, was acquitted. Made some candles. N. Wylie & Uncle Jno Wylie dined with us. Read Greek lesson. Wrote letter to Walsh in camp. Retired.

Wednesday, October 30, 1861

Rose late, felt very weak and full of pains. May God afflict in love and correct in Mercy. Held worship and prepared for school. Scarcely able to walk at night. Read Greek lessons, very weary. Read Bible, retired early tonight, 9 1/2.

Thursday, October 31, 1861

Father dug his potatoes. This is the last day of October! How rapidly the time passes away. I am hastening to the grave, the house appointed for all the living. Rose at 6, had worship, read Horace, went to school. Scarcely able to walk. Received letter from Joe Moffatt. Did not study at night. Violin &c.

Friday, November 1, 1861

Another month has been ushered in. Months seem very short. Time flies rapidly. Life with all its pains & troubles will soon be gone. Rose late. Held worship. Read Horace, went to School. Heavy rain all day & night, did not go to school in evening; too weak to walk. Worked on staff.

Saturday, November 2, 1861

Rose late this morning. Oh that I was free from pains but they are the wages of sin. Read Bible. Went up home to the Shop, worked on my Manassas walking stick. Helped mother to make some candles. Did nothing at night, to bed at 10.

Sunday, November 3, 1861

Another holy Sabbath has come. Oh that I was able to spend it as I should, viz., in preaching the glorious gospel. But my heart is too much on things of the world. Rose late, unable to go to Hopewell. Father & William & Isaiah went. Mr. Hemphill did all the preaching. Brice's family is sick.

Monday, November 4, 1861

God is long suffering and kind to such sinful creature as I am. Rose late. Had no school this week on account of my health. Oh that I could live more temperately and eat less than I do. Worked on my stick. Went down to depot to play guitar with Brenecker &c.

Tuesday, November 5, 1861

Time is rolling away rapidly. A few more years and life will be gone. How diligent should I be! Worked on walking stick. Went up town. Paid Carrol $30.00 for my coat. Went to depot at night to play. Mrs. Moffatt called at home but did not stay long.

Wednesday, November 6, 1861[4]

Rose early this morning. Held worship. Varnished my stick. Went up home, shaved, then up to the Bank. Mr. Hemphill was not there, went to Mrs. Gaston's, saw Mrs. Moffatt. She and Mr. H. left for Due West. I sent Belle Grier some music; sent Joe Moffatt flannel drawers & shirt. Went to Dr. Wylie to fix sewing machine. Went up home after tea. Called at depot. Began a letter to Mag Moffatt.

Thursday, November 7, 1861

Rose very late this morning. Sat up too late last night. Held worship. Wrote at Mag's letter. Worked on stick and Sister Sarah's bell. Went to Mrs. Hemphill's to fix her machine. Had singing at night. Wrote more letter. Called at Mr. McCormick's.

Friday, November 8, 1861

John Simpson brought Sallust for me. The month is rolling away. Rose in usual health. Held worship and read Bible. Went up town, bought some Muriatic acid to fix Mrs. Hemphill's machine. Waited on train. Saw Worthy's Reg. of Georgia's Vol. going to Va. Wrote at Mag Moffatt's letter &c, to bed at 11.

Saturday, November 9, 1861

Rose early this morning. Had severe pain in back & thigh. Held worship. Read Bible. Father came over and gave me the sad news of the Federals defeating us at Port Royal.[5] Never spent such an uneasy day in all my life. Finished my stick & Mrs. H's machine & a letter to Mag. Felt badly. May God not forsake us.

Sunday, November 10, 1861

The Lord has preserved me in life to spend another Sabbath. But my mind was too much engaged in the war which is going on in our once happy country. May God in mercy put a stop to the cruel war. Went up home and spent the day with Father and Mother. God forgive my sins.

Monday, November 11, 1861

God in his abounding love has preserved my life another day. Rose in better health than usual. Read Horace and went to school. Unfit to study on account of the war, O that it was ended. Called in evening to see Mrs. H's sewing machine. Read Homer & Xenophon at night.

Tuesday, November 12, 1861

Rose in good health, read Bible, held worship, prepared lessons for school. Went to Academy. O that the war was ended. May God have mercy upon us, we feel our dependence on Thee, O Lord. Studied Greek & Latin. Grier was sick at night. Played violin. Broke a chimney of lamp. Wrote letter to Joe Moffatt.

Wednesday, November 13, 1861

Time waits for none of us. We should all live in preparation for death. Rose in good health, except pains in legs. Read Bible and studied lesson, went to school. Played violin. Talked to Isaiah about going to the camp. May God bless our armies.

Thursday, November 14, 1861

Time rolls away like a stream. Life is but a shadow, it soon does pass away. Rose in good health. Prepared lessons for school, Bro. Isaiah said his last lesson in Sallust before going to Charleston. Oh that the war was ended. May God defend us. It is hard for me to teach school.

Friday, November 15, 1861

Wrote letter to Moffatt Grier at night. The month is half gone today. "The turbid stream of life is waning." This day has been set apart by the President of the Confederacy for fasting and prayer. May the people humble themselves in dust and ashes, O my Soul, mourn over thy Sins. Did not go to church, sore ankles. Stayed with father &c.

Saturday, November 16, 1861

Rose in good health. Read Bible. Ran 146 pistol bullets. Shot Mr. Baird's shotgun & loaded it with balls. Varnished my staff. Fixed Mrs. Melton's clock and father's. Played violin. Talked with Sister and Isaiah about the War. Father and Mr. Harris came down at 8 o'clock at night to get me to preach. Studied sermon until 12.

Sunday, November 17, 1861

The holy Sabbath has dawned again. Oh that I could spend the day aright. Rose in good health. Studied sermon. Preached for White from John 11:35 with some ease. Oh for more grace and wisdom. Elihu and family came up from Hopewell. Elihu is on his way to Charleston. God grant us peace.

Monday, November 18, 1861

A day long to be remembered. Rose in good health. Had worship. Studied lessons. Gave Elihu & Isaiah all my money $12,00[?] to go to the war on. Talked until 11 o'clock & came to depot to see Culp's Company leave for Charleston for the war.[6] Sorry to part with Elihu & many dear friends. May God protect their families & save us all. Received letter from Joe Moffatt. Read lessons, &e.

Tuesday, November 19, 1861

Time is very precious. We are responsible for every moment. O teach me to number my days that I may apply my heart to wisdom. Rose in good health. Prepared lessons for school. Wrote letter to Captain Strait about Joe Moffatt's gun.[7] Play violin &c.

Wednesday, November 20, 1861

In mercy God has preserved my life another day although I am an unprofitable servant. Rose early and in good health. Studied lesson and went to school. O that God would grant us peace. Went to depot at night to play with Breniker on violin.

Thursday, November 21, 1861

O how rapidly time flies; this day one year ago I crossed the Allegheny mountains, very cold & snow fell. My life has been spared another day. Rose in health. Went to schoolroom. Teaching idle children is laborious work. Dug pindars, eat them at night.

Friday, November 22, 1861

God in mercy is sparing my unprofitable life. Another week has gone & all my deeds are recorded for eternity. Oh God forgive my sins. Rose in health, held worship &c. Prepared for school. My mind is not fit to study. Oh that the war was ended. May God in mercy bring it to a close. Played violin and went to singing; rain prevented ladies coming out.

Saturday, November 23, 1861

The time is short. Life is fast running out. I am hurrying to the grave. Rose early and blessed with health. Read Bible &c. Went up home. Sister Sarah moves up home today. Carried violin & books &c up. Arranged "Faded Flowers" for piano for Belle Grier. Went up town, read Bible, talked of war. Sewed Palmetto on Isaiah's hat.[8]

Sunday, November 24, 1861

In mercy God has permitted me to see another Sabbath day. It is a precious privilege yet I do not improve it as I should.

May God grant me grace to spend the Sabbath aright. Held worship, read Bible. Went to Presbyterian Church, heard White preach. Read Boston's 4-fold State. Called at William's. Felt dull at night. Eat potatoes.

Monday, November 25, 1861

Just one month until Christmas. Time is passing away like a dream. Oh that peace was restored to our afflicted country. Rose early, studied lessons; went to Academy. To depot at 11 to see Bro. Isaiah leave for the war. May his life be preserved. Went home with Miss Alexander to Mrs. Melton's. Called on them at night.

Tuesday, November 26, 1861[9]

Another day has passed away. Rose in good health. Father was sick this morning, better in evening. Prepared lessons. Went to school. David Hemphill commenced Geometry. Mary Blanks came up. Worked on a glove, played violin, parched pindars; read lessons, retired at 11.

Wednesday, November 27, 1861

My life and health have been preserved another day. Rose early this morning, prepared lessons for school. Received dispatch that Henry Smith was dead & remains would be in Chester on tomorrow.[10] Sad news to his parents. Wrote letter to Mr. Baird. Father has a bad sore on his leg. Went up town &c.

Thursday, November 28, 1861

Rose in good health this morning. God has restored my health. May I be thankful and bless his name always. Prepared for school, read Greek & Latin; received letter from Joe Moffatt, one of my best friends, glad to hear from. Studied lessons at night. Went up town, bought another plaster for my back. O that the war was over.

Friday, November 29, 1861

My week's work is finished. My health has continued to improve. Prepared my usual lessons &c. Went up town from school to Singing at night but few out; had a pleasant time with the ladies, Bell Hemphill &c. Went home with Miss Char. Bradley.

Saturday, November 30, 1861

Another month has passed away. My unprofitable life has been spared, God is good to the unthankful and to the evil. Worked on stick for old Mr. Walker. Moved up some of Sister's things: clock, bureau &c. Played violin, went to P.O. Wrote letter to Rev. J. R. Castles; regulated clocks, read newspaper &c. O for peace.

Sunday, December 1, 1861

Chilly December has commenced its round, may God have mercy upon our Country and stay the cruel war. May He give me life, health & strength of body and mind. Rose in health, held worship. Went to Union with Mother. Mr. McDonald preached from Ps. 50.15, returned home, little cool & muddy. Retired at 9.

Monday, December 2, 1861

My life and health are continued. God is good to the unthankful and to the evil. Rose early at 4 o'clock, felt dull. Studied lesson. Went to school, heavy rains. Called at Dr. Wylie's about bees. To P.O. Jos. Johnston spent night at father's. Read Latin & Greek. Worked on gloves & retired at 11 o'clock.

Tuesday, December 3, 1861

The time is short, the days are few and evil. God's mercies never fail. Rose in good health. Prepared for School. Whipped John Hemphill and Peter Wylie for fighting. Oh that the war would come to an end. Worked on my gloves. Studied Greek and Latin. Retired at 11.

Wednesday, December 4, 1861

Man that is born of a woman is of few days and full of trouble. Rose in good health. Prepared usual lesson. Went through with all the lessons before dinner, dismissed at 2 P.M. Worked on my gloves in evening. Studied and played violin. Elihu came up to go to camp.

Thursday, December 5, 1861

Health is still continued to me. Great is God's mercy towards me. Rose at 6. Held worship. Forgot Secret prayer! God forgive my ingratitude. Talked with Elihu. Went to school. Finished by 2 o'clock P.M. Read papers, played violin, worked on gloves. Oh that peace was restored!

Friday, December 6, 1861

Cold December is passing away. Life is but a strife, a bubble, a dream which is soon forgotten. Rose in good health. Prepared lessons. Held worship &c. Went to school, dismissed at 2 P.M. Worked on gloves; went to Singing at night until 10. Worked on gloves till 12. Very tired and sleepy.

Saturday, December 7, 1861

Another week has passed away and numbered with the things that were. Rose at 6. Had worship. This is a world of strife and contention. Father corrected Servants this morning. Sarah said she was going home! Went to Dr. Wylie's for bees, put them in gum. Fixed buggy. John Hamilton came up from camp.

Sunday, December 8, 1861

The Sabbath is a day of rest, a feast for the Christian in this world of sin and trouble. Rose early. Held worship, felt unwell, unable to go to church. Father and Mother went to Union. William came home from his father-in-law's. Retired at 10. Too much of the day spent in sin.

Monday, December 9, 1861   — very warm

Another week's work has commenced. Rose early and in good health. Had worship. Studied Horace lesson. Went to school, opened with prayer, read a chapter. At the request of the School suspended until after M.E. Conference. Came home, worked on gloves. A Methodist Minister Wood came to father's to remain during Conf'. Worked on gloves.

Tuesday, December 10, 1861   — warm

The month is rolling on, it will soon be gone. Our days are swiftly passing, we will soon reach the 'Port' called '*Heaven*'. Rose early and in good health. Worked on gloves. Wood held worship. Went to depot. Mr. Sharp came on train. Chester is full of Methodists this week. Retired at 11. O for peace.

Wednesday, December 11, 1861

God's mercies are new every day. Rose early and in good health. Mr. Sharp conducted worship, the Methodists are unacquainted with the Psalms of David. Finished my gloves. Went up Street in evening. Went by church at night, Rev. Lester preached from Gen 4.10, good sermon. Great change in weather.

Thursday, December 12, 1861

Great fire in Charleston.[11] Rose early and blessed with health. How great is God's goodness to me an unworthy creature! Read Bible &c. Went to Methodist Church, Rev Mood[?] preached. Revs. Pennington & Sherril came on train, stopped at father's. Went to church at night. Rev. John Picket preached a wild sermon from Rev. 22.13.

Friday, December 13, 1861

Blessed be the Lord for goodness to me. Rose in usual health. Read Bible &c, prepared from Conference. Heard sad news of an awful fire in Charleston. Great excitement. Many left Conference for Charleston, their homes having been burned. May God bless the poor Sufferers! Revs. Evans & Lester addressed the Sabbath School Society.

Saturday, December 14, 1861

Time is fast rolling by. Another week has passed into eternity. Blessed with health. Read Bible &c. Went to Conference; very much interested. May much good be done. Went to Church in evening. Parsons preached a good sermon from I Cor 1.7. Picket addressed Miss. Soc.

Sunday, December 15, 1861

The month is half gone, how swiftly time passes away! Another Sabbath has come again. God has given the day for our souls to grow in divine life. Went to Pres. Church. Whiteford Smith preached an excellent sermon from Jno. 4.10; Jas. Stacy in even. from Phil. 1.23. Went to Methodist at night. Shipp D.D. preached a good sermon from 2 Tim 2.15. Had some loud praying.

Monday, December 16, 1861

God's mercies fail not, hence I am not consumed. Rose in good health. Read Bible &c. Went to Conference Room. Very much interested in Methodists this week. Went to Church at night. Rev. Franks preached from Psa 19-7. Great excitement, too much I think. Father went down to old place, to kill hogs.

Tuesday, December 17, 1861

Rose later than usual but in good health. Great is God's mercies to me. Read Bible, but too hastily. Went to Con' which closed at 10 1/2 A.M. Bp Andrews, D.D. made some touching remarks at the close. All the ministers left, on trains. Chester is somewhat still after the Con'. Such is life!

Wednesday, December 18, 1861

The goodness of God is greatly displayed towards me his ungrateful servant. Rose in general health. Studied the Scriptures &c. Played violin. Rode out to Chisolms Sale. Bought nothing. Pork(?) sold for 28 cents gross. Went to Singing at night. Went home with the ladies. Beautiful moonlight!

Thursday, December 19, 1861   — Went to Singing at night. Stopped at depot.

My health is good. Rose rather late. Held worship. Read Bible &c. Fixed up the kettle to make mush for the hogs. Went over to Mr. Melton's to see the ladies. Miss Jane Ratchford, Misses Wright, Miss Ida came down, first time I've seen her in 2 years. Went down to train with Miss Ratchford &c.

Friday, December 20, 1861

Rose in good health. Conducted worship. Read Bible &c. Wrote letter to Isaiah and mailed it. Went up town. Went to Singing at night. Little boys were rude. Walked home with Miss Charlotte Bradley. Saw Robert Hemphill. Played at depot for him and David; hunted Crocket Stringfellow's Store key.

Saturday, December 21, 1861

Rose later than usual, felt dull. Conducted worship. Read Bible &c; oh for more wisdom from above! More love for the truth as it is in Jesus. My heart is too cold! Changed my bees. Played violin. Went to depot to meet Mr. Baird but he did not come. Went to P.O. Read news. Fixed Grier's violin. Went down to Wm's.

Sunday, December 22, 1861

This life is subject to continual change. Life is a checkered scene. Rose early, in good health. Held worship. Father and Mother went to church at Union. Heard of a defeat of the 6th Reg. S.C.V. in Virginia.[12] Sad news, many friends killed & wounded. Mr. Baird came home from Charleston. Went to depot; too rainy for preaching at the Methodist Church.

Monday, December 23, 1861

Rose late, blessed with health; held worship. Read Bible. Oh for more grace. Went down to depot; more favorable news from the late fight. Went up to P.O. Bought corn for Sister Sarah. Played violin. Called on Miss Ida Melton & Miss E. Alexander at C. D. Melton's.

Tuesday, December 24, 1861

Rose in good health. Held worship. Read Bible &c. Went up town to apply for the Female School. Mr. Hemphill (Esq.) could give me no definite answer. Fixed Grier's violin — played violin. Went to Singing at night. Boy very rude. Went by printing office. Retired at 11.

Wednesday, December 25, 1861

Another Christmas has come, the year has passed away like a dream. Spent last Christmas in the mountains of Virginia, Second Creek. I am at home but the country is drenched with the blood of our best men. Went down to Sister Mary's, bought candies for children. Took a bad cold.

Thursday, December 26, 1861

Rose late; cold no better. Held worship — talked a while. Went to Aunt Malinda Martin's and took dinner. She has a bad cold like myself. Went over to Elihu's; all well — gave boys crackers and candy. Went to bed early. Held worship. Called on Mrs. Fergerson. Retired at 9.

Friday, December 27, 1861

Rose before sun, cold no better, prevented from having worship. May God forgive my neglect of duty. Examined Elihu's potatoes, moved them upstairs — read papers — started home — stopped at Joe Wylie's. Bought corn (30 bu70). Went to Sing, good class. Mr. Ran Poag and Jim Brawley treated the class. Looked at the darkies "dance".

Saturday, December 28, 1861

By the grace of God I am what I am. My life and health are continued. Rose early, held worship, went up to bank. Borrowed $25.00 from Mr. Harris, a friend to me, bought more corn. Went to P.O., letter from Isaiah. Read papers, played violin. Settled with darkies for corn. Mr. Baird and Sister went down to Fishing Creek.

Sunday, December 29, 1861

The Sabbath is a day of rest appointed by God for man's spiritual wellbeing. Yet it is often spent in idleness. This is the last Sabbath of 1861; 52 Sabbaths with all their blessings are gone. Went to hear White preach. Have a bad cold, felt very dull. Mr. Baird came home.

Monday, December 30, 1861

Rose in general health, cold some better. Held worship and read Bible &c. Went down to depot, and to P.O., read papers. Oh that the war was at an end. Played violin & piano. Worked with Mr. Baird's pistol. Talked. Studied the 121st Psalm, retired at 11.

Tuesday, December 31, 1861

Rose in good health, excepting the cold. God has granted my prayer. He has preserved my life unto the close of another year. Held worship night and morning, read epistle to Philemon at night. Went up town with Mr. Baird, returned, helped him to pack up his box for Camp. Assisted him to carry his trunk to depot and bid him adieu. Oh God, I beseech thee to restore peace to the country! Worked on Mr. Baird's pistol in evening; played violin & piano. Studied Greek grammar. Thus ends 1861 with all its cares and tears and wars. Many, many have had to part with the loved ones at home for the tented field, many have fallen in defence of their country. God has been with us thus far, may He continue to bless us with victory over our cruel enemies. Here I will erect my '*Ebenezer*' saying, The Lord has helped us hitherto.

Notes

[1] The company formed a part of the 23rd South Carolina Volunteers.

[2] On October 21, Union troops suffered a disastrous bloody defeat at Balls Bluff, a short distance from Leesburg, Virginia. Union losses totaled 921 men to only 155 for the Confederates.

[3] Reverend W. R. Hemphill was one of the professors at Erskine College which due to the war had now closed its doors for lack of students and faculty, most of which had joined Confederate service.

[4] Jefferson Davis is elected President of the Confederate States of America. Previously, he had been serving provisionally.

[5] Flag Officer Samuel Dupont led a flotilla of Union men of war against the Confederate defenses of Port Royal, South Carolina, causing the surrender of the Confederate garrison. General Thomas Sherman landed 12,000 Union forces to occupy the Hilton Head and Port Royal area.

[6] Captain John R. Culp commanded the local company raised in Chester which became Company A, 17th South Carolina Infantry. The destination of the company was actually Camp Hampton, Columbia, South Carolina.

[7] Captain Gilbert M. Lafayette Strait commanded Company B, 6th South Carolina Infantry, stationed at this time in Centreville, Virginia.

[8] The Palmetto tree symbol generally identified South Carolina soldiers.

[9] A convention in Western Virginia approved a constitution for the new state of West Virginia.

[10] Henry Smith was a member of the Company A, "Chester Guards," and died of disease in camp at Centreville, Virginia.

[11] A calamitous fire swept the business district of Charleston on December 11. The fire burned most of the district from King Street to the Cooper river.

[12] A sharp engagement took place in Dranesville, Virginia between the Confederates, including the 6th South Carolina and the Pennsylvania Reserves. Many of the 6th South Carolina were shot by mistake by their own men. The engagement was more a draw than a Confederate defeat.

Chapter 5

"The Spirit of Prayer"

The new year of 1862 promised little in the way of peace for Simpson and his family. Yet, he clung to the daily routine of life in Chester, South Carolina, as an escape from the dreaded verities of war. Unfortunately, War came to his life in South Carolina and demanded his return to Virginia, this time to attend to sick family and to return soldiers lost to disease to their home for burial.

There was no glory in the side of war Simpson was to see in early 1862, only the suffering of soldiers far from their homes, some who would die without firing a shot.

Wednesday, January 1, 1862

I am this day a monument of God's loving kindness, long suffering and tender mercy. I am permitted to see another year commence its round. Who knows its changes and difficulties! None but He who rules over all things in heaven and earth. It is well that the future is concealed from our mind. Yet we are disposed to inquire what will take place during the incoming year. None but the Omniscient eye of God can see the end from the beginning. Man is prone to search the Almighty's ways. But the Scriptures tell us that His ways are past finding out. Nothing is hid from his eyes, everything is opened and naked unto the eyes of Him with whom we have to do. Every action is noted down by the Almighty. And we must give an account for everything done in the body, that is, everything done in this life. May I always remember that the deeds of this year must all be accounted for at the Day of Judgment, the great day of final reckoning.

Arose this morning in good health. Read the first chapter of Hebrews. Worked on Mr. Baird's pistol. Read newspapers etc. Oh that the war was over! May God grant peace, and influence our enemies to be at peace with us.

Thursday, January 2, 1862

Time is rolling away, life is rapidly passing on to an end. Man is of few days and full of trouble. Arose early this morning. Read Bible, man's only guide in this world. Worked on pistol (R. Poag's). Went down to the train; to Singing at night. Father is absent to fix a gin.

Friday, January 3, 1862

Much of my time runs to waste. Oh, that I would be more careful how I spend each moment. I too often forget that life is very short at best. Arose in good health. Held worship. Killed father's hogs. Stayed at shop. Went to Singing; walked home with Misses Virgy and Mag Alexander.

Saturday, January 4, 1862

My heart is full of evil and that continually. Oh, for a new heart and a right spirit. Innumerable blessings today and during the past week. Arose in good health, cold much better. Father came. Read papers. Played violin, etc. Called on Miss Mag Alexander at C. D. Melton's. Retired at 10.

Sunday, January 5, 1862

The holy Sabbath has come again, the first in 1862. Oh that I was a useful laborer in Christ's work, but I, alas!, am a drone in his vineyard. May He remove me as a cumberer of the ground! Arose in usual health. Read Bible, etc. Read Meikles' "Secret Survey". Very unpleasant, rain and freezing.

Monday, January 6, 1862

Cold and cloudy, ice on the trees for the first [time] during the winter. Arose early and in good health. Thanks to God for his great mercies. Held worship. Read Bible, etc. Wrote off "Faded Flowers" [music] of Miss Bell Grier's. Played violin, learned "Sounds from Home". Assisted father to calculate the worth of Amy McNinch's house. Read the Scriptures and retired. God bless our land.

Tuesday, January 7, 1862

Still cold and cloudy. Rose early, read Bible. Oh for the Spirit of wisdom — of prayer and supplication. My heart is cold and too much concerned about the world. Read papers, played violin, made pen for Sarah's hog. Went down to depot at night to play with Brenecker, then to Mr. Melton's with Ran Poag to see ladies.

Wednesday, January 8, 1862

Blessed with health. God's mercies renewed every day. Oh that men would praise the Lord for His goodness, etc. Rose late. Conducted worship. Read Bible but with too little care. Put pigs in the pen — went to shop, fixed pump, shelled corn — read papers. Went over to Mr. Melton's, took violin and guitar; had a very pleasant time — retired at 11.

Thursday, January 9, 1862

Rose late this morning. Blessed with health. God be praised for his goodness & mercy. I'll not abuse his kindness. Still cloudy but warm & raining. Held worship. Read Bible. Went to depot. Saw Miss Alexander, Mrs. Melton & Miss Virgie. Made trough for pigs. Read papers. Received letter from Mr. Baird. Went over to Mr. Melton's for my violin. Talked to ladies; played violin for them. Fed pigs and to bed at 10.

Friday, January 10, 1862

The Lord is long-suffering and kind to me, but I am very ungrateful. Rose early in good health. Made trough for pigs, etc. Went down to depot. Played violin with Brenecker on the fife. Mr. Hemphill & Mrs. Moffatt came up on train, glad to see them. Went up town, looked at S. Mill's machine. Went to sing at night. Retired at 10. Father received despatch, about Wm Simpson[1], very sick.

Saturday, January 11, 1862

Another week has passed away. Many are the sins of the week. May God forgive me, oh for more grace to serve him day and night. Rose early. Read Bible etc. — put floor in pig pen. Went down to depot — thence to Mr. Hemphill's to see Mrs. Moffatt. Came back to depot with Rev. W. H. Wm Dickey came up sick. Went back to H's. Mr. (H) came over to shop with me. Fixed troughs in pig pen. Went to depot at night. Retired at 10.

Sunday, January 12, 1862

God in mercy has spared my unprofitable life to see another holy Sabbath day. Oh that I would spend the day in manner becoming a real zealous Christian. Rose late. Conducted worship. Read Bible, went down to Depot to see if any message came about Wm Simpson. None came. Set out on up-train to Richmond with Cousin Elizabeth, Wm's wife. Reached Charlotte 3 1/2 and left at 7 P.M.

Monday, January 13, 1862

Left Charlotte last at 7 pm, traveled all night. God preserved us from all danger. Reached Raleigh at daylight. Took train for Weldon thence to Petersburg and then to Richmond. Arrived in safety. God be praised for care over us. Stopped at Manchester at 6 pm. Found Wm Simpson living & improving, put up at hotel. Went to hospital after supper.

Tuesday, January 14, 1862

Rose late in good health, thanks to God for his mercies. May I not abuse the riches of his goodness. Engaged in secret prayer. Oh for the spirit of prayer and supplication. Went down to depot. Sent despatch home. Wrote letter to father. Moved from hotel to hospital, had prayer in room with William.

Wednesday, January 15, 1862   — Snow

Another day has passed away and many souls have gone to meet their final Judge. We all must give an account of deeds done in the body whether good or evil. Rose in good health, thanks to God for his mercies. May he have mercy on all the sick here. Went over to Richmond, visited the Capitol. Bought breakfast at eating saloon; cold & rain. Wrote letter to Rev. McElwee of Lexington, Va.

Thursday, January 16, 1862

God's mercies never fail. He is good and kind to the unthankful & to the evil. May I not forget him and abuse his goodness. Rose late. Ate breakfast at 10 am. Read Bible, went to Richmond — visited the Tredegar foundry[2], etc. Eat oysters — made me sick. Received telegram to go home to see Father, injured by horse running away with buggy Sabbath.

Friday, January 17, 1862

Rose early this morning to go home but cars would not stop at Manchester. Very much disappointed. Went back to hospital, received another despatch that Father was better and for me to go see Dixon Wylie at Huguenot Springs[3]. Read papers. Went over to Richmond bookstores &c. Visited brass foundry, cloth factory, &c.

Saturday, January 18, 1862

Another week has rolled away. God has spared my unprofitable life. Oh that I had the spirit of my divine master. Rose early this morning. Eat no breakfast, took the Danville train for Huguenot Springs to see Dixon Wylie, arrived at hospital 1 pm, but found him a corpse; having died last night.[4] How sad a sight! No loved one near him.

Sunday, January 19, 1862[5]

Sabbath the blessed day has come and gone but it has not been spent as it should have been, but I hope I may be forgiven the sins of the day. Rose late, engaged in secret prayer for a few minutes. Had no opportunity for religious exercises. Oh that the war was ended. Put Dixon Wylie in coffin, took remains to Richmond. Went to S.C. hospital[6]. William Simpson improving.

Monday, January 20, 1862

Rose early this morning. Read Bible. Breakfast at 9 1/2 a.m. Went to Richmond, put charcoal around Dixon Wylie's coffin. Dined at 3 pm. Had remains taken to Petersburg depot. Went to P.O. got transportation for myself & corpse & passport. Bought song "By gone hours" and pair of shoes, price $9.00. Sent despatch home and returned to S.C. hospital. Heavy rain — dark walk.

Tuesday, January 21, 1862

Rose at 4 AM. Took leave of Cousin Wm Simpson at hospital. Went to Petersburg depot, had Dixon Wylie's remains put on cars, left at 5 o'cl. Breakfast at Petersburg, had to pay 75 cents. Had a safe journey, rode all night. Breakfast at Kerr's Hotel, Charlotte. Thanks to God for his care over me.

Wednesday, January 22, 1862

Took breakfast at 8 1/2. Had corpse put on Cars & left for Chester at 9 AM, arrived at 12, delivered corpse to Samuel Wylie. I deeply sympathize with him and his relations in their sore bereavement. Oh that the war was ended. Reached home at 1 pm, found Father very badly injured but improving. He was very sick at night. Sat up with him all night.

Thursday, January 23, 1862

Rose late, with bad cold and cough. Conducted worship. Oh for the spirit of prayer and supplication! Father was much better — may God restore him to health and strength. Read papers, took a sleep, very dul, cold, rainy day. Mr. Ran Poag and Sam McNinch came to sit up. I went to bed after worship. Cold & cough no better.

Friday, January 24, 1862

Time is rolling on. Oh that this war would come to an end, that peace may soon return to our land. Rose late, felt very bad. Weather very inclement — rain & sleet. Sister Mary went home. Isaiah took her & Grier down in buggy. Father some better, may God be merciful to us as a family.

Saturday, January 25, 1862

Another week has come to an end. My days are running on to an end. I should live as the wise and not as the fool, redeeming the time. Rose late, cold not much better. Read Bible &c. Read papers. Isaiah came home. Mr. Harris & Walker came to see Father who is some better. Went to bed with bad cold.

Sunday, January 26, 1862

The Sabbath has come once more. Last Sabbath I was at the Huguenot Springs where there seemed to be no Sabbath at all. This day has been more quiet and Sabbath-like. Not able to go to church. Read Bible and Meikles works. Spent the day very pleasantly. Oh that Sabbath was rightly observed in camps. Mr. Harris & McNinch sat up.

Monday, January 27, 1862

Rose early, cold some better. Conducted worship. Read Bible &c. Messers White called to see Father, who is not so well this morning. Went up town, bought some cloth for Mr. Baird's pants. Stopped at Depot to attend Capt Walker's funeral but his remains were left at home. Made shelter for hogs & cows. Went to bed with very bad headache. Father better.

Tuesday, January 28, 1862

Another day has been recorded; life is short, Man should remember his days are like the grass. Rose early, conducted worship. Read Bible &c, read news &c. Made a bran for the pigs . Received letter from Rev. W.M. McElwee with $150. Wrote letter to Sister Mag Moffatt. Played piano. To depot. Ran Poag came up at night. Isaiah made some envelopes, I made one.

Wednesday, January 29, 1982

Rose in general health. Cold some better. Conducted worship. Read Bible &c. Read war news. Oh that the nations would beat their swords into plowshares &c and learn war no more. Played piano; learned "By gone hours", pretty song. Wrote letter to Joe Moffatt & note to Bell Grier. Sent her "Faded flowers". Retired at 11 with very bad cough.

Thursday, January 30, 1862

The month will soon be gone. Oh that the War would end with

it! Rose late, rested badly last night. Conducted worship. Oh for the spirit of prayer & supplication. Read Bible and read Astronomy (Long. & tides). Went to P.O. Heavy rain. Uncle John Fennell came to see Father, dined with us. Lewis assessed our property today. I began knife to cut envelopes. Read papers, played. Sold old John to Green Simpson for $30.00.

Friday, January 31, 1862

Another month passed away! Many are the changes which have taken place since it began. Many souls have been summoned to the bar of God to give an account of their stewardship. God has been kind to me, an unprofitable servant. Conducted worship & read Bible, papers, music. Isaiah left home for the Camp! Worked on knife to cut envelopes. Rain today. Saw Rev. McDonald[7] at depot.

Saturday, February 1, 1862

I am permitted to see another month commence its round. May God preserve my life & health & keep me from all evil. Rose early, conducted worship, read Bible. William went to muster. I stayed in shop and worked on my envelope knife. Finished it and cut 20. Dined with Mrs. Melton who had a large dining party; went to sing, walked home with Miss Virgie Melton.

Sunday, February 2, 1862

Rose late. It is sinful to lie so late on Sabbath morning. I should rise earlier than on other days. The Sabbath is more important than any day of the week. It shows that my heart is not right— too much concerned about the world. Rose with the mumps, eat breakfast with difficulty. Read Bible & Meikles Works.

Monday, February 3, 1862   — Rain today —

Rose late. Badly off with the mumps on both sides. Could scarcely eat anything. Not able to conduct worship, could hardly talk. Sat in house all day. Oh for health! Read Bible &c & papers. Mr. White called, on his way to Camp. Worked with my envelope knife. Colonel McDaniel, Esqr. Lipsey, and Rev. White called to see Father. Mumps still raging.

Tuesday, February 4, 1862

Sun came out today for the first time in 2 or 3 weeks. I love to see the merry sunshine — it makes the heart rejoice. Not able to hold family worship. Read Bible and engaged in secret prayer. Wrote a notice of Dixon Wylie's death. Dr. Wylie called to see Father who is improving. Difficulty in the Academy (H. Strong) today. Gill Wyle cut Martin Kee in the side, a narrow escape of his life. Wickedness is very bold these days.

Wednesday, February 5, 1862

Rose late. Mumps somewhat abating. Could eat with less pain. Read Bible & engaged in secret prayer. Sat in parlor all day— floor was washed today. Read some Hebrew. Played violin — not musical with the mumps. Read news. Worked with my knife. Received letter from Miss Belle Grier. Mrs. Sledge called. Father still better.

Thursday, February 6, 1862[8]

Mumps are retreating. I am not at all sorry, they are not pleasant company. Rose late. Read Bible &c. Sat by the fire all day. Still rainy and damp. Read news, played violin and piano. Commenced reading Mason DD on open communion. Read until 9 o'clock. Oh that the war was over & the soldiers all at home.

Friday, February 7, 1862

Still raining. Oh for clear weather. But God is, ruler of heaven and earth, it is not for me to complain at his doings. Mumps much better. Rose late. Read Bible etc. Read news and Dr. Mason. James Wylie called to see me about his son's death. Went down to shop. Worked on my knife. Melton Esq. called to see father.

Saturday, February 8, 1862[9]

Rose late. Another week with its cares and troubles is gone — a week long to be remembered by me. God is still sparing my unprofitable life. May I no longer abuse his mercies — almost well of the mumps. Read Bible &c. Rain continues. Read Dr. Mason, Telescope &c. James Hamilton came up from Camp. Heard of Ft. Henry's fall in Ky.

Sunday, February 9, 1862

"No day like this day hath appeared." This is the day God made for man's spiritual well being. Rose late, felt very well, but was taken with a severe attack of the colick in evening. How frail is man! Liable to sickness and death at any moment. Read Bible & Meikles works. Oh for Grace and peace on earth.

Monday, February 10, 1862

Rose in good health, thanks to God for his great goodness to me an unworthy creature of his hand. May I not abuse his mercies. Conducted worship, read the 1st Chap. of Acts at worship. Read 2 chapt. in Proverbs. May I increase in wisdom. Went down to Shop, worked on knife and cut 169 envelopes. Rev. R. W. Brice dined with us, pasted envelopes at night — retired at 11.

Tuesday, February 11, 1862

The days are rolling away, life is rapidly passing, death is another day nearer. May I be prepared for that day. Rose in health. Praise to God, conducted worship &c. Completed envelopes. Shaved, went up town, got Mr. Baird's free school money. A good many of the 6th Reg[iment] came home. Moffatt Grier passed down, but I was sorry not to see him.

Wednesday, February 12, 1862

The turbid dream of life is waning, "the Strife will soon be o'er". God is lengthening out my days and giving me health & strength. Read Bible and engaged in secret prayer. Oh for the spirit of prayer and supplication. Went up town, called at bank. Bought bottle of Woods' hair restorative. Waited on cars, began another knife &c. Planted strawberries.

Thursday, February 13, 1862

God's mercy never fails, hence I am not consumed. What shall I render to my God for all his kindness shown? Rose early — held worship, read Bible etc. Went in buggy to James Wylie's, dined with him. Called at Rev. Brice's, returned home at dusk. Found Mr. McDonald at father's. Rec'd letter from Joe Moffatt. Mr. McDonald conducted worship.

Friday, February 14, 1862

Much of my time has run to waste — Oh that I was more diligent in Spirit serving the Lord. Blessed with health, yet I abuse God's mercies and forget Him who gives life and all things. Cousin Wm Simpson came home today. Stopped at Father's. I cut some envelopes. Went to sing but few out. Had watch fixed.

Saturday, February 15, 1862

The month is half gone! The time seems short indeed. Oh that the war was short and near to an end. But God will defend all his children. He is my help and Shield. Rose in health &c. Read Bible and prayed to God in secret. Went to shop and worked on knife. To depot; a soldier got his arm broken and hurt otherwise. Read papers, victorious at Ft. Donelson. Bought barrel of molasses at 68 cents gal.

Sabbath, February 16, 1862[10]

Man's days are vanity. The place that knoweth us now will soon know us no more. May I be prepared for death for it is appointed unto all men once to die. Blessed with health another day. Much of the day was spent in idleness, mind too much on the world. Read Bible etc. & Boston's 4-fold State & Telescope.

Monday, February 17, 1862

The lamp of life is still permitted to burn. Rose in usual health. Read B &c. Wrote letter to Mr. Baird & Mr. Clawson. Went up town, got medicine for Isaiah. Called at Bank. Lipford paid me for school ($4); bought 2 1/2 lbs butter for Mr. Baird. Sent it by James Hamilton. Heard of another victory at Ft. Donelson. Thanks to God for his goodness. Worked on knife. Heavy rain.

Tuesday, February 18, 1862

My days are vanity. But life and health are still granted to me. May I not forget the Giver of all good. Rose late, conducted worship; went to shop, worked on knife. Sad news of fall of Ft. Donelson and surrender of Nashville & 13,000 Confed. prisoners.

God deliver us from our cruel enemies. Went to depot, bought 18 lbs tobacco for $4.50 for Mr. Baird. Read news. Oh that the war was ended. Oh God send us peace from above.

Wednesday, February 19, 1862

Rose early. Sister Sara sick with sore throat. Conducted worship. Read Bible &c. Mended the winding chain of my watch. Went to depot, saw Jane Hemphill & son Robert. Went up town, read papers. Bought pocket knife at Poag's, price $1.40. Finished envelope knife. Talked with Dav Hemphill & Jas. Brawley. Yesterday's news not satisfactory. Bought old Lewis a knife, price 75 cents. Remained at mill til 7 o'clock.

Thursday, February 20, 1862

The wise man says "There is a time to be born and a time to die" but he does not say there is a time *to live.* Thus he teaches us to set light of all earthly things. Life is vain & full of trouble. Blessed with health. Good news from west, news of the 18th false. Saw a man from Columbus, messmate of Mr. Baird's bro. Sun came out. Beautiful day.

Friday, February 21, 1862

God's mercies never fail. It is my privilege to sing of mercy as well as judgment. God is afflicting the nations of the earth for their sins. Conducted worship. Read Bible. Oh for wisdom and spiritual understanding! Went to Methodist Church, heard Picket preach. Worked on pistol. To Sing at night.

Saturday, February 22, 1862

Rose late, blessed with health. Cloudy & some rain. Read Bible, the only source of comfort in time of trouble, but I am too careless about study of its great truths. Worked on Jim Brawley's pistol. To Depot. Elihu came up sick with jaundice.[11] Sister Mary & Calvin brought Grier home. Went over to see C. D. Melton. Went up to Ordin's Office with Sister M. Talked with her until 11 o'clock. Oh for peace! God is King of all the earth.

Sunday, February 23, 1862

The quiet and holy Sabbath was ushered in with a bright & clear sky — beautiful day! Conducted worship and engaged in secret prayer. May the Holy Ghost sanctify my heart and prepare me for heaven. Elihu and Mary & Calvin started for home. I read Boston's 4-fold State. To Church, heard Pickett — not much edified. Read Ps 102 with Scott's notes. Oh for wisdom & peace on Earth, but in heaven there is rest and peace.

Monday, February 24, 1862

Another clear day, not a cloud to be seen. Oh that the political heavens were as calm and serene. But the Lord God omnipotent reigneth, let the earth rejoice. Conducted worship. Read Bible & prayed in secret to God. To shop, worked on pistol; finished it. To depot, read news &c. Made toy for Grier out of an old clock. Received letter from Mr. Baird. All well in camps.

Tuesday, February 25, 1862[12]

Rose early, blessed with health. God's loving kindness is everlasting. Conducted worship, engaged in secret prayer. Went up town. Bought bottle No. 6 for father and a riding bridle. Went to Fishing Creek. Called at Mrs. Moffatt's and dined. Went by Mary's but did not get down, went on to Elihu's — found him improving. Sat up until 11 o' clock. Mary & Mrs. Jas. D. Hamilton were at Elihu's.

Wednesday, February 26, 1862

Rose late, had a good night's rest in the old homestead, the place where I first beheld the light of day; I have left the scenes of my childhood, could those days but come again. With their thorns & flowers I would give the hopes of years for those by-gone hours. Went down to the old mill — all is still as the grave. Left my birthplace at 10 a.m. Called at Aunt Malinda Martin's, they are sick with measles. Stopped at Mrs. Moffatt's. Went home in a heavy rain.

Thursday, February 27, 1862

God's mercies fail not. His loving kindness is everlasting. Conducted worship &c; wrote letter to Isaiah in Charleston. Took letter to P.O, bought plasters for Nelson. Waited on trains. Uncle John Fennell dined with us. Fixed the Depot clock, price $2.00. Finished Jim Brawley's pistol, price $2.50. Went to Singing School. Read Bible and retired to rest.

Friday, February 28, 1862

"A little more sleep" is too often my cry. Oh that I was more diligent in business, fervent in spirit, serving the Lord. Conducted worship. This day is appointed by President Davis as a day of Fasting, humiliation and prayer before God.[13] May the Southern Confederacy receive many blessings from the Lord of Hosts. Went to Union, clerked, returned home, commenced letter to Joe Moffatt.

Saturday, March 1, 1862

God has preserved my life during another month. May his mercies be continued this month. Thousands have been killed on the field of battle since the first of February. Oh God it is time for Thee to work; assist us in our time of need. Conducted worship. Finished letter to Joe Moffatt. Went to fix Mrs. Robinson's sewing machine. Read Telescope. Worked on Mrs. Simril's machine.

Sunday, March 2, 1862

The Sabbath has returned again. God is giving me greater opportunities to prepare for the world of retribution but I am guilty of enormous sins beyond number. Rain prevented from going to Union, went to hear White. Read Bible and Telescope & Boston's 4-fold State. Wasted part of the day in sleep.

Monday, March 3, 1862

Rose early. Blessed with good health. Thanks to God for his great goodness. Conducted worship and went up town. Fixed Mrs. Simril's machine, price $2.00, also Ran Poag's watch. Played violin & piano. Elihu came up and spent the night. Talked late. Retired at 11. Father is still improving. God's mercy is sure.

Tuesday, March 4, 1862

The loving kindness of the Lord, Oh how free! O how great. Permitted to see the light of another day. May God watch over me and my country & deliver us from our foes. Read Bible, man's only comfort and guide in this world. Wrote letter to Isaiah, Elihu, to W.W. Boyce; to P.O., to train; marked a few pigs, fixed knife, cut a few envelopes; read news. John Lyle came from camp.

Wednesday, March 5, 1862

When I contemplate the heavens with all its shining orbs I am compelled to say, Lord what is man that thou art mindful of him or the Son of man &c. His bounties are lavished upon me every day. Rose early, conducted worship &c. Went up town. Bought Middleton a pair of shoes, $4.00, 25yds of cloth for negroes, $5.60. Played piano & cut envelopes out of wall paper.

Thursday, March 6, 1862

Rose in usual health, thanks to God for his mercies. Read his word and sung his praise. But alas, how languid are all my devotions. I sin even in my prayers. Folded envelopes. Killed & cleaned Sarah's hog, the first in my life. Went to depot. Glad to meet Mr. Baird from Charleston. Cut more envelopes. Played piano and violin. Read Mother Goose.

Friday, March 7, 1862

Time is ever moving — life is wasting away — much of my time is spent in sin. Conducted worship &c. Went to shop, worked at sundry things. Went to depot, talked with Major Lowry who asked me to take a school in his neighborhood. Mr. McDonald & John C. Burns came up. McD spent the night. Went to sing. Called on the class for money. Sat up until 12 o'clock.

Saturday, March 8, 1862

Rose in good health. Conducted worship. Mr. McDonald examined us all about an hour on the means of grace and salvation. To shop. William went to father-in-laws. Rev. Picket called at shop. Tempered the blades of envelope knife. Worked on the engine. To barber shop; hair trimmed. Bought cravat, $1.00. Played with Brenecke & Pride. Saw Moffatt Grier at depot on way to his grandma's.

Sunday, March 9, 1862

Another day of rest has come. This day was appointed for man's spiritual as well as temporal welfare — but it is spent in mere idleness. Went to Union today on horseback with Mr. Baird. McD preached from Prov. 22.6. Went with Moffatt — glad to meet my old friend — talked of old times in Due West. Read Cummings works. Conducted worship.

Monday, March 10, 1862

Rose late. Blessed with health — thanks to God for his mercies. His loving kindness is everlasting. Conducted worship. Talked and played with children. Played "Bygone Hours" for Moffatt Grier. Set out for home, carried two letters of Moffatt — one to his *beloved one*, the other to his sister Belle. Elihu left for Charleston. Went up town, stopped at depot. Ran Poag gave me an eye glass. Rain today. Wrote a note to M. Belle Grier.

Tuesday, March 11, 1862

Rose in good health. "Oh that men would praise the Lord for his goodness &c." Conducted worship morning and evening. Sent a note and piece of music "Bygone Hours" to Miss Belle Grier. Went down to depot. Read news. Worked on John Allen's gun. Commenced another envelope cutter. Smoked pipe, made me sleepy. Mrs. Melton called.

Wednesday, March 12, 1862

Time is rolling away, the month is nearly half gone! Life is short, yet I spend much of my time in idleness and folly. Rose as usual. Conducted worship night and morning. Worked on engine and knife. To depot then to P.O. Soldiers left for Virginia. Oh that war was ended. Bed at 11.

Thursday, March 13, 1862

My life and health are still continued. God's loving kindness is everlasting, yet I am an unprofitable servant. Rose early, conducted worship night and morning. To shop, worked on knife. To depot — met Moffatt Grier, a dear friend of mine. Read papers &c, retired at 11.

Friday, March 14, 1862

Rose in excellent health. Thanks to God for his daily kindness unto me. Conducted worship night and morning. To shop, worked on knife. Began a fancy book box. Moffatt Grier called to see me. Played violin and piano. Thought of olden times in Due West. To Singing — no one came. Stopped at depot, played violin. Moffatt & others left for Virginia. God bless them!

Saturday, March 15, 1862

Oh, that nations would be at peace and learn war no more. God is afflicting the nations for sins and rebellion against his authority. Conducted worship morning and evening. Heavy rain at noon. Went to shop. Worked on box. To depot. Saw a soldier (Mills) on route to the Miss. To P.O. Letter from Hon. W.W. Boyce. Read papers &c; played violin.

Sunday, March 16, 1862

God's loving kindness is everlasting. Oh, that men would praise the Lord for his goodness &c. Rose late. Blessed with health; how ungrateful I am. Conducted worship night & morning. Read Bible etc. Sister Sarah gave birth to another child today. Read Boston's four-fold State. To depot to hear news from Newbern, N.C.

Monday, March 17, 1862

Permitted to spend another day; great opportunities for improvement & usefulness are extended to me but much of my time is spent in folly and Sin. Conducted worship but my devotions are cold and languid. Worked on book box. To depot, saw Joe Brice on train. Oh that wars were unknown to mankind!

Tuesday, March 18, 1862

War is now both a science and an occupation. It is the great business of the day. May God soon turn wars into peace. Rose as usual. Conducted worship. Went to shop. Worked on box. To depot; six cars of soldiers for Virginia went up. Wrote letter to Elihu. Played violin. Mrs. Melton called. Read Bible. Retired at 10.

Wednesday, March 19, 1862

The month is waning, life is passing, death is approaching. These are weighty considerations. Blessed with health. Conducted worship. Went to shop. Up town bought locks for box. Worked on box. Read paper. Heavy [rain?] in evening. Flora and Calvin came up. Went to Poag's store. Retired at 10.

Thursday, March 20, 1862

Had not God been merciful to me a sinner, I would have been cut down as a cumber of the ground. I can never realize my obligations to the Author of my being. Conducted worship night & morning. Went to Poag's store, bought cassimere suit, vest (marseiles), pants, shoes, 7 pairs socks, overshoes; in all $24.60. Finished box except for glueing. Went to depot at night with Mr. Baird; played guitar.

Friday, March 21, 1862

Life is still continued. God is lavishing his mercies on me although I am unthankful and evil. Rose early. Conducted worship. Went to shop; to depot. Mr. Baird left for Char. S.C. Saw Gen. Pillow[14] on train and Winestock from Due West. Went to church but there was no singing, too cold. Stopped at Depot; played violin &c.

Saturday, March 22, 1862

Great responsibility rests upon every man in this life. His happiness in the world to come depends upon his actions here. Rose in good health. Conducted worship night & morn. Went to shop; to depot. Saw Hood & others from Newberry. Went to P.O., read Telescope and news. Played violin. Read Bible; retired at 10.

Sunday, March 23, 1862[15]

Sabbath has come with its usual quietness and untold blessings to man and beast. Rose in health, conducted worship; read Bible, engaged in secret prayer. Went to Union on horse. Mr. McDonald preached a good sermon on Job 22.21. Went to Uncle John Fennell's. Spent the night. Very cold. Retired without reading &c. Meditated on my bed of God's mercies.

Monday, March 24, 1862

Rose early in good health. Thanks to God for his mercies. Breakfast. Went to Wylie Store, bought silk thread. Came home with James Hamilton. Went to Shop; to Court House. Came back to the train. Saw Jim Brice en route Va. Went up to P.O. Saw Major Lowry about school. Worked on box. Talked of going to War. Went to see Mr. Brawley — very sick. Sat up until 2.

Tuesday, March 25, 1862

Rose in good health. Thanks to God for his kindness to me. I am an unprofitable Servant. Read Bible &c. Went to Shop. Worked on box; glued up part of it. Sharpened knife. Went to depot. Soldiers passed up. Met with my dear friend Joe Moffatt on his way home from Due West; also Bradey and old col boy. Consulted father about going to the war.

Wednesday, March 26, 1862

Rose early, conducted worship, engaged in private devotions, but I am too cold. Went up town, bought clothing for the War. Stopped at depot. Soldiers passed up. Oh that the War was turned into peace. And soldiers were returning from the War. Played violin, fed bees. Went over to Mrs. Melton's at night. Had a pleasant time with Miss Mag Alexander. She ... [?] some pretty songs for Ran Poag and myself for the last.

Thursday, March 27, 1862

Rose early, blessed with health. Thanks to God for his mercies. Conducted worship, etc. Went up town. Settled with Ran Poag. Went down to Fishing Creek to see my relations & friends for the last time it may be. Called at Aunt Linda Martin's. Could not cross creek to Elihu's. Saw Margaret at Creek. Went to Sister Mary's for dinner. Called at Mr. McDonald's; to store & Mrs. Moffatt's. Sorry to leave her and Joe, my dearest friends.

Friday, March 28, 1862

Rose early, conducted worship and prepared for leaving home. This is a world of parting and pain. Packed up my napsack for the war. Dined; took leave of the loved ones at home. Sad! Sad!! to leave home. Took train with Ran Poag and Wm Gaston for the Army. Shopped a few hours in Charlotte. Took cars again for Raleigh, travelled all night. God is good.

Saturday, March 29, 1862

The protecting hand of the Almighty has been displayed in my behalf. My life and health have been preserved although I am sinful and an unprofitable servant. Travelled all night from Charlotte to Raleigh, N.C. Missed connection. Stopped in Raleigh at Yarborough Hotel. Had a dul time — visited the Asylum. Well pleased. Eat a chick. Walked about. Had prayers at night, &c.

Sunday, March 30, 1862

The holy Sabbath has come again with its untold blessings, but I have not spent the day as it should have been. Rose early at the Yarborough Hotel in Raleigh N.C. Took the cars for Richmond, trains very much crowded. War is a fruitful source of many evils. May God say to the troubled waves "Peace be still." Reached Richmond, Va., at 3 PM. Thanks to God for preserving care and goodness. Stopped at Spotswood Hotel. Had prayers & retired.

Monday, March 31, 1862

Rose in good health. Thanks to God for his mercies from day to day & month to month. March with its cold bleak winds has come to a close. Rose late at the Spotswood Hotel, eat breakfast, had prayers with Poag and Gaston. Moved to Lumkins house, a very indifferent place. Secured pass to Gordonsville. Walked the city, visited a gunshop, agreed to take a job. Had earache. Had prayer and retired.

Notes

[1] William Simpson, cousin to John H. Simpson.

[2] The Tredagar Iron Works was a major weapons producing factory for the Confederacy.

[3] A Confederate hospital was located in Huguenot Springs, Chesterfield County, Virginia.

[4] Wylie was a member of the Pickens Guard, 6th South Carolina Infantry.

[5] The battle of Mill Springs was fought in Kentucky, resulting in a Union victory which created the first crack in the Confederate defenses in the west.

[6] The South Carolina Hospital was established for the care of South Carolina soldiers in a building near Mayo's Bridge, Richmond.

[7] Laughlin McDonald, minister to congregations in Chester and York Counties, South Carolina.

[8] Surrender of Fort Henry to Union forces, opening the Tennessee River to an advance from the north.

[9] Capture of Roanoke Island, North Carolina by Union forces, allowing the Union fleet to enter the sounds of eastern North Carolina.

[10] Surrender of Fort Donelson on the Cumberland River to a Union army commanded by General Ulysses S. Grant. The state of Tennessee now is exposed to the invading Union armies.

[11] Many of the soldiers in Virginia were succumbing to illness, and were allowed convalesence leave to regain their health at home.

[12] Nashville, the capital of Tennessee is captured by Union troops.

[13] Davis issued periodic proclamations of fasting to bolster Southern morale in times of crisis.

[14] Brigadier General Gideon J. Pillow, was relieved of his command after abandoning Fort Donelson on March 11.

[15] Confederate forces under "Stonewall" Jackson are defeated at the battle of Kernstown, Virginia, but succeed in holding Union troops in the Shenandoah Valley.

Chapter 6

"A Shadow Which Quickly Passes Away"

The spring of 1862 seemed to be a time of trial for the Confederacy. Union victories secured land on all the borders of the new nation. Even in Virginia, where the promise of victory seemed so great after First Manassas, the Confederate army was compelled to fall back to the Rapidan River line, abandoning Northern Virginia to Union occupation. Yet, the spirit of the Southern soldiers was unbroken. Reverend Simpson continued to minister to the needs of his family and friends in S.C and Virginia, himself undaunted by the Union victories.

The prevailing feeling in the South seemed to be that a few large battles would soon be fought in Virginia and elsewhere in the South which would determine the outcome of the war. Simpson would be close to the lines of battle when that happened. He would not bear arms for his native land, but Simpson worked ten hour days making guns in Richmond to assist his country the best way his conscience would allow.

By the end of June, Simpson would have participated in two battles, Seven Pines and Gaines Mill. Each would sweep death to his friends and family in the 6th South Carolina Infantry and Orr's Regiment of Rifles, thus demonstrating the reality of Civil War. Despite the closeness of death in war, Simpson remained steadfast in his belief in God and his country.

Tuesday, April 1, 1862

Another month has passed away. Life is like a shadow which quickly passes away. May God watch over me and my dear country during this month. Rose early, had prayer, went to Central Depot. Took train for Gordonsville — arrived in safety at 2 PM, changed cars for Orange, reached camp at 5 PM. Glad to see all my friends. Had severe headache. Slept with Gaston's mess. Saw several old col.[college] boys &c.

Wednesday, April 2, 1862

The loving kindness of the Lord is everlasting. Rose late in camp, with earache, but in general health. Read Bible, had prayers in Gaston's mess at night.[1] Visited the Catawba Guards[2]. Saw some kindred friends, talked &c, wrote out diary. Moffatt Grier was put in guard house for the first time. Went to Poag's mess. Retired in health with Moffatt and Wm Brawley.

Thursday, April 3, 1862

God's mercies never fail, hence I am not consumed. Rose late, blessed with health. Eat breakfast, read Bible, took a walk with Moffatt Grier. Sat about in tent until 2 PM, and set out for Orange C.H.[Court House]. Waited on cars for Gordonsville but none came. Eat supper. Walked 9 miles to Gordonsville with Atkinson. Arrived 1 1/2 a.m. Woke up R.R. Hemphill[3] in his tent and he got me a bed very kindly.

Friday, April 4, 1862[4]

Rose late, blessed with health, somewhat fatigued from last night's walk. Eat breakfast, took a walk with Robt. Hemphill. Went to Passport Office; got a pass, went back to Robert's tent. Waited for cars. Left Gordonsville at 5 PM; reached Richmond at 8 PM. Stopped at Monumental Hotel, a poor house. Thankful to God for his protecting hand from day to day. May he soon restore peace to our land.

Saturday, April 5, 1862

Rose late at the Monumental Hotel. Engaged in secret prayer to God; but my devotions are cold and languid. Oh, that the Holy Spirit may descend and rest upon [me]. Left hotel before breakfast. Went to the Everett House to get boarding. Eat breakfast and dinner, did not like the place. Looked around for another. Stopped at the Capitol House, board $8 per week. Read Bible &c. Retired.

Sunday, April 6, 1862

Rose late. Slept away part of the Holy Sabbath. Oh that I could spend the whole day in spiritual exercises and in preparation for the rest that awaits the people of God. It is great comfort for Christians to know that there is rest, eternal rest!! beyond this world of strife and war. Went to depot to see S.C. soldiers en route for Yorktown.[5] Met with McDaniel and others at hotel. Went to First Pres. Church. Heard More D.D. from Num. 14.24 & Hoge at night from Luke.

Monday, April 7, 1862

Rose early. Blessed with health. Thanks to God for his mercies to me. Read Bible, engaged in prayer. Went to Adams gun shop and began to work. Heard of a glorious victory at Corinth, Miss.[6] Thanks to the God of nations for his assistance in overthrowing our enemies. May he continue to crown our arms with success. Engaged in prayer at noon. Very tired at night. Bought ink & pen staff. Retired at _____. May God bless my native land!

Tuesday, April 8, 1862

God's mercies never fail. He is good to me beyond reckoning. I am unthankful for his kindness. Rose early, blessed with health. Read Bible &c. Went to workshop — worked 10 hours — very tired at night. Wrote letter to Sister Sarah. Sat up until 11, retired. May God watch over me & my country.

Wednesday, April 9, 1862

This is a world of strife and suffering. I am a pilgrim and a stranger looking for a better country. There is a land of pure delight, where saints immortal reign [from hymn by Issac Watts]. Rose early, health good, thanks to God for his goodness. Went to work at 7 without reading the Bible! May God forgive me. Soldiers came into my room, prevented me from writing letter to Mrs. Moffatt; read, prayed to God & retired at 10.

Thursday, April 10, 1862

God is the ruler of the Universe and the Arbiter of Nations. Earthly empires may fall & decay, but God shall endure forever. "He changeth not, neither is weary" hence "I am not consumed". Rose early, had no opportunity to enjoy reading God's word and communion with him, soldiers in room. Worked 10 hours, very tired at night.

Friday, April 11, 1862[7]

The week is drawing to a close; life is wasting away. Oh, that I could spend each moment in advancing my Maker's glory but my heart is evil & that continually. Oh, for a new heart! Read Bible but not much advantage, wicked soldiers in my room all the time. Blessed with health. Thanks to God, may he continue to bless me and my country.

Saturday, April 12, 1862

My life and health are continued from day to day. God is good to the unthankful and to the evil. Rose at 6 o'clock. Read Bible, had no opportunity for devotional exercises. Oh, may my heart all day long hold communion with God my Preserver and Redeemer. Worked hard all day. Glad when evening came. Stopped at 4:30; bought pants, $6, vest $5. Hunted boarding. Became acquainted with some ladies.

Sunday, April 13, 1862

The blessed Sabbath has come with all its privileges and advantages. Rose late. Read Bible and engaged in secret prayer. Went down to Exchange. Saw Walker[8] from 6th Reg. Went to First Pres. Church; heard Dr. More at 11 from Phil. 2.5-8; heard Dr. Hoge at 8 PM, good soldier of Jesus Christ. May the world soon be converted & brought to the knowledge of Jesus Christ, retired at 10.

Monday, April 14, 1862

Permitted to see the light of another day. God's loving kindness is everlasting. Oh that I did properly appreciate His care & love towards me. Rose early. Read Bible, engaged in secret devotion to my maker. Worked full 10 hours – very tired. Wrote some – read Bible and retired at 11. God bless my country. Received letter from my dear Father – good news from home.

Tuesday, April 15, 1862

The month is half gone and so is my life in all probability. May God give length of days & his grace to support me through life & at death. Rose early, engaged in secret prayer. Went to work, felt very feeble & bad. Did not work afternoon – took a sleep – refreshed. Met with John Millen & others at hotel. Walked with them. Hunted boarding, failed. Wrote on Mrs. Moffatt's letter. Prayed, retired at 10.

Wednesday, April 16, 1862

Rose early. Blessed with health; had a good night's rest. Engaged in prayer but my devotions are cold & languid. Oh for more grace to serve God aright. Worked all day. Saw a great number of soldiers pass Main Street. Saw Alston Chaplan of 6th S.C. V. Wrote to Mrs. Moffatt. Read Bible and retired at 10.

Thursday, April 17, 1862

Rose late; not in as good health as usual. God is afflicting me for my sins. May He have mercy on me and grant me health of body & mind. Had diarrhea last night. Worked only 2 hours today; bought some No. 6. Saw 6th Regiment & Battalion[9] leave on boat for Yorktown. May God be with them. Wrote to Mr. Grier for Moffatt. Wrote to Belle & Jane. Read Bible & prayed to God &c.

Friday, April 18, 1862

My [life] is like a shadow, this world with all its vanities & follies will soon pass away. Thanks to God for a hope of a better inheritance through Jesus Christ. Rose early, read & engaged in prayer. Worked as usual. Very tired. Received letter from Sister Sarah. Wrote an answer. Good news from home. Thanks to the all wise and good God for his mercies.

Saturday, April 19, 1862

Another week's work is done, life and health still continued. I should be profoundly grateful for the blessings I enjoy. Read Bible, my guide and comfort. Prayed to God for his blessings on me, the Church and country. Quit work 4:30 PM. Walked about. Wrote letters to Sister Sarah and Mrs. Melton. To Congress, saw Hon. W. W. Boyce & Col. Orr.[10] Read Bible &c, retired at 12.

Sunday, April 20, 1862

The holy Sabbath has come once again, an emblem of that eternal rest which is prepared for the faithful. May God forgive wherein I have failed to remember the Sabbath day to keep it holy. Rose late, this is one sin. Read Bible, engaged in secret prayer for myself, Zion, and my country. Committed the 1st Psalm. Heard Dr. More in the morning from Phil 2.9,11, read Bible in evening. Thought of home and friends.

Monday, April 21, 1862

Another week's labor has begun. My life and health are continued through the mercy of a kind and beneficent Father. Rose at 6:00. Read part of 2d Psalm. Worked as usual. Oh that all the workmen were pious men. What an awful thing to live with wicked men and devils forever! Went to War department. To music store. Played violin. God bless my country.

Tuesday, April 22, 1862

He who preaches up War is a fit chaplain of the devil. War is the direst curse that sin brought into the world. War is death in every form. Oh, that God would be pleased to send peace to this land! Rose early. Engaged in prayer worked as usual. Bought 35c of coffee and a Greek testament, $1.50. Read Matt. 1. Wrote diary, read Bible and prayed, to bed at 10.

Wednesday, April 23, 1862

Rose as usual. Engaged in prayer. Oh what a comfort it is to make known our wants to God who is ready to hear and answer prayer! Worked as usual. Saw Orr's Reg. S.C. V.[11] enroute to Fredericksburg. Met with Due West friends: Point Lindsay, Jim Malone &c, glad to see friends of my college days. Saw Capt. Gaston at hotel. Walked with him &c.

Thursday, April 24, 1862

Heaven is still smiling upon me. Thanks to God for his untold blessings. Read Bible, communed with My Preserver and Redeemer Oh for the Spirit of my Master. Worked as usual. Walked over to Church hill hunting for boarding. Played piano for some ladies. Read as usual, retired to rest. God bless my native land!

Friday, April 25, 1862[12]

Home Sweet Home! Oh for some quiet spot to call "My home". But this is not my resting place, there is a "better land". Blessed with general health. Read Bible &c. Worked as usual on pistol hammers. Walked over to Church hill to get boarding &c. Read novel "Julia Home". Bible, to bed at 11.

Saturday, April 26, 1862

Another week's work is done. I am glad tomorrow is the Sabbath of rest and a day of spiritual improvement. Rose early, engaged in prayer in my bed; read a verse or two from Bible. Worked as usual. Received 13.50 cents. Saw soldier from Newberry, S. C. [Davis], walked with him to Exchange. Wrote note to R.R. Hemphill. Read some for a doctor &c.

Sunday, April 27, 1862

The holy Sabbath has dawned again on this tumultous world. Oh that universal peace and purity prevailed throughout the world. Read the Scriptures, engaged in secret prayer. Went to Exchange Hotel. Saw Robert R. Hemphill, John Millan. Walked with Robert to Dr. Hoge's church. H. Hoge D.D. at 8 PM in More's church. Parted with R.

Monday, April 28, 1862

God's mercy never fails, hence I am not consumed. Of all his creatures I am the most ungrateful and unworthy. Yet he deals not as I have sinned. Rose later than usual. Read Bible. Went to work. Felt rather dul with a slight headache. Went to bed early, read Bible, engaged in prayer.

Tuesday, April 29, 1862

The time is short, but eternity oh how long! And I must be happy or miserable during its endless cycles. What a solemn thought! May God's grace be sufficient for me. Rose, engaged in secret prayer &c. Worked as usual. Happy to meet Cousin Dav Simpson in the workshop. Went out to Camp Winder with him, returned.

Wednesday, April 30, 1862

This day closes another month with all its solemn realities. May God forgive all my sins and follies and may my future months be marked by greater advancement in holiness. Read Bible &c. Worked two hours A.M. Went to P.O. Received letter from Father. Went with Coz Dav Simpson out to his camp. Sold him my oil cape. Saw Rev. C.B. Betts,[13] talked &c. Worked even. Went to hotels, etc. Wrote letter to Joe Moffatt.

Thursday, May 1, 1862

Another month has commenced. Oh God continue my life and health during pleasant May of blooming &c decked with flowers. Began the month in the enjoyment of great blessings, engaged in prayer. Worked as usual. Went round to hotels looking for friends but saw none. Got the Christian Observer. Read it at night &c. Commenced boarding with Mr. Jones.

Friday, May 2, 1862

Oh how rapidly time is passing, life is very short. Oh what a blessing to have a hope of eternal life of happiness and peace. This alone can make this life desirable. Rose early. Read a verse or so in 2nd Psalm, engaged in prayer. Worked as usual. Rev. C. B. Betts came into the shop. Bo't Hebrew gram. & bible, $3.00.

Saturday, May 3, 1862[14]

Received letter from Livie Grier, glad to see it; he has not forgotten me. Another week's work is finished. Saturday night has come. Thanks to God the Giver of every good and perfect gift. He gives me life and health. Rose early. Engaged in prayer. Read Psalm. Worked as usual. Lost 1 hour in looking for better pay. Studied Hebrew. Wrote letter to Danville about work. God return to us again.

Sunday, May 4, 1862

The blessed Sabbath has come again. Wasted some of its precious hours in bed. Read Bible. Rev. C. B. Betts called and dined with me, left his trunk in my care. Talked until 11, went to Episcopal Church, heard an excellent sermon from Jno. 1.12. Went to

Hoge's church, heard More D.D. from Luke 21.19. To More's church at 8 PM, heard Hoge from Ps 48.14.

Monday, May 5, 1862[15]

Began another week's work enjoying God's mercies. Rose early. Read a small portion of Scripture, engaged in prayer. Worked as usual. Very tired at night. Played piano and violin in music store. Studied Hebrew grammar. Read Bible, communed with God.

Tuesday, May 6, 1862

Rose early, blessed with health. "Oh that men would praise the Lord for his goodness &c" Read the Bible night and morning. Met with Rev Boggs at American Hotel. Took a walk with him. Studied Hebrew at night. Worked hard all day; tired at night, retired at 11. Oh, for peace.

Wednesday, May 7, 1862

God's mercy never fails. Blessed with health. Worked as usual; lost a half hour in going to P.O., received no letters. Oh that I had company in Richmond, I am lonely, a stranger and a pilgrim on this earth. May God return to us as a nation and deliver us from our foes.

Thursday, May 8, 1862

I am an object of God's care and protection. His mercies fail not, hence I am not consumed, he gives me life and health. May He not withhold his grace & spirit from me. Worked as usual, lost one hour to look for friends from the 6th Reg S.C. Vol. Very tired at night. Saw a Miss. Col's (Mott)[16] remains. Went down to Rockets. Saw 330 prisoners from Wmsburg.

Friday, May 9, 1862

Received letter from Mr. Baird at Char. N.C. Rose early. Thanks to God for his goodness, his loving kindness, Oh how free! Read Bible, communed with God, but my devotion is very cold. Worked until dinner, all the men went to Rockets to fill boats with stone to obstruct the River.[17] Walked with Lipsey. Met with Sloan, an old Due West friend; talked late with him, etc.

W. Moffatt Grier, 6th regiment of South Carolina severely wounded at the Battle of Williamsburg.

Saturday, May 10, 1862

I am an unworthy creature constantly enjoying God's blessings and yet live in forgetfulness of Him, who daily loads me with his benefits. Worked hard all week. Glad my work is finished, tomorrow is the day of rest, the best of all the week. Thanks to God for mercies. Heard that Moffatt Grier was wounded.[18] Wrote to Livie Grier.

Sunday, May 11, 1862

The Christian Sabbath is always hailed with joy by the followers of Jesus. It is an emblem and a foretaste of that everlasting rest which remains for the people of God. Went to More's (D.D.) church. Heard him from, 2 Chron. 4.9-10 in morn and from Ps. 48:14. Oh that the world was converted to God, then peace would return to earth.

W. Moffatt Grier, D.D. Erskine College President 1871-1899 (statue on Due West campus).

Monday, May 12, 1862

Time is hurrying on, the turbid dream of life is waning. Oh, that peace like a river would flow through the land. Read Bible night and morn but my reading is not very profitable. Worked by the piece, made $3.92. Very tired at night. Received letter from Rev. C.B. Betts. A letter is a welcome visitor. To bed at 10.

Tuesday, May 13, 1862

Rose early in good health, thanks to God for his daily benefits. I am unworthy of his kindness. But his loving kindness, oh, how free. Worked as yesterday, made $3.09. Tired at night. Read Bible &c. Received letter from Mr. Grier, glad to hear — a dear friend. I am lonely here and confess that I am a stranger & a pilgrim. Commenced a letter to Belle Grier.

Wednesday, May 14, 1862

Rose at or before 6. Blessed with good health. Received letter from Joe Moffatt. God does not consult my merits in the bestowment of his gifts, his mercy fails not. He crowns me with his goodness. Worked hard. Oh, that I was converting swords into plowshares &c. Glad to meet Rev H. T. Sloan[19] at Exchange Hotel and Capt. Strait.[20] Heard from Moffatt Grier. Sent dispatch to his Father and Grandma that he was doing well.

Thursday, May 15, 1862[21]

Rose early, health good. May God's grace be sufficient for me. Did not work much today. Great excitement, the enemy's gunboats attacked our batteries, but were driven back. May God deliver us in the day of trouble. Fixed a pistol for a soldier. Went down to the Va armory with some pistols. Finished letter to Miss Belle Grier.

Friday, May 16, 1862

"Oh that men would praise the Lord for his goodness &c". I believe that men often entirely forget their Creator. Although I call upon him, yet my devotion to him is cold and dead. Oh for a new spirit. Worked 1/2 hour, forgot that it was fast day. Went to

Dr. Hoge's church, heard an excellent exhortation. Read Flemming's in evening.

Saturday, May 17, 1862

It seems that [God] is more gracious & kind to me than anyone else I know. He gives me far more than I deserve. His loving kindness is everlasting. Worked as usual. Blessed with health. Went to music store, played violin and piano. Another week's labor is done. Made $17, lost nearly two days. Thanks to God for his mercy.

Sunday, May 18, 1862

The weeks are so short that they seem but days. Would that I could spend each moment in preparation for the eternal rest, where war and death never enter. Went to P.O. Met Sam McNinch from Chester. Received letter by mail from Sister Sarah. Went to Dr. Hoge's church, More D.D. preached, Dan 3.25. Hoge[22] in More's church at 8 P.M. Mark 12:34.

Monday, May 19, 1862

In the good providence of God my life and health continue the same as usual, except a rising of some sort on my finger. I am always blessed beyond my merits. Did not work much today, yet made $4.50 on pistols & a spur. Studied Hebrew and read Bible. Made salve for my finger. May peace soon return to our land.

Tuesday, May 20, 1862

Did nothing today but walk about, finger very painful. Slept late, up last night with my finger. Read Bible. But oh how little am I interested in the Words of divine truth! Oh for the spirit of wisdom, prayer & supplication! Walked down to Rockets, watched the steamboats sailing about — beautiful sight!

Wednesday, May 21, 1862

No work today, finger but little better. Enjoyed myself with my good friend R. R. Hemphill; bought some pies. Walked down to Rockets, sat down and talked of old times and our dear friend Moffatt.[23] Saw Capt. Gaston at the Exchange. Talked with [him] about Moffatt Grier. Wrote letter to R. C. Grier, D.D.[24] Bought four cigars, 25 cents, for the first in my life for my own use.

Thursday, May 22, 1862

Still enjoying the favor of God, who never consults merit in the bestowment of his gifts, but according to his loving kindness which is everlasting. Read God's word, man's only comfort and guide. Went over to Manchester,[25] saw some friends. Found Ran Poag at the Ladies Hospital.[26] Miss Baird of Manchester gave me "Gay and Happy", a song. Heard that Joe Moffatt & Patton had passed through on discharge for home. Sorry not to see them.

Friday, May 23, 1862

My days are like the weaver's shuttle, and every day's deed is recorded in the book which is to be opened at the Great Day for which all other days were made. Read Bible and engaged in prayer but my heart is cold and too much set upon earthy things. Played piano at bookstore, learned "Gay and Happy". Went to see Ran Poag. Saw Maj McClure[27] just from Chester with a letter to Ran Poag. Wrote letter to Father, went over to Man., sent it home by Sam McNinch.

Saturday, May 24, 1862

Another week has passed. Saturday night is here, tomorrow is the holy Sabbath of rest, the best of all the week. Rose late. Read God's word, His promise is: Call upon me in the day of trouble and I will answer thee &c. Went to shop, no work, then to Lester's shop to see about work. Called on Ran Poag morn and evening; bought sundries for him per week. Thanks to God for goodness manifold.

Sunday, May 25, 1862[28]

The blessed Sabbath is gone. I have heard some good sermons, had great opportunities for spiritual improvements. [Heard] Dr. More in morn and even. from Jno 14.1 and Heb 11.6; Dr. Hoge at 8 P.M. Oh that the Holy Spirit may impress the truth upon my heart and sinners everywhere. May the Word "be as the fire &c." Read Horne on Psalms. Visited Ran Poag at the Ladies Hospital.

114

Monday, May 26, 1862

Rose early. Thanks to God for his care over me from day to day and week to week. Yet I often forget him and treat Him with ingratitude. My heart is cold. Oh, that the spirit might breathe into my dead soul a new life. May I not be ashamed of the Gospel of Christ. Visited Ran Poag; went on to Winder Hospital[29], exchanged my watch for a Yankee coat with a soldier in Ladies Hospital. Talked, read Bible. Retired 11.

Tuesday, May 27, 1862

May I so deal with temporal things that I may not fail of eternal things. There is great danger of being too much concerned about the things of time. Rose early. Blessed with health. Work[ed] today on pistols. Went to see Ran Poag. Called at the Exchange Hotel[30] to see Mr. Bratton. Read Bible. Oh for the spirit of prayer and supplication.

Wednesday, May 28, 1862

The Bible is a mine, rich and inexhaustible in its treasures, yet how few "Search the Scriptures". It is a sealed book to many. I read it with too little zeal and desire for spiritual wisdom. May the Holy Spirit descend upon my dead heart. Worked on pistols. Fixed up an old clock. Went to see Ran Poag at the Ladies Hospital. Oh, that war may soon end and may God deliver us from our enemies.

Thursday, May 29, 1862

"Still trust in the Lord and do good, so shalt thou dwell in the land." This is a divine injunction with a precious and encouraging promise to all. May I not trust in my own strength either for temporal or eternal things. Rose early. Thanks to God for his mercies. Worked as usual. Saw 4 or 5 Regs. pass the streets. Called on Ran Poag – he had a chill today.

Friday, May 30, 1862

God's love to fallen man is immeasurable and everlasting. Oh, that men would give praise to God for his goodness and for his wonderful works to the children of men. Rose late. Blessed with health. Worked a little. Packed up all the machinery for Lynchburg. Very heavy rain, thunder. Called on Ran Poag. Rain prevented me from leaving. Eat supper with him and spent the night. Had prayers &c.

Saturday, May 31, 1862[31]

Rose early, read Bible and engaged in prayer. Called on Ran Poag. Started for camp of 6th S.C.V. Overtook it on the march for the battlefield of Seven Pines. Followed Captain Gaston until he told me to go to Dr. Gaston and assist in carrying off the wounded. The fight commenced about 2 P.M. with 6th S.C.V.[32] Soon the dead contest became general. Earth and heaven seemed to jar and tremble with the continual roar of battle. Shells came near me but never bursted. Carried Robt. B. Hemphill,[33] Wade Brice, Gaile Mills & others to the surgeon's quarters. Remained in the Yankee camp all night amidst the groaning and dying and dead. Drank Yankee coffee with Mim Fudge. Did not sleep during the whole night.

Captain J. Lucius Gaston, 6th South Carolina killed at the Battle of Seven Pines.

Dr. James McFadden Gaston surgeon 6th South Carolina Infantry.

Sunday, June 1, 1862[34]

Never shall I forget last night — remained on the battlefield all night, amidst the dying and the dead. Found the bodies of Captain & Billy Gaston.[35] Went after ambulance but the fight began again and was not able to get them until evening. Took them to Rich., had them encased. Went back to Surgeon's quarters. Slept on the ground, had no supper. Thus ended the 1st battle of June 1862.

Monday, June 2, 1862

Came to city with Drs. James & Brown Gaston. Went to Undertaker, Mr. Belvin. Looked at the coffins. Went out to Camp of 6th Reg. to see Dr. Gaston. Called on Robt Hemphill, Scott Wilson & others. Left Robt at 11 P.M. Went to Depot with remains of Gastons en route for Chester. Took boy Charles with me. Slept 3 hrs. at depot with corpse.

Tuesday, June 3, 1862

Left Richmond at 5 A.M. with remains of Gastons, rode on open car to Petersburg, Conductor refused to take remains on morning train. Had to wait until evening train. Met Mr. McMorris going home with remains of John McMorris. Took evening train to Weldon; went on to Will. N.C. with Mr. McMorris, traveled all night. Engine gave out, very much delayed. Thanks to God for his preserving care.

Wednesday, June 4, 1862

On the cars from Weldon to Wilmington until noon. Sent dispatch to Jas. Hemphill. Heavy rain. Slept in depot with soldiers from Ala. on their way home with the remains of dear friends who fell in battle. War is the sum of all evils: it brings death, sorrow and grief to every home. Oh, for peace once more.

Thursday, June 5, 1862

Rose early, blessed with health. Oh the loving kindness of God. Oh how great! Oh how free. Took cars for Kingsville, eat breakfast on the way, had a pleasant ride. Saw an alligator for the first time in a swamp. Reached Kingsville in the night, took supper, slept in depot for 3 hours, thanks to God.

Friday, June 6, 1862

Took the cars for Col. S.C. Conductor at first refused to take the corpse on the train but I persuaded him to do so. Reached Col. at 6 A.M. Met T. Howze. Went on to Chester with him at 1 P.M. Ate dinner at home and accompanied the remains to Cedar Shoals for burial. Rode with Mr. Hemphill. Opened Capt. Gaston [casket] to get some hair for Mrs. Gaston. Spent night with Dr. Gaston.

Saturday, June 7, 1862

Rose early, conducted worship, eat breakfast, set out for Chester with Mr. Hemphill and Mrs. Jane H., arrived at 11 A.M. Dined at home in great haste. Took the cars for Charlotte to take Mrs. H. to Richmond to see Robert. Stopped at Kerr's hotel, took train to Raleigh at 5 P.M. Traveled all night.

William H. Gaston, 6th South Carolina Infantry killed at the Battle of Seven Pines, Cedar Shoals ARP, Chester, South Carolina (grave site).

Sunday, June 8, 1862

The Sabbath finds me on the R.R. cars, not the place to spend the holy Sabbath but I feel that I am engaged in an act of necessity and mercy. War subjects us to many sore evils. Had a safe journey to Richmond. Took Mrs. Hemphill to the hospital. She wept when she met Robert who was mortally wounded.

Monday, June 9, 1862

My life is in the hands of a merciful Father who deals not with me according to my sins. Rose late, somewhat refreshed. Engaged in reading the Scriptures and prayer. Visited Wm Brawley[36] at Bird Island[37] Hospital. Called on David Dickey[38], found him very low. Called on Robert Hemphill, talked with his mother. A mother's love is deep and lasting as life itself.

119

Tuesday, June 10, 1862

Time is rolling on and carrying many to their long home. But God is sparing my unprofitable life. Oh that I was truly thankful for the mercies that I enjoy. Rose early, left hospital, came to my room, slept until eight; read Bible, engaged in prayer. Went to hospital on Main between 25 and 26 [Sts.].[39] Found David Dickey dead. Visited Robert Hemphill. Went with Dr. W. Brice to see Wade at Gen. Hospital.[40] God bless the wounded soldiers.

Wednesday, June 11, 1862

Life is full of trouble and anxieties. I would not exchange my hopes for heaven for all that this vain world can give; its joys are fleeting and vain. Received letter from Livie Grier. Went with Dr. Brice to General hospital to see Wade and others. Sat up with Robt. latter part of night. May God bless and comfort the wounded.

Thursday, June 12, 1862

Thankful for health and strength, many are wounded and sick and dying but I am enjoying the blessings of God. Sat up with Robert Hemphill, may he be prepared to meet his God. Commenced letter to Livie Grier. Dr. More called to see Robert, conversed with him about his prospects for the future world of retribution. Robert gave us all evidence of a good hope.

Friday, June 13, 1862

I am happy to know that there is a better world than this. There is nothing but sin, death, and sorrow here below. Sat up all last night with Robert Hemphill. His days are nearly ended. Oh that he may meet his God in peace. I watched his sinking, heaving breast and closed his eyes in death at 10 P.M. He died trusting in Jesus as his Savior. Sat up all night.

Saturday, June 14, 1862

I have no claim on God's mercy yet He is lavishing his blessings upon me every day and night. While thousands die around me, my unprofitable [life] is still preserved. Sat up all last night. Went early to Belvin's to get zinc coffin for Robert Hemphill's remains,

Robert Hemphill, brother of Margaret Hemphill Gaston and John Nixon Hemphill, died from wounds received at the Battle of Seven Pines.

had them encased. Went to see Wm Brawley. Put corpse on train and went as far as Weldon. Mrs. H. and C.L. Brice were left by the cars at Richmond.

Sunday, June 15, 1862

Oh that 1 could spend the Sabbath as it should be but I have to spend the day on the R.R. Left Weldon with Mrs. Hemphill and Brice. Saw for the first time Jeff Davis[41] on the cars to Raleigh. Left Raleigh at 5. Traveled all night. Thanks to God for his preserving care. Slept very little. Heavy rain in evening, air quite cool at night.

Monday, June 16, 1862

The month is half gone, life will soon be over. Thanks to God for his mercies past number and may I not abuse them. Reached Charlotte about daylight. Went to Kerrs Hotel with Mrs. Hemphill and C.L. Brice. Put corpse and baggage on train. Reached Chester at noon. Went on to Cornwels T.O. Went on to funeral at Hopewell. Came home on horseback. Called on Mrs. Melton. Saw Ran Poag and Res White.

Tuesday, June 17, 1862

Home again! Home Sweet Home. Oh that the war was ended. Thanks to God for his goodness — felt dull. Looked at my bees. Called on Mrs. Brawley, Mrs. Hemphill, Mr. Ed McClure. . . [dim ink] . . Went down to depot; received book box from Brenecke. Looked at Father's grapes and pears. Played violin and piano. Talked with the loved ones at home. Played with Grier. Read Telescope.

Wednesday, June 18, 1862

Rose early. Conducted worship. Engaged in secret prayer. Oh for a new heart! Opened a can of tomatoes, well preserved and nice. Went up town. Received money ($ 9.00) from Mr. Hemphill, and boxes from Sheriff McDonald. Prepared to leave home. Called on Mrs. Melton & Misses Virgie and Mag. Took leave of the loved ones at home. Left for Charlotte on evening train, travelled all night to Raleigh.

Thursday, June 19, 1862

God has preserved my unprofitable life thus far. Reached Raleigh too late for the Weldon train. Went on to Goldsboro, lay over until 8 P.M for the train from Wil'ton. Goldsboro is a dull place. But there is no pleasant place in this world of sin and sorrow and death. Traveled all night, no sleep to refresh tired nature. There is a better world than this, thanks to God.

Friday, June 20, 1862

God's mercies never fail; his protecting hand was around me last night. Reached Petersburg too late to take morning train. Had a wearisome delay. Sent a dispatch to Joe McDonald Brice. Trains taken up by soldiers en route for Richmond — rode in baggage car.[42] Arrived Richmond 6 P.M. Went to Bird Island Hospital. Brought a trunk for Wm Brawley. Saw John and Dick Graham at depot.

Saturday, June 21, 1862

Time is rolling on. The war will end sooner or later . . . Oh that all were prepared to meet their God in peace, then all would be well, come what may. Read Bible, engaged in prayer. Went to see

Brawley, Caldwell and Raider, all doing well. Went over to Camp of 6th Reg. S.C.V . Delivered letters. Saw Boggs about the lost horses. Returned to city. Saw Drenner &c. Went bathing with Jim Brawley in James River. Sat up with Willie.

Sunday, June 22, 1862

The holy Sabbath has come again, but it does not look like the quiet Sabbaths of yore. War is destructive both to spiritual and temporal happiness of man. Engaged in prayer, read God's word but my [heart] is too much concerned about the things of this world. Went with Jim Brawley to First Presbyterian Church, heard Burrows, D.D. Took a nap in evening. Too late for service in Dr. Hoge's church. Stopped in Bird Island Hospital.

Monday, June 23, 1862

The days pass away like evening shadows. Oh that I like a dove could fly away and be at rest. Eat breakfast at Capitol house. Visited St. Charles Hospital[43], saw Caldwell and Rader. Took cars to Petersburg at 3 P.M. Went to Robert Taylor's 20 miles from Petersburg. Got off cars at night in the road. Walked a mile. Found R.D. Taylor at father's about 10. Talked about the lost horses at Battle of Seven Pines.

Tuesday, June 24, 1862

Rose late. R.D. Taylor wanted me to drink with him. Eat breakfast, took a walk; talked a while, then went to Hicksford depot. Very lonely waiting on the train, arrived in Petersburg. Went to S.C. hospital[44], took cars for Richmond with N.C. troops. Rode on an open car during a heavy rain. Went to Byrd Island Hospital. Sat up with Wm Brawley. Very tired, oh for rest and peace.

Wednesday, June 25, 1862[45]

Rose early, God is never unmindful of my wants. Oh (if) I could praise Him aright. May his grace be sufficient for me. Eat breakfast. Engaged in prayer. Went out to 6th S.C.V. Met Rev. Boggs on street. Saw Tom Polhill of the 48th Ga. on a march. Ate dinner with Robert Poag. Went to Orr's Reg[46]. Glad to see my dear friends, Livy, John, Robt, Win & Point[47]. Eat supper with them.

Reg. rec'd orders to march. I went with Livy, carried his blanket and canteen all night. Slept a little before daylight with Livy and Robert.[48] Livy stood march very well. God bless the soldier.

Thursday, June 26, 1862[49]

Did not sleep much last night; rose early. Livy and I took a walk to the well; washed our faces, sat down and talked, bought cakes and pies. I went to Barnes' Reg.[50] to see David Simpson. Expected to return to Richmond, but the Brigade received orders to march. I carried Livy's blanket, crossed Chickahominy. Enemy shelled us but God shielded us in the day of battle. Livy and I slept together in a ditch. We told each other what to say to our friends if either should fall.[51]

Friday, June 27, 1862[52]

Aroused before daylight by the roar of artillery. Started at early dawn to meet the enemy. I carried Livy's and Robt. H's blanket. Saw battleground of Elyson's Mills covered with the slain. The enemy left knapsacks and everything in their retreat. Found coffee and sugar in their camps. I kept close to Orr's Regiment. Was in great danger at Gaines Mill. Was exposed to the heaviest of enemy's artillery. But thanks to God for his protecting arm. Frank Clinkscales[53] was killed near me. I got lost from the Reg., found them just before the fatal charge.[54] The sound of the musketry was terrific. Slept at the hospital for two hours.

Saturday, June 28, 1862

Rose early and went to hunt for my friends. Found the Reg. in the pines beyond Gaines, but some were missing, among them my dear friends Livy and Poinsett Lindsay. Went on to the battlefield to search for the wounded and killed. Found Livy first. Cold in death he fell in defense of his country. Shot through the head. Found Point shot through the neck lying in the open field. Found an axe and shovels; commenced digging a soldier's grave for Livy. Robt. Hemphill and Wm Lindsay came and assisted me to bury them until I could get coffins to take their remains home. Went to Richmond. Got four coffins. Returned to the temporary hospital. Slept with John Hemphill. Oh the horrors of war. May God deliver us in the day of trouble.

Enoch Washington Pruitt, ARP Cemetary, Due West, South Carolina (grave site).

Sunday, June 29, 1862[55]

The Sabbath has dawned upon this awful scene. The ground is covered with the wounded and dying. Eat breakfast with Jno. Hemphill on Yankee coffee. He and I were busy ministering to the wounded. I became exhausted. Went over to camp to get a wagon to go for the remains on the battlefields; had some difficulty in getting one. Dr. Gaston tried to take it from me to haul the wounded. Some of Com. G and a boy and Mr. Graham assisted me to take up the remains about sunset in hearing of sound of artillery; took up the remains of Livy, Point, Enoch Pruit[56] and Geo. Ritchey.[57] Too late to get to Richmond. Stopped at camp, slept with Jno. & Robert & Win. I missed Livy and Point. They are gone to that land of rest where there is no sound of war.

Monday, June 30, 1862

Set out from camp with the bodies to Richmond. Eat breakfast at Richmond. Belvin had but two zinc coffins. Put Livy's and Point's remains in them. Assisted the workmen to make the other

Rev. Isaac Livingston Grier,
Company G, Orr's Rifles killed
at the Battle of Gaines Mill.

two. Got them finished about 5 P.M. Put remains in them; had difficulty in getting Pruit's body in the coffin. Pressed it in with my hands and feet. Called on Mr. Caldwell at St. Charles.[58] Got money from him. Went to depot to see about the remains. Slept at depot all night; very tired, worked hard all day. Thus ends June.

Notes

[1] Captain James L. Gaston, commanding Company F, 6th South Carolina Infantry.
[2] Company A, 6th South Carolina Infantry, raised in Richburg, South Carolina.
[3] Member, Company G. Orr's Rifles.
[4] The Union army of George B. McClellan begins a movemnt toward Yorktown and up the Peninsula. The siege of Yorktown begins the next day.
[5] Confederate troops were shifted in early April from the Rapidan River line to confront George B. McLellan's army on the peninsula at Yorktown.
[6] The battle of Shiloh, or Pittsburg Landing, Tennessee. After a great initial success, the battle resulted in a Confederate defeat.

[7] Fall of Fort Pulaski, Georgia to Union troops, blocking the Confederate port of Savannah.

[8] Captain F.T. Walker, commanding Company A, 6th South Carolina Infantry.

[9] The 6th South Carolina at this time consisted of only seven companies enlisted for the war, and was technically a battalion. The regiment left the Rapidan line on April 6, and once in Richmond used the James River for easy transportation to the Yorktown line.

[10] William W. Boyce and James L. Orr, congressmen from the Edgefield and Anderson S.C. districts, respectively.

[11] Orr's Regiment of Rifles or 1st South Carolina Rifles, came to Virginia from the Charleton area as part of move to reinforce the Confederate forces defending Richmond.

[12] The city of New Orleans surrenders to a Union fleet, opening a portion of the Mississippi River to Federal shipping.

[13] Rev. Charles B. Betts, received his theological training at Erskine Seminary and was ordained in May 1855. He was chaplain of the 6th South Carolina Infantry until it was reorganized and at this time was chaplain of the 12th South Carolina.

[14] The Confederate defenders of the Yorktown line, including the 6th South Carolina, withdraw under cover of night towards Richmond.

[15] Battle of Williamsburg, Virginia, where the 6th South Carolina is heavily engaged in holding back McClellan's army.

[16] Colonel Christopher H. Mott, of the 19th Mississippi Infantry, killed in action at Williamsburg, May 5, 1862.

[17] With the loss of the Yorktown line, the threat of Union vessels coming up the James River to Richmond seemed very real, and obstructions were prepared to block the river from any such attempt.

[18] William Moffatt Grier was severely wounded and captured in the battle of Williamsburg, May 5, 1862 as a member of the 6th South Carolina Infantry. In 1871 at age 28, Grier succeeded his father as president of Erskine College.

[19] Reverend Henry T. Sloan, chaplain of Orr's Rifles.

[20] Captain and Doctor G. Lafayette Strait, Company A, 6th South Carolina Infantry.

[21] Battle of Drewey's Bluff, where Union ironclads and other ships were repulsed by Confederate batteries on the James River, saving Richmond from assault from the sea.

[22] Dr. Moses D. Hoge, minister of the Second Presbyterian Church, was one of the most famed church orators of his time.

[23] Moffatt Grier.

[24] Father of Moffatt and Livy Grier, former president of Erskine College, professor at the Theological Seminary in Due West and pastor of Due West Church.

[25] Manchester was a suburb of Richmond on the south side of the James River.

[26] Presumably the former Richmond (Baptist) Female Institute, or General Hospital Number 4, equipped with beds for 300 patients.

[27] Major J. J. McClure, Quartermaster of the 6th South Carolina Infantry.

[28] First Battle of Winchester, Virginia, fought, in which "Stonewall" Jackson defeated the Union forces of Nathaniel Banks.

[29] The Winder Hospital complex would become one of the largest hospitals in the city and was located at the west end of Cary Street.

[30] One of the finest hotels in Richmond, equipped with polished brass gas lights.

[31] Battle of Seven Pines, Virginia. Confederate forces under Joseph Johnston succeeded in suprising Union troops under George B. McClellan, overrunning their camps in an attempt to drive the Union army from Richmond.

[32] The regiment was instrumental in breaking the Union line on this day, defeating several Union lines of battle.

[33] Hemphill was wounded in the first charge on the Union line, and was more easily recovered from the battlefield.

[34] On the second day of battle, the Union army counterattacked and drove the Confederates from all they had taken the day before, winning the battle. Union losses totaled 5,031 men, while Confederate losses amounted to 6,134 men.

[35] The two brothers were killed in the fourth charge by the regiment that day. The battle ended for the day (June 1, 1862) shortly after the charge.

[36] William H. Brawley of the 6th South Carolina Infantry lost an arm in the May 31 attack on the Union camps.

[37] Byrd Island Hospital, or General Hospital Number 3 held 225 paitients and was located at south end of 9th Street, on the James River.

[38] Dickey, a member, Company A, 6th South Carolina Infantry, received his mortal wound at Seven Pines.

[39] General Hospital 22, or Howards Factory Hospital, a former tabacco factory with capacity for 110 patients.

[40] Also known as the Almshouse hospital, General Hospital Number One was the first of the large city hospitals, and held room for 50 patients.

[41] President of the Confederate States of America.

[42] The South was concentrating troops from the eastern seaboard to Virginia, to provide reinforcements to General Robert E. Lee's army at Richmond.

[43] The St Charles Hospital, more commonly known as General Hospital Number 8, held at least 460 patients, and was the former St Charles Hotel.

[44] The South Carolina Hospital was located in a cotton warehouse near Mayo's bridge.

[45] On June 25, the Confederate army around Richmond, now commanded by Robert E. Lee, began an offensive that was designed to drive the Union army away from Richmond. This campaign would become the Seven Days battles.

[46] Orr's Rifle Regiment, part of Gregg's Brigade, was poised on the north side of Richmond, ready to begin Lee's great counteroffensive which resulted in the Seven Day's Battles.

[47] All mentioned were members of Company G, Orr's Rifles. Isaac Livingston Grier, Erskine College, Class of 1860, Graduated with First Honor; John L. Hemphill, Erskine College 1858, licensed as a minister, April 1861; his brother, Robert R. Hemphill, Winfield W. Lindsay, A. Poinsett Lindsay.

[48] The regiment camped near Meadow Bridge over the Chickahominy Creek.

[49] The battle of Beaver Dam Creek on this day is the first attack by the Confederate army and resulted in a repulse to Lee's army.

[50] 12th South Carolina Infantry, commanded by Colonel Dixon Barnes.

[51] Livy told me to tell his father and mother and all that he hoped to meet them in a better world than this and that he died trusting in Jesus as his Savior. [Original Note from diary]

[52] The battle of Gaines Mill on this day was the result of Confederate pursuit of the Union forces north of the Chickahominy. Despite heavy losses, Lee's army swept the Federals from the field.

[53] Clinkscales, a classmate of Simpson at Erskine College and former member of Company G, Orr's Rifles, was then assistant surgeon of the regiment when killed by an artillery round.

[54] Orr's Rifles was ordered in a frontal assault to break the Union position behind the creek at Gaines Mill. The attack was a bloody failure, and cost the regiment 319 casualties of 537 men in the attack, one of the highest rates of loss in the entire war.

[55] The Seven Days battles swept on as Lee drove the Union army to the James River, and ended on July 1 with the Battle of Malvern Hill. Simpson remained behind in the backwash of the campaign, tending to the dead and wounded.

[56] Enoch W. Pruitt, Company G, Orr's Rifles, killed in the charge at Gaines Mill.

[57] George B. Ritchey, Company G, killed in the charge at Gaines Mill.

[58] The St. Charles Hospital, or former St. Charles Hotel, held room for over 400 patients and was located on the corner of Wall and Main Streets.

Chapter 7

"I WOULD NOT LIVE ALWAYS"[1]

The horrors of war were now all too real for John Simpson. Losing some of his closest friends to war, Simpson was determined to bring home the bodies of his companions to their families and bury them in the soil of their native state, South Carolina. In a unique way, he saw the war as few southerners did, from the homefront, hospital and battlefield, from camplife to burial ground, from the small towns of upcountry South Carolina to the seemingly teeming cities of Raleigh and Richmond. And yet, Simpson never faltered in his duty to God, family and friends. The future bore little promise of a peaceful end to the War. Only hardship could be seen in the future months.

Tuesday, July 1, 1862

Another [month] has commenced. May God preserve my life and enable me to serve Him, my Creator and Benefactor. Left Richmond with the remains of Livy Grier, Point Lindsay, E. Pruit, Geo. Ritchey and Capt. Moore.[2] Made connection at Petersburg; left for Weldon at 8 A.M., ate breakfast at Petersburg. Reached Raleigh at 4 P.M. Made connection and left for Charlotte, traveled all night. God is merciful towards me an ungrateful creation.

Wednesday, July 2, 1862

Arrived safely in Charlotte. Slept a little on the cars, eat no breakfast. Put remains on cars and left for Chester at 9 A.M. Reached home at 12. Dined at hotel. Went on to Columbia. Put Capt. Moore's remains off at Blackstock. Stopped at Janey's hotel; took remains to G&CRR Depot. Saw Brother William – he went up to hotel with me. He returned to his boarding house. I retired to rest.

Thursday, July 3, 1862

Aroused early by my old friend Jim Lowry and Bro. William. Eat breakfast. Lowry and I took the cars together. Had a pleasant ride to Cokesburg. I reached Donalds at 2 1/2 PM. Met the friends of the deceased soldiers with a sad heart. Felt unwell; rode with Joe Moffatt to Due West, a place dear to me but the cause of my return is very distressing to me and my friends. Oh what a sad scene when I entered Mr. Grier's house; everyone seemed to be overcome with grief at my approach. *Livy is no more.* Walked with Jamie to the graveyard. God forbid that I should witness such a funeral again. Oh! this is the horrors of war![3]

Friday, July 4, 1862[4]

Rose late, felt very unwell. Eat very little breakfast. Sat in the house. Mrs. Lindsay, Bonner and Pressly came up to see me. I felt very lonely. Where are the friends of my college days? My old room is still familiar; but I no more hear the voice of Livy. He sleeps in the churchyard. Talked with the children. I thought of those old happy days gone by.

Saturday, July 5, 1862

Still unwell, but thankful to be among the best of my friends. Dr. Grier's house is like home to me. Mr. Cowan, Messrs. Bonner and Pruit called to settle with me the expenses on the remains of their friends. Went over to the Hemphill's,[5] dear to me by many ties of friendship. Talked of War. Walked down to P.O. and shoeshop. Saw many friends.

Sunday, July 6, 1862

The ever-blessed Sabbath I love to see. Many happy Sabbaths I've spent in Due West. Sat under the familiar shade trees around my old room; but where are old associates? Livy has gone to spend an eternal Sabbath with the firstborn above. Moffatt, John and Robert are away battling for home and liberty. When will all meet again around this sacred place?

Went to church. Mr. Patton[6] asked me to sing, but I was too unwell. Mr. Grier preached a good sermon, as he always does, from

*Rev. Isaac Livingston Grier,
ARP Cemetery, Due West, South
Carolina (grave site).*

1 Thes. 4:13. I saw Wick for the first time in the pulpit. Went to prayer meeting in the evening. Said questions with the children as did in the days of yore. The first I recited the Shorter Catechism since I left college.

Monday, July 7, 1862

More unwell than before – not able to travel as I expected to do today. Lay sick all day with diarrhea, in my old room. It made Mrs. Grier weep when she came into the room. Recollections of Livy rushed into memory! She treated me like a mother and she will be remembered as long as my memory lasts. Walked out and talked to the children.

Tuesday, July 8, 1862

Health improved. Thanks to God for his great mercy. Remained in the house until noon. Went down to Female College to hear examination[7] of Senior Class in which was Belle Grier[8] and all the Due West girls. They stood a good examination. I was introduced to Miss Morse, the music teacher. Heard her play "Home Sweet Home" variations, &c. Heard the class repeat their musical exercises and I sung bass for them. Glad to meet with the Due West girls. They are all grown to be ladies. They are all dear to me. I have had many happy hours with them during my college days. I hope they will be useful in life and be blessed with good husbands.

Wednesday, July 9, 1862

Still improving; rose late, read Bible etc. Talked with Mr. Grier. I always enjoy his company. Went down to church to attend Second Commencement in Due West.[9] Heard some good compositions from the Class. Mr. Hemphill delivered the annual address; Mr. Bonner[10] the Bac. The ladies did credit to themselves and their teachers. I sung bass in two tunes with the girls. Glad to meet with my old friends once more on such an occasion, but I did not enjoy myself as in days gone by. Saw Wickel, examined his wooden foot. He took a walk with Sis. I walked with Laura, Lois and Jane. Slept with Joe. Settled with Mr. Grier. Dined with Mr. Bonner. Bid farewell to Miss Morse and Miss Lillie Wideman and Feenie.

Thursday, July 10, 1862

Rose early, prepared to leave my friends. Went over to Mr. Hemphill's. Bid his kind family farewell. I did not eat much breakfast. Felt sad in leaving. Bid adieu to Mr. Grier & family with heavy heart. Went to depot with Mr. Gallaway, Joe Moffatt with Kennedy. Met Miss McQueson & many of the school girls at depot. Took cars with Miss Ettie P., Miss Cameron & her sister. Had a pleasant time with them on the train to Newberry. Reached Col. in time for the evening train to Chester. Reached home at 10 o'clock at night. Thankful for the care & protection of a kind heavenly Father. Home Sweet home.

Friday, July 11, 1862

Rejoiced to see my home once more. But this is not my home forever. This world can not give a house free from sorrow and death. There is a land of pure delight, "there is a rest for the people of God". Eat peaches, went up town; wrote diary; looked at my bees. Read newspapers & played violin & piano "Home Again".

Saturday, July 12, 1862

Rose late, conducted worship around the old family altar, a place ever sacred to my memory. Sister Sarah & I went down to Sister Mary's with Grier. I stopped at Mrs. Moffatt's, found her grieving about poor lost Livy. But I gave her great comfort when I told his last request to his father and mother. I went to Sister Mary Burn's.

Sunday, July 13, 1862

Sabbath has come and is hailed with joy by every true child of God. Today he holds sweet communion [with] his Father & thinks of that glorious abode where Sabbaths have no end. Went to church in Mary's carriage. Heard Mr. McDonald preach, sung for him. Dined with Joe Wylie & returned home. Conducted worship & retired to rest.

Monday, July 14, 1862

"Home Sweet Home" I must leave thee again with all thy comforts. Yet I have no home on this earth. I am a stranger & pilgrim here below. Rose early, conducted worship, eat breakfast; went over to Mrs. Melton's, bid them goodbye. Eat dinner, went to cars. Saw Gen Magruder[11] at hotel. Took cars to Charlotte. Took boxes to sick soldiers & trunks to John Hemphill's mess — traveled all night.

Tuesday, July 15, 1862

My life is in the hands of a kind heavenly father who doeth all things well. Traveled all last night from Charlotte to Raleigh, arrived at Raleigh in time for the train to Weldon, had to lie over at Wel. on account of boxes. Cars were overloaded, had a lonely delay. Oh for constant companion. Read Bible, my only companion in trouble. Read Alex Smith; did not stop at any hotel; eat my lunch from home.

Wednesday, July 16, 1862   (Found $17 at Petersburg)

Traveling is no pleasure in time of war. Left Weldon about 3 A.M. Had all my boxes, trunks, bundles &c put on the cars; arrived in due time in town, Petersburg. Had great trouble with the boxes but I expect trouble everywhere. Arrived in Richmond at 11 A.M. Had boxes and trunks taken to the Capital house. Met Lathan

135

on street, he told of Matt Latimer's death.[12] I went to see Mrs. Latimer, found her in great affliction. Met J. R. Ellis.[13] Went to Orr's Reg. with him. Glad to see my friends but Livy is not there. He has left this world of tears and sorrow.

Thursday, July 17, 1862[14]

Spent this day lying and walking about Camp with Robert, John, and Winfield, my best friends in the War. Oh that I was in a land of rest and peace; but life is very short, let me improve every moment. Eat breakfast, dinner, and supper with the boys, enjoyed their good things I brought from home. Saw Johns, my old classmate. Read Bible. Win told me his courtship at night. We alone sat up late and talked on various things.

Friday, July 18, 1862

God's mercy and loving kindness are everlasting. My life is in his hands. He is the ruler and disposer of all things. Rose early this morning. Camp life is not like home, yet it is not wholy destitute of comfort. Read Bible. Eat breakfast. Went to the 6th Reg. S.C. V. Found the Reg. absent on picket. Talked to my friends. Returned to Richmond. Met Lathan on the way. Stopped at the Capitol house.

Saturday, July 19, 1862

Rose early. Eat breakfast. Walked down to Book Store. Bought 2 Greek Tes[taments] for John and Robert Hemphill and other articles. Bought a pie for my dinner. Went to Gen. Winder and Sec. of War about going after Moffatt Grier,[15] they sent me to Gen. Lee; went to his headquarters but he was not present. Returned to Richmond. Met Jim Lowry[16] on street. We came out to Orr's Reg., tented with John Hemphill.

Sunday, July 20, 1862

Rose late. Read Bible. Eat breakfast. Win L. returned from picket. Talked and read tracts and Bible. Jim Lowry preached for the Reg. I closed with prayer. Talked a while, showed Lowry the way to Moore's Reg.[17] Sat up with Moses Smith;[18] he was not rational all the night. Oh that wars would cease and peace return to our land. God deliver us in this the day of trouble.

Monday, July 21, 1862

Dined with Gus Lee. Rose early in Camp. Took a walk, eat breakfast with J. Hemphill's mess. Talked with the boys about old times, those happy hours spent in Due West. Many have passed away and are free from the ills of this world. Sat up with Moses Smith in a church converted into a hospital. Oh, the evil of War! The Sanctuary is desecrated, homes are destroyed by its fearful march.

Tuesday, July 22, 1862

God's mercy is displayed towards me. I am living at the expense of his goodness, thousands are falling but I am preserved. Eat breakfast in Orr's Regiment with John H. &c. Walked to Richmond, engaged two coffins. Very tired, had a sore foot. Saw Robt Poag and L. Caldwell and Jim Lowry. Went out to Orr's Reg. Spent night with John H's mess. Slept with Dave Wilson, eat supper with Capt. Agers.

Wednesday, July 23, 1862

Oh that men would praise the Lord for his goodness &c. Rose early, blessed with health, more than I deserve; eat breakfast, read Bible. Walked to Richmond. Went to Belvin's undertaker. Saw Robert Poag & L.Caldwell, hunted for a wagon from 6th Reg. – met Wm McClure, took two coffins out to Reg., eat supper with Capt. Agers. Slept with Dave Wilson.

Thursday, July 24, 1862

Rose very early. Eat breakfast with Robert McCormick and set out for the 30th of June in company with Jim Lowry, J. Lipsey, Crosby, R. McCormick & Jaggers to get the remains of Sam McAliley and Capt. Crosby.[19] Pickets forbad Lowry & Lipsey to pass out. The rest of us went on and succeeded in getting the bodies, put them in coffins with charcoal. I carried them on to Richmond. Received letter from Mr. J. N. Young.[20] Went to Banner Hospital,[21] found Jim Young at the point of death, sat up with him until 10 and saw him pass in triumph the Jordan of death.

James H. Young, Company G, Orr's Rifles, ARP Cemetery, Due West, South Carolina (grave site).

Friday, July 25, 1862

Slept in Banner Hospital but did not sleep much. Another friend and college mate has passed away. But I hope to meet him again. He died in triumph. Let me die the death of the righteous and let my last end be like his. Went to the undertakers, got a coffin, packed the body of Jim Young. Went to Petersburg with the remains of Sam McAliley & Capt. Crosby. Doctor Tate took the remains of Jim Young to Due West.

Saturday, July 26, 1862

Saw Elihu at Weldon last night. Traveled all night. Very tired; missed connection at Raleigh. This is a world of disappointment. Took freight train with the corpse – had a dull, wearisome, rough ride without dinner. A lady on the road gave me a pie & cakes. Eat supper at Com(pany) Shops; took passenger train for Charlotte.

Sunday, July 27, 1862

Sabbath signifies *rest*; the day should be spent in spiritual exercises and communion with God. But I have to lament that I cannot enjoy the ordinances of God's appointment. Oh, that war would cease forever. Oh that Noah's dove would return bearing the olive branch of peace. But all things shall work together for good &c. Took night train for Chester. Dr. Tate went on to Due West. I sent a present to my dear little friend Jane Grier. Reached home at one o'clock at night. Home again, there is no place like home. Took remains off the cars.

Monday, July 28, 1862

Rose late. Thanks to God for his preserving care. Home again! Eat breakfast. Looked at my bees. Played with Grier. Went to Sam McAliley's funeral at Purity, rode Jno. for McClure. Met with Mrs. & Miss McAliley, gave her Sam's ring and a lock of hair. They were overcome with grief but were profoundly grateful to me for my service. Called at the Bank. Met Ida Melton at Depot; took tea with Mrs. M.

Tuesday, July 29, 1862

Rose early and in good health. Conducted worship around the old family altar. The family is scattered but we will meet in heaven where there will be no more parting. Isaiah and I took some honey and altered some boxes. Went down to depot, Jim McAliley gave me a check of 250.00 dol. on Chester bank. Eat peaches with Miss Virgie. Saw Ran Poag.

Wednesday, July 30, 1862

Time passes away like a shadow. Man's days are like a weaver's shuttle. Rose early, conducted worship. Worked with my bees. Went up town & called on Mrs. Hemphill & Mrs. Brawley. Miss Mary played for me. Returned home. Packed up my baggage – told Mrs. Melton & family goodbye. Parted with the loved ones at home. Took cars for Charlotte, missed connection. Had my hair cut. Slept with Mr. Harris at Mansion house.

Thursday, July 31, 1862

Left Charlotte on 3 o'clock morning train for Raleigh. On cars all day and until 10 o'clock at night. Arrived in safety in Weldon. Had an unpleasant trip. Cars very much crowded with soldiers. Reached Raleigh in evening at 5, took train for Weldon. God watches over me in the house and by the way.

Friday, August 1, 1862

Took the cars this morning at 2 but the train did not leave for Petersburg until 7 A.M. Delayed on the way. Met two trains. Saw Mr. J. N. Young from Richmond on the passenger. He was surprised and so was I. He gave [me] 40 dollars to pay remainder of the expense on Jim Young's remains. Saw J. H. Peoples in Petersburg. Left on 4 o'clock train of conscripts. Reached Richmond at 4 . Stopped at Capitol house. Called on Bob Poag, L. Caldwell. Paid Belvin $140. Read Bible. Retired to rest.

Saturday, August 2, 1862

Rose early. God is daily loading me with his benefits, yet I am guilty of atheism, for I often forget Him and abuse his mercies. Went out to the 6th Reg. S.C.V , took trunks to Major McClure. Dined with the Quarters M. Met Jim Lowry, went over to new camp. Went with Sam McDill,[22] Moffatt Wylie[23] to the 17th.[24] I went to the 23rd. Spent night with Mr. Baird.[25]

Sunday, August 3, 1862

This day I am 28 years old; my days are passing away, Oh that I could spend them to the glory of God! I must confess my great unfruitfulness and wonder that I am not cut down. Heard Chaplain of 23rd preach from Heb. 7.25. Walked to town. Called on Maj McClure at Linwood and John Chiles[26] at a private. Went to Winder hospital to see Elihu, eat supper with him.

Monday, August 4, 1862

May God assist me to live a more useful life, to be more devoted to his service. He preserves my life from day to day and from year to year. Rose late, read Bible. Went to bookstore. Returned to P.O. Received letter from my highly esteemed friend R.C. Grier. He sent a letter to Moffatt; I gave it to Gen. Winder. Engaged a coffin for Sam Millen's body.[27] Came out to 23 Reg. Slept with Mr. Baird in camp.

Tuesday, August 5, 1862

Rose late, eat breakfast. Started for Richmond. Heard that the brigade had received marching orders to meet the enemy.[28] Returned to camp. The 17th & 23rd were ordered out. Mr. Baird was on guard duty and did not go. Dined with Mr. B. Set out for Richmond – met Yankee prisoners to be exchanged. Rode some in an ambulance. Stopped at the Capital house. Very warm.

Wednesday, August 6, 1862

Rose early. Eat breakfast. Set out for Winder hospital but met Elihu on street and turned back. Called on John Childs. Showed Elihu and Smith Ketchins around the city. Went down to meet the exchanged prisoners but did [not] meet Moffatt Grier – returned to Richmond in an ambulance. Stopped in Capital house.

Thursday, August 7, 1862

Rose in good health. Thanks to God for his goodness to me from day to day. Looked for Moffatt Grier. Went over to S.C. hospital to see John Hamilton then to Camp of 23rd, found Reg. absent to attack the [enemy] on Malvern Hill.[29] Eat dinner in Camp and set out at 3 o'clock to find the Reg. Walked 8 miles, found 17th & 6th & 23rd two miles this side of Malvern Hill. Twenty-third returned to Camp. I slept (with) the 6th in the open field.

Friday, August 8, 1862

The 6th S.C.V. began the march for camp at early dawn. Joe Pedan and I went to the 23rd Reg. Mr. Baird, Harvey McDill went to the 6th. I went to Richmond to look for Moffatt Grier, did not see him; dined with Major McClure. Walked until my feet were blistered. Weather is oppressive. Walked out to 6th Reg. Slept with Capt. Strait;[30] supper with Capt Craford.

Saturday, August 9, 1862

Rose early. Set out for Richmond before breakfast; eat at Linwood house. Walked the street. Met Rev. Hinton, John Chisolm. Glad to meet Jim Brice from Fort Delaware. Heard from Moffatt Grier. Sent a letter to Mr. Grier by Jim Brice. Rode to Camp of 6th with Dave Wilson, Hinton and Chisolm. Eat supper with Tom Brice. Enjoyed his fruit from home.

Sunday, August 10, 1862

Rose in good health on a bright Sabbath morn. But the day loses its quiet and holy appearance in Camp. Regiments are moving, artillery is constantly rolling causing a noise like the troubled sea. Eat breakfast with Tom Brice. Chisolm and I went to the 17th. Heard its Chaplain preach. Saw Elihu and Mr. Baird. Dined with Mr. B. Returned to the 6th. Supped with Tom Brice. Slept with Captain Strait. Rain fell in the evening. Wrote a letter to Moffatt Grier.

Monday, August 11, 1862

Excessively warm. Rose early. Eat breakfast with C. S. Brice. Went to More's Reg.[31] Saw Jim Lowry – then to Quartermaster. Returned to Camp. John Chisolm and I came to Richmond with some baggage. Looked around for work and boarding. Dined with Mrs. Russells on Brd St. Went to depots to see if our friends had gone to Gordonsville.[32] Put up at Capital house with Chisolm.

Tuesday, August 12, 1862

Rose in good health. May I not abuse the goodness of God. Yet I must confess that I often forget him & break his law. But His mercy fails not. Went to Central R.R. Saw Elihu and Mr. Baird. They left for Gordonsville at 10. Returned to Capital house.

Walked about with John Chisolm. Heavy wind, dust and rain. Wrote letter to Father by Rev. Hinton.

Wednesday, August 13, 1862

Time goes rapidly by, life is short. Man is like the grass. He soon decays and becomes the food of worms. Rose early. Read 2 chapts. in Genesis, breakfasted and went to Belvin's. Got a pine coffin and set out with J. C. Chisolm to 7 Pines to get remains of Sam Millen. Paid $10.00 for a wagon. Called on John Childs – bought a pipe.

Thursday, August 14, 1862

My life is preserved, how great is the goodness of God. Oh that I could serve him according to his benefits to me. Rose early in good health. Went to Central R.R. Met the 6th S.C. Vol. on its way to reinforce Stonewall.[33] Went to Ins' of hospital with Lunt Wylie and others. Passport to Petersburg to look for Moffatt Grier. Returned on Government train. Trip cost me 60 cents.

Friday, August 15, 1862

Rose early. Slept last night in the Capital Square, bedbugs drove me from my bed in the Capital house. I took the grass in the open air. Eat breakfast at Res. Went to Winder hos' with Joe Chisolm. Called on Mr. Ould[34] about the exchange of prisoners. Went to Belvin's, put remains of Sam Millen on train for Petersburg on evening train. Met old Cason at Weldon. Wrote letter to Moffatt Grier and one to his father.

Saturday, August 16, 1862

Left Raleigh on the morning train for Charlotte. Great change in the weather – quite cool. Had a safe journey to Charlotte, made every connection, took train for Chester, put corpse on cars for Smiths TO, found no one to receive them, left them at TO. Went on to Chester. Found all asleep, opened parlor windows, slept on sofa all night. Home! Sweet Home!

Sunday, August 17, 1862

Health is good, home again, thanks to God for his care and protection. Walked into the dining room to the great surprise of

Mother and Isaiah eating breakfast. I had breakfast, talked a while; set out for Fishing Creek Church to attend funeral of Sam Millen, eat dinner with Mrs. Millen. Went to Sister Mary's, eat supper then over to Elihu's and spent night.

Monday, August 18, 1862

Rose early at the old homestead, the dear old place, my native home. Took a walk about the old familiar shop and barn. How still!! How noiseless!!! Where are the friends of my youth? Went over to Sister Mary's, thence to Mrs. Moffatt's. Got Moffatt Grier some clothing. Reached home at dinner. Went up town, called on Mr. Hemphill, Mrs. Gaston and Wm Brawley. Relish[ed] peach pie for dinner and supper.

Tuesday, August 19, 1862

This world is full of changes, I must leave my home again. Conducted worship. Eat breakfast. Finished letter to Joe Moffatt. Went up town, received $187.00 from Dr. Cornwell. Left $100 with Isaiah, ate watermelons, peach pie, probably for the last time this season. Took leave of the loved ones at home. Set out for Richmond. Met Ran Poag at Lewis' TO; was introduced to Miss Rader. Left Charlotte for Raleigh.

Wednesday, August 20, 1862

A kind providence has watched over me thus far on my journey. Reached Raleigh in time for train to Weldon. Eat breakfast on cars. Ran Poag bought watermelon. Slept on train. Reached Petersburg, made connection to Richmond and in safety at 6 PM; eat a snack at depot. Stopped at Capital house. Eat peaches and called on Mr. Ould about the next exchange. Heard good music.

Thursday, August 21, 1862

Rose early in usual good health of body and mind. Oh that I could love and serve God for his great loving kindness towards me; eat breakfast. Ran and I called on Mrs. Henningser; took her some fruit, then to the St. Charles. Called on Miss Terry and gave her some fruit. Called on I. N. Lewis. I went to the Auditor office.

Dined on the last of our lunch from home. Went to see the Merrimac. Talked with Lan Milan.

Friday, August 22, 1862

This is a world sorry and troubled. Many are the afflictions of the righteous. Rose early. Went with Ran Poag to depot. Sorry to part with him. Read Bible and a tract, Prepare to Meet Thy God. Wrote diary in the Capitol. Went to Winder hos' to see McNinch boys – found Jno. McN., their father, at the grave of one and the other at the point of death. May God sustain the poor afflicted father.

Saturday, August 23, 1862

Rose early and in good health. God's mercies are inexhaustible and his love is everlasting. Went out to Winder hospital to see Mr. McNinch, his son Sam is at the point of death. Went to Central R.R. – returned to Camp Winder. Sam McN died at 11 A.M. Promised to take his remains and his brother's home. Brought the bereaved father into town. He gave me $90. Showed him the Capitol. Got a passport for him.

Sunday, August 24, 1862

Rose at 3 A.M. Took Mr. McNinch to depot, got tickets for him and secured a seat. Returned to room, took a nap before breakfast. Did not sleep much last — the bedbugs nearly drove Alex Wylie and myself out of the room. Went to Winder hospital. Saw Sam McNinch buried. Took a long sleep. Went to First Presbyterian Church to prayer meeting, in evening at 2nd Pres. Church. Called on Johnson and McDaniel at St. Charles.

Monday, August 25, 1862

Rose late, bell rang for breakfast. Read Bible and P. Young's "Night Thoughts." Went to P.O., received letter from Bro. Elihu in hospital at Lynchburg. Went to the 2d Auditors office. Called to see Robert Ould about exchange of prisoners. Wrote letter to Sister Sarah. Bought watermelon for $2.00. Lt. Wylie[35] eat with me. He treated me ice lemon. I bought 3 lb. smoking tobacco. Sent letter home by J. H. McDaniel.[36] Retired at midnight.

Tuesday, August 26, 1862

God is daily lavishing his favors upon me. I should be grateful and live a life devoted to His service. Permitted to see the light of another day. Eat an early breakfast. Saw Mr. Ould's clerk about exchange of prisoners. Took cars for Lynchburg to see Brother Elihu sick in hospital. Down train ran off track, delayed 8 hours, without dinner or supper.

Wednesday, August 27, 1862

Reached Lynchburg 4 o'clock this morning. Eat breakfast at Cabel house. Took a walk. Went to hospital to see Elihu. Found him doing well able to walk the Streets. We walked all over Lynchburg. Had splendid view of the Peaks of Otter. Oh the mountains! how vast. Called at Adams gunshop. Looked at the foundry making shells, etc. Wrote letter to Father. Eat and slept in Warick hospital with Elihu.

Thursday, August 28, 1862[37]

Rose early and in good (health). Elihu went with me to the depot. I was sorry to leave him so far from home. But we are all in the hands of God at home and abroad. I secured a se[a]t, paid $1.50, soldiers. Eat loaf and butter for breakfast. Had a safe journey to Richmond, passed over the highest bridge I ever saw. Arrived at 4 P.M. Met Jim Walker on st, eat watermelon with Wylie and Johnson. Witnessed militia drill in Capitol. Received letter from Joe Moffatt. Saw Mr. Wilkes. Called on Mrs. Darby at Col. Hotel.

Friday, August 29, 1862

Blessed with health. Eat breakfast, dinner and supper in the Capitol Square on bread and butter. Called on Mr. Ould. Al' Wylie and I bought three boxes of tobacco on Broad Street. Treated to a nice watermelon by Wylie. Engaged three coffins. Received letter from Sister Sarah. I neglect too much to read God's word, may He not withdraw his spirit from me.

Saturday, August 30, 1862

Another month will soon be gone. Oh that the God of all the earth may soon bring an end to the War which is now filling the land with mourning. Read Bible. Wrote letter to Elihu and Mr. Baird. Bought 1 lb butter at market. Found charcoal dust for corpse. Called on Mr. Ould. Eat melon with Lt. Wylie. Bought bread for the Sabbath. Read and prayed and retired.

Sunday, August 31, 1862

Rose later in usual health of body and mind. Eat breakfast in the Capitol Square. Read Bible, prayed &c. Alex Wylie and I went to Dr. Moore's church, heard a good sermon. Returned to the Exchange Hotel and dined. Went to prayer meeting at 2nd Ba[p]tist. Went to passport office for passes. Eat lunch in Capitol Square, another month has ended – thanks to God&.

Monday, September 1, 1862

September begins cool and pleasant. My health through the mercy of God is good. I pray He may watch over me at all times. Rose early. Alex Wylie left for the Reg. I feel lonely. Went to Mr. Gannon's, the undertaker, to get up the remains of John and Sam McNinch and W. J. Darby. Saw Mr. Wilkes. Expected to start to Raleigh with remains. Called at Major Ould's office. Heard prisoners were coming up. Sent dispatch to Isaiah to wait one day longer.

Tuesday, September 2, 1862

Rose early. Went to American hotel and was rejoiced to find my dear friend Moffatt Grier fast asleep. Did not waken him for some time. But I could not keep from disturbing his rest to welcome him home in Dixie. Took him to hospital; had him discharged. Got all his papers for him and started home with him and remains. Made the connection at Petersburg and Weldon. Ate supper at Wel.

Wednesday, September 3, 1862

Reached Raleigh in safety and in time for the train to Charlotte. Came near being left and hurt in getting on cars. Made very good time all day. Dined at Com. Shops. Bought some cigars. Reached Charlotte in due time. Met Isaiah at Depot. He took remains on to Chester. Put up at Kerr hotel. Eat supper and retired to rest. Moffatt and I thankful for success & preservation on our journey home!

Thursday, September 4, 1862

"The Lord is on my side! I will not fear: what can man do unto me." This is the language of every true Christian. I hope it is not presumption for me to utter such words. Rose early, left Charlotte on 9 o'clock train in company with Cols. Pratton and Fourney for Chester. Arrived in due time. Met Mrs. Moffatt and Mr. Hemphill at the depot. All rejoicing over the return of my friend Moffatt. Eat a lunch on cars with Moffatt from Mrs. H. Saw Knight, old student, on train. Reached Col. in safety. Stopped at Janey's. Bought a gold pen, $8.50.

Friday, September 5, 1862

Moffatt and I rose early in good health. God has been with us. Praise the Lord, for his merciful kindness is great toward us. We are permitted to go on our way; no difficulty, no calamity has befallen. Left Col. on morning train for Donalds. Dined at the ladies table at Greenwood. Reached Donalds in due time. Met Mr. Grier, Jane and Calvin with a carriage. Arrived safely in Due West. Witnessed a happy soldier's return. All wept for joy. A great contrast between this and my last visit to Due West. I brought the dead before, but Moffatt is alive.[38] Glad to meet my friends. Mrs. Grier was much affected. Slept with M.

Saturday, September 6, 1862[39]

Another week has passed by. Many have gone the way of all living. But my unprofitable life has been continued. Rose very early. Mr. Grier and Joe Moffatt set out for Cedar Springs to attend Presbytery. I enjoy myself with the children. Took a walk up the street with Moffatt and children. Met Mrs. J. McMorris. Mrs. Pressly, Young Lindsay and Miss McQuerns called to see Moffatt and myself. Miss Nannie M. sent Moffatt some peaches.[40]

Sunday, September 7, 1862

The Sabbath has come, the blessed day, an emblem of that eternal rest, the heritage of the peace of God. Spent the day with Mr. Grier's family. Read the Bible. Oh, that I could spend every Sabbath as quietly as this. Had a prayer meeting and conducted the exercise – made a few remarks. Sat on the porch and talked with the family until worship. Read the 119 Psalm and retired to rest. Thanks to God.

Monday, September 8, 1862

Rose quite early, as was my custom in the days of yore. Those happy days are gone. Conducted worship – took a walk with Moffatt to Livy's grave. Walked over to Mr. Hemphill's, talked with Bella &c. Mrs. Grier killed a turkey for dinner, invited Mrs. H. to dine. Rode with Mr. Young to his house, talked with Mrs. Young and Lizzie. Called Mr. Pressly, Mrs. Lindsay and Bonner. He gave me 5.00 dollars to buy tobacco. Mr. Young gave me a pair of shoes. Mr. G. & Joe returned from Presbytery. John Brison came with them.

Tuesday, September 9, 1862

Rose early. Did not sleep well. Moffatt had to get up during the night. Packed up to leave Due West once more. I am always reluctant to leave the place I have spent so many happy days. My dearest friends are in D. W. Bid farewell to Mr. Grier and his kind family. Moffatt went with me to Newberry to see Miss Nannie. I saw them meet. Oh it was, a happy scene. I was sorry to leave my dear friend Moffatt. I went on to Cpl. Met with Branard McClure who told me that Mr. Baird was wounded in the foot.[41] Reached Chester at 10 P.M. Met Sister Sarah and many others at depot. Ate a lunch and set out for the scene of battle in company with Dr. Ready and A. White. Travelled all night. Blessed with health and preservation of life.

Wednesday, September 10, 1862

Traveled all last night and all the day. God in his kindness has preserved me on my journey. May I always put my trust in Him who doeth all things well. Reached Raleigh in time for train. Formed an acquaintance with Miss Vict. Murden at Raleigh; took charge of her to Richmond. Reached Weldon at midnight. Heavy rain fell. Left for Petersburg at 3 A.M.

Thursday, September 11, 1862

Arrived safely in Petersburg. Procured passports of Miss Murden, Dr. Ready &c for Richmond. Made every connection and reached

Richmond at 11 A.M. Eat dinner. Bought $500.00 worth of tobacco for Mr. Bonner from Mr. Hartwell on Broad Street. He gave me a nice pipe. Wrote letter to Moffatt Grier, Dr. Ready &c. I changed lodging to the Linwood house. Oh for home and peace again.

Friday, September 12, 1862

Rose very early. Went to Central R.R. depot. Took train for Rapidan.[42] Cars very much crowded. Slept on the way. Reached Rapidan at 4 P.M. Very loath to leave the cars and travel on foot 20 miles to Warrenton. Walked all evening and all night, carried a box and carpet sack. Stopped in a deserted house out of a heavy rain. Reached Culpepper Courthouse at midnight. Slept a little and set out at 2 A.M. for Warrenton on foot.

Saturday, September 13, 1862

I never shall forget my trip to Warrenton on foot. Travelled all last night. Glad to see daylight come once more. Was much in love with the moon for her silver light. Began to get very weary. Met my friend J. L. Hemphill on foot as I was going to Culpepper; turned him back with me. Reached Warrenton at 2 P.M. It was the desired haven to me. I was well nigh exhausted. I was called to mourn the loss of my dear friend Ran Poag. He died on Wednesday night. It is sad to part dear friends. He has left this world of toil and trouble. Heaven is his home. I hope to meet him in that happy place. I found Mr. Baird at M. Spilman's – a very kind man. Saw Scott Wilson & others wounded.

Sunday, September 14, 1862[43]

The blessed Sabbath has come again. I spent last Sabbath very quietly and pleasantly in Due West. But now I am far away amid scenes of bloodshed and all the horrors of war. Went about the hospitals in Warrenton, and almost every house is one.[44] Oh, that such scenes were gone never to return. Saw Joe Martin[45] and many others.

Monday, September 15, 1862

The time is rolling away rapidly. September is half gone. "We take no note of time but mourn its loss." How wicked for nations to consume months and years in horrid war. Rose late. Dressed Mr. Baird's[46] wound. Wrote letter to Sister Sarah. Went to hospitals to see my friends. Took Scott Wilson, Brant J Martin, Thos. Smith, Jno. White some luxuries. War is the most direful curse a people can suffer.

Tuesday, September 16, 1862

Oh how swiftly the moments fly! My days are like a weaver's shuttle. Rose early this morning. Dressed Mr. Baird's wound. Finished Sister's letter. Wrote diary. Talked with John Hemphill and Mr. Baird. Spent the day in the room, read paper and took a good nap. Sat up late. Commenced letter to my friend R. C. Grier. Retired at 11.

Wednesday, September 17, 1862[47]

Life is but a strife and as the grass which soon withers. Rose at usual hour. Eat breakfast, dressed Mr. Baird's wound. Took some nice pudding to the hospitals. Dr. Ready called on Mr. Baird. I went upstairs to see a wounded soldier. Heard Miss Molly Spilman[48] play the piano and played some for her. John Hemphill sang with me.

Thursday, September 18, 1862

Oh that the war was at an end! May peace and prosperity once more return to this once happy land. Rose in good health. Dressed wound as usual. Dr. Ready gave John Hemphill some brandy; he and I drank a toddy. Was introduced to the Misses Bramham from Albemarle visiting their wounded brother at Mr. Spilman's. Went around to see my friends in hospital.

Friday, September 19, 1862

Time passes away rapidly with me although I am far from home. But I am among kind friends. Dressed Mr. Baird's leg. Went around to the hospital. Saw surgeon amputate a man's thigh. The evil of war is incalcuble. Went in the parlor and talked with the ladies. Wrote letter to Sister Sarah. Finished one to R. C. Grier. Retired at 11 o'clock.

Saturday, September 20, 1862

Another week has passed and is numbered with the past. The time is short. This life of pain and sorrow will soon end. There is a life of eternal joy and peace in heaven where the weary are at rest and the wicked cease from trouble. Dressed Mr. Baird's leg. Played piano for the ladies and talked with them. Visited hospitals. The wounded are improving, although many will never see their home on earth. May God be merciful to them and prepare them for an entrance into the joys of a heavenly home beyond this vale of tears.

Sunday, September 21, 1862

Another Sabbath of rest has come. I am blessed above many of my fellow creatures! Great privileges are granted unto me. Rose at the usual time. Dressed Mr. Baird's leg. Went to the Baptist Institute. Heard a long sermon from Pollok, D.D. on Jno. 16. 7-11. Took a nap in evening. Read Bible. Retired at 10 o'clock. Oh! that I spent the Sabbath in preaching the unsearchable riches of Christ. May my divine Master not turn me out of His vineyard nor cut me down as a cumberer of the ground!

Monday, September 22, 1862

Rose early. Did not sleep well for the rats. Dressed Mr. B's leg. Went in house to bid Miss Gillie Braham goodbye. Went to see Scott Wilson and Brant. Sent dispatch to George McMaster. Called on Joe Martin &c. Gave Mr. Baird some lobelia – it made him very sick. Fixed my bed out of an old chair. Mr. Baird very sick. Read Bible and retired.

Tuesday, September 23, 1862

This is a world of trouble. "Man that is born of a woman is of few days and full of trouble." Rose early. Dressed Mr. Baird's leg. Waited on him all day, he is not doing as well as he has been. Had a slight chill and fever all day. Went to different hospitals. Received telegram from Thos. Smith's mother. Talked with Jno. Hemphill on prayer &c and those pleasant prayer meetings we had in Due West during our happy days at college. Oh that we could enjoy such blessed privileges now!

Wednesday, September 24, 1862

Weeks seem as short as days, time rolls so rapidly. Rose at usual hour. Dressed Mr. Baird's leg. Dr. Shelton called in the morning; Dr. Holland in the evening. Went to town. Scott Wilson and Brant started home. Got some sweet spirits of Nitre for Mr. B. Called on Blain at Warren house. Talked with Miss Sallie Braham and Flora Spilman. Read a fast-day sermon by O. S. Barton. My health is excellent, thanks to God for his great goodness. Mr. B. is not doing so well. May God be merciful to him and restore him to health and strength. Read Bible at night. May the blessings of peace soon return to our once happy country. Mr. Baird received a letter from Sister Sarah, dated September 16, 1862.

Thursday, September 25, 1862

The days go by like a shadow. God is good and kind to me far beyond my deserts "But if thou O Lord should mark iniquities &c". Rose early, dressed Mr. Baird's leg. Went for Dr. Frazer who said Mr. B was very sick with typhoid. May God spare his life and bless the means used in his restoration. Had a severe headache, went to bed early after reading and praying. Mr. Baird is delirious and does not know what to say, his mind is so much affected by the fever. May God who controls all things preserve his life and permit him to return to his wife and children.

Friday, September 26, 1862

Rose in good health, thanks to God for his goodness. Mr. Baird is very sick; Dr. Fraser thinks his condition very critical. But I pray that God will spare his life and permit him to return home again. Went to the dispensary, gave medicine all day. John Hemphill sat up until two at night. Called on Jim McCormick who is very sick. Read Bible and engaged in secret prayer. The blessing of the Lord maketh rich and He addeth no sorrow with it. Oh for the spirit of prayer and supplication.

Saturday, September 27, 1862

Another week has departed and has been numbered with the things of the past. I am one week nearer my journey's end. It is so comforting to know that there is a life of endless joy and peace.

Mr. Baird is very near the gates of death, may God spare his life. Went to dispensary — bought peaches. Sent a telegram to Sister Sarah; sorrowful news for a wife to hear. Mrs. Reno called to see Mr. B., gave him a lemon. Mrs. Spilman and Mrs. Bramham also called. Dr. Fraser called morning and evening. The ladies are very kind to Mr. B. I went upstairs to assist Mrs. Bramham with her paralyzed son. Called to see Joe Martin &c.

Sunday, September 28, 1862

Time in its rapid march has brought around another holy Sabbath. It is so ordered by divine providence that I cannot preach the everlasting gospel nor attend the services in the church below. Waited on Mr. Baird who is growing worse, I fear his days are numbered. May God be his support in the hour of death.

Monday, September 29, 1862

Who can tell what will take place during this week. Many will be called to the judgment bar of God to receive their final reward. James McCormick died this evening. I called to see him but he was speechless. I regret that I did not converse more with him on his hopes for the world to come. Mr. Baird is growing weaker, fever very high. The Yankee cavalry came into town today. They made desperate charge upon an unarmed village. I commenced a letter to Mr. Bonner but the Yankees stopped me. John Hemphill and I fixed Mr. Baird's bed and dressed his leg. Sat up with him; he is still getting weak. Sent a dispatch to Sister.

Tuesday, September 30, 1862

Rose at 3 A.M. to sit up with Mr. Baird. He is still delirious and very low. Oh may God restore his mind before he dies! John Hemphill and I are very much fatigued by sitting up every night. Gave Mr. B. an enema. His bowels acted and continued running off all night. John and I had a heavy task all day and night. The Yankees all disappeared last night. A portion of Confederate cavalry came into town. I called on Joe Martin on my way to dispensary. Jim McCormick died this morning; was buried this evening. *Bella! horrida Bella!*[49]

Notes

[1] Captain J. Michael Moore, 6th South Carolina Infantry, killed in action on June 27, 1862 at the battle of Gaines Mill.

[2] From Job 7:16, the text used by Dr. R.C. Grier at the funeral of his son, Livy Grier, July 3, 1862.

[3] The bodies of Lindsay, Grier and Pruitt were buried on July 3, in Due West and Abbeville, while Ritchey was buried the following day in Greenville.

[4] Simpson was quite a celebrity in Due West, and was constantly asked for news of the battle and of the local men by their families. According to a letter of July 15, "Simpson was so exhausted with the trip that he was not able to return for a week, but was busy talking all the while. People from all around flock to hear him speak of the battle." Letter of Lizzie Young to Cousin Jim, July 15, 1862, Young Family Papers, South Carolina Historical Society.

[5] Dr. William R. Hemphill, professor of Latin at Erskine College, and father of John L. and Robert R. Hemphill.

[6] Dr. Edmund L. Patton, Class of 1846 and elected President of Erskine College in 1859.

[7] The class was examined in three areas: Botany, Evidence of Christianity, and Mental Philosophy.

[8] Isabella Grier, younger sister of Livy Grier.

[9] Due West Female College was founded in the fall of 1859 with the first class beginning in Jan 1860 with a faculty of four.

[10] Rev. John I. Bonner, D. D., president of Due West Female College 1859-1881.

[11] John Bankhead Magruder, was blamed for much of the failure to destroy the Union army in the Seven Days Battles. He was accordingly transfered to the Trans-Mississippi theater of operations, and left Virginia in mid-July.

[12] Lieutenant B. Milton Latimer, Company G, Orr's Rifles, died of wounds received in the charge at Gaines Mill.

[13] James R. Ellis, Sergeant, Company G, Orr's Rifles.

[14] The regiment was camped at Laurel Church, on the River Road seven miles from Richmond.

[15] Simpson was attempting to obtain a pass to cross the Union lines and bring Moffatt Grier back from Williamsburg, where he lay wounded in Union hands. General John Winder was provost-marshal for the City of Richmond.

[16] James Robert Lowery, graduate of Erskine College in 1858, ordained as minister in March, 1862, went as a missionary to the Confederate Army in Virginia in July, 1862.

[17] Colonel John S. Moore's 2d South Carolina Rifles.

[18] James Moses Smith, Company G, Orr's Rifles.

[19] Captain J.M. Crosby and Samuel L. McAliley, both of Company I, 6th South Carolina were killed in action on June 30, 1862 during the Battle of Fraysers Farm.

[20] Rev. John N. Young, held the chair of Mathematics and Natural Philosophy at Erskine College, from 1839-1881. His nephew, James A. B. Young, was a member of Company G, Orr's Rifles.

[21] Banner Hospital, or General Hospital Number 12, was a former tobacco warehouse holding over 250 patients and stood at 19th and Franklin Streets.

[22] Company D, 17th South Carolina Infantry.

[23] Company D, 17th South Carolina Infantry.

[24] The 17th South Carolina Infantry arrived in Virginia on the 24th of July from the South Carolina coast. The regiment was part of a Brigade composed of the 17th, 18th, 22d, 23rd Infantry Regiments and Holcomb's Legion, which came together to Virginia.

[25] Al Baird, 23rd South Carolina Infantry, brother-in-law to J. H. Simpson.

[26] John H. Childs, Company G, Orr's Rifles.

[27] Samuel Millen, Company A, 6th South Carolina Infantry, killed in action at Seven Pines, May 30, 1862.

[28] The two regiments went on a reconnaisance to the Union position at Malvern Hill, but suffered no casualties.

[29] The Confederate advance was meant to ascertain if the Union army was moving from Malvern Hill.

[30] Captain G. L. Strait, commanding Company A, 6th South Carolina Infantry.

[31] Colonel John V. Moore's 2d South Carolina Rifles.

[32] On August 9, Stonewall Jackson fought the battle of Cedar Mountain, near Gordonsville.

[33] Lee began to shift his army to Jackson near Gordonsville as the Union army at Harrison's Landing also shifted north by river.

[34] Robert Ould, Confederate commisioner of exchange of prisoners of war.

[35] Osmond Alexander Wylie, Company F, 6th South Carolina Infantry.

[36] Possibly Lieutenant James H. McDaniel, who resigned his commision on July 29, 1862 from Company H, 24th South Carolina Infantry.

[37] The Battle of Second Manassas begins, and ends on August 30 in a great Southern victory. At great cost, Lee drove the Union army back into Washington.

[38] See Diary entry for July 3, 1862.

[39] Buoyed by the victory at 2d Manassas, Lee took his army north into Maryland. On this day, he occupied Frederick, Maryland.

[40] Moffatt Grier later married Nannie McMorries.

[41] This wound occurred at the battle of 2d Manassas, August 30, 1862.

[42] Rapidan was the foremost station still linked to Richmond on the Orange and Alexandria Railroad.

[43] The Confederate army was still in Maryland, fighting a rear guard action on South Mountain and investing the Union garrison at Harper's Ferry on this day.

[44] These hospitals were filled with the Confederate wounded from the battle of 2d Manassas.

[45] Joseph Martin, Company A, 17th South Carolina, wounded seriously at 2d Manassas, August 30, 1862.

[46] His Sister Sarah's husband.

[47] On this day was fought the battle of Antietam, which resulted in Lee withdrawing the Southern army back into Virginia.

[48] Daughter of Judge Edward Spilman, one of the prominent men of the town.

[49] From the *Aeneid* by Virgil, meaning War ! Horrible War!

Chapter 8

"MAY GOD GIVE STRENGTH IN THE HOUR OF DEATH"

As the summer of 1862 ended in Virginia, so ended in a forceful way any idea of an early end to the War between the States. Almost every Southern family was in some way touched by the searing fire of war, and the harsh realities of the conflict now set in across the newly founded country. In the case of John Hemphill Simpson, the war no longer mattered as far as winning or losing. He was now in the backwash of battle, tending the grievously wounded men of Second Manassas, including his own brother-in-law. These duties of mercy were perhaps worse than any duty encountered on the battlefield, watching the slow and painful death of a loved one.

And yet, the war was certain to continue, as Lee's army returned to Virginia to carry the conflict into the fall in Virginia, leading to yet another major battle at Fredericksburg.

Wednesday, October 1, 1862

Mr. Baird is much worse. We got no rest last night scarcely. I sat up the latter part of the night. Slept 3 hours. Went for Doctor before breakfast. Gave Mr. Baird opium to check his bowels. There seems no hope of his recovery. May God give strength in the hour of death. Sent a sad telegram to Sister Sarah. May God's grace be sufficient for her in this her day of trouble and misfortune. God is her only refuge in the day of trouble. May she find comfort in His great and exceeding precious promises. Took a refreshing nap before dining. Dr. Fraser called morning and evening. Read Bible and engaged in secret prayer.

Thursday, October 2, 1862

Life is dear to man, he clings to the last lingering hope. Al Baird is wasting away, God's will towards him be fulfilled. May his soul grow stronger and stronger as his body grows weak. God is his refuge, his strength and everlasting portion. I felt very much fatigued; lay down early. The longer I live the more I am convinced of the vanity of this world. There is nothing below to satisfy the unworldly soul. There is nothing true but heaven – there our joys will be full and eternal.

Friday, October 3, 1862

Rose at 5 to wait on Mr. Baird who still is lingering on the very border of life. Will the Lord not spare his life? God's will be done. Gave him some tincture of lobelia and No. 6 which caused him to revive during the entire day giving some signs of a return of mind. We are all in the hands of God who doeth all things well. There is nothing too great for His almighty arm. His mercy is great toward those who fear Him and His loving kindness is everlasting. I made a poultice of charcoal for Mr. B's leg and applied it. Mrs. Reno, Mrs. Bramham, Mrs. Spilman, Miss Sallie Bramham and Frances Spilman all came up to see him.

Saturday, October 4, 1862

The morning dawns. Saw a glorious sunrise: "The heavens declare the glory of God &c". Mr. Baird's days are fast coming to an end. John Hemphill and I sat up all night. Received dispatch from Sister Sarah. Mr. Anderson arrived this evening, brought letter from Sister. Mr. Baird did not know him. Doctors have no hope of his recovery. May God comfort him in the hour of death, and may God be a husband to his wife and be her support in the day of trouble. Mrs. Spilman and Mrs. Bramham came in to see Mr. Baird. John and I sat up all night expecting him to die.

Sunday, October 5, 1862

I have seen the sun rise and set again but many a spirit has left to meet the judge of all the earth. Mr. Baird breathed his last breath at 5 minutes past 8 A.M. He died calmly and without a struggle or a groan. John Hemphill and Anderson washed and dressed the body. I went to the shop to get his coffin. Took the body down to the shop and packed it with charcoal. Went to see Captain Witherspoon, found him very low. His wife and mother are with him. I had the bodies of J. H. Bigham, Ran Poag and Jim

Confederate Hospital used by John H. Simpson, Warrenton, Virginia.

McCormick. John H. and I slept in the parlor. Our trouble with Mr. B. is over, he has gone to a land of pure delight where saints immortal reign.

Monday, October 6, 1862

Rose early, had a good night's rest, the first in 3 weeks. Packed the remains at the cemetery. Returned to Mr. Spilman's, took a last look at the old room – long to be remembered. Bid adieu to Mrs. Spilman with a sorrowful heart; also to Mrs. Bramham and Miss Sallie B. and Miss Florence Brent. I never can forget Mr. Spilman and his family for their great kindness to Mr. Baird during his sickness. May God bless and prosper them. John Hemphill went down town with me. I gave him 30 dols. and was very sorry to part with him. I left for Culpepper with Mr. Anderson. We travelled all night favored by the light of the moon.

Tuesday, October 7, 1862

Reached Culpepper about daylight. Took a short nap in the Cars. Eat breakfast at Mrs. Jones. Put the corpses on the cars, had hard work; paid 4 dollars for help, nothing can be done with money. Glad to get on the cars once more. Arrived in Gordonsville at 10 A.M. but could not put the remains on the morning train. Had to lie over all day. Very dull place to stay. Eat supper with some soldiers of the 23 S.C. V. Slept in a boxcar with the QM of the 44th Ala. Had a good bed. Sent four dispatches home containing sad news. Lord, not my will but thine be done.

Wednesday, October 8, 1862

Rose early. Had a good night's sleep, the first in three weeks. Put remains on 6 P.M. train. Paid $30 for transportation to Richmond on four bodies. Slept on the cars. Reached Richmond at 12 A.M. Ate dinner at the American. Borrowed $50 from Newton Lewis. Procured passports, etc. and left Richmond for Petersburg on 3 P.M. train. Cars are very much crowded with soldiers sick and wounded. Travelling is very unpleasant indeed. The cars smell like a hospital. Left Petersburg at sunset – been very fortunate in making connections. Thanks to God for his preserving care and great goodness to me.

Thursday, October 9, 1862

Left Weldon this morning at 1 A.M. Got to sit in the ladies cars and had a chance to sleep some. Reached Raleigh in time for train to Charlotte. A Georgian had to leave his son's remains, being so offensive. Dined at the Shops. Saw Kirkpatrick on the Cars. Reached Charlotte in time for train to Chester; another corpse, was left at Charlotte, too offensive, but mine was put on. Reached home at 12 at night. Met Sister Sarah at the door almost overwhelmed with grief. The dispatches failed to get to Chester in time. No one knew I was coming. Oh what a night of sorrow! May God's grace be sufficient for the bereaved widow. May she be resigned to His sovereign will & Say "it is good that I have been afflicted."

Friday, October 10, 1862

Rose late, did not sleep much. We are all in the furnace of affliction.[1] May God correct in mercy and chasten in love. And may we not despise the chastening of the Lord nor faint when we are rebuked of Him; He doeth all things well. Father went to Union to have a grave dug. Mrs. Hemphill and Mrs. Gaston and Miss Kate Gaston called to see us, to express their sympathy for us. I went up town, called on Mr. Harris. He settled for expenses on Jno. McNinch's sons. Retired early. Conducted worship. Isaiah went to John Bigham's &c.

Saturday, October 11, 1862

Rose early. Blessed with good health. God's loving kindness is everlasting. What shall I render to the Lord for all his gifts to me? Conducted worship and started to Union with Sister and the children in the buggy to commit to the tomb the dear remains of Mr. Baird, a kind husband and father. Went to Sister Mary's – spent the night. But God has promised to be the widows 'stay and orphan's' help. They that truly seek the Lord shall not lack any good thing. It is well to have a kind and merciful God as our refuge in the day of trouble. "If the righteous scarcely be saved, where, where shall the wicked and the ungodly appear?"[2]

Sunday, October 12, 1862

The Sabbath is a welcome day to the Christian. It is a *rest* to the people of God, an emblem of that eternal *rest* prepared for the followers of Jesus. Conducted worship, heavy rain prevented Flora and me from going to Neeleys Creek. Spent the day at home. Felt unwell, taking cold with a slight headache.

Monday, October 13, 1862

God is good and kind to the unthankful and to the evil. If thou O Lord shouldst mark iniquity, who could stand? but yet with him is forgiveness that thou mayst be feared. Went over to Elihu's on horse with Flora, dined and worked on cards &c. Returned to Sister's and set out for Chester. Called at Mrs. Moffatt's. Saw Mr. McDonald at store. Reached home at dark.

Tuesday, October 14, 1862

"Home again". God is with me in the house and by the way. Felt very unwell, took some antibilious powders—made me sick. Commenced a letter to Mr. W. R. Hemphill. Worked with my bees. Not doing well. Gathered castor beans. Cold is growing worse. Elihu came home last night from Virginia.

Wednesday, October 15, 1862

Time is rolling on, waits for no plans of man. Conducted worship. Cold no better. Finished and sent off letter to Mr. Hemphill, Due West, and received one from him about Jno and Robert and expressing his sympathies for us in our affliction. Looked at an old spinning jenny at the shops. Began a letter to Joe Moffatt.

Thursday, October 16, 1862

Cold still very bad, but am thankful it is no worse. I always consider myself blessed far beyond my merits. Conducted worship but my devotions are cold and lifeless. Oh for the spirit of prayer and supplication, of truth and wisdom. Finished letter to Joe Moffatt. Worked on spinning jenny. Sharpened saws and card. Wrote out diary at night. Had my photograph taken by Elliot.

Friday, October 17, 1862

Rose early. Cold no better but rather worse. Conducted worship, read the Bible. May the spirit teach me to understand the truth. Worked on machine; succeeded in getting it to spin very good yarn. Called on Mrs. Melton and Miss Ida. They were busy making molasses. Wrote diary at night; read Bible and prayers, etc.

Saturday, October 18, 1862

Rose early, cold no better; very much stopped up. Read Bible, conducted worship. Worked on machine – went up town; got my pictures. Very well pleased. Looked at an old spinning jenny of Alexander's. Played violin. Called at William's. Gave him a likeness. Called on Mrs. Gaston and Mrs. Hemphill. Great excitement about the smallpox. A soldier was left at depot with them. I received letter from Mr. Hemphill. Went to depot to see if he would come up on train but he did not come. I met the soldier with the smallpox but walked around him. Read *Telescope*.

Sunday, October 19, 1862

It was my blessed privilege to hear God's word preached today for the first time in many months. Mr. McDonald preached an excellent sermon on Eph 2.10. Oh that all the soldiers were at home to the truth expounded to them. Cold some better. Drove Mark to Union, dined at Joe Wylie's. Brought Martha up to William's, late getting home. Glad to meet my good friend Mrs. Moffatt at church. Gave Sister Mary my likeness, also one to Elihu's wife.

Monday, October 20, 1862

The time has come again for me to leave my dear home to go to the seat of war in Virginia. Rose early, prepared to leave. Walked over to see Mrs. Melton. Happy to meet with Misses Mag and Ada M. Went uptown. A great many fathers and mothers called to send letters and clothing to their sons in the Army. Great is the love of parents for their Sons in the army. They occupy the greater part of their time in preparing things for their comfort. But many are bereaved of the loved ones and weep over the things left behind – memorials of those gone before to a land of rest.

Tuesday, October 21, 1862

Oh how memory brings back the actions and looks of our dear departed friends. "A song or a tune or the time of year, Strikes the cord of reflection and moans in the ear." Travelled all night. Missed connection in Raleigh. Johnston Woods and Jno. Stringfellow stopped for dinner and breakfast at a private house. I hope never to stop in Raleigh again. I had a severe headache, felt very bad, often thought of home and loved ones. Left on evening train for Weldon, reached it at midnight. Secured seats in train for Petersburg. God has watched me all my life. His loving kindness is everlasting.

Wednesday, October 22, 1862

Slept very little last night, suffered very much from the headache. We never think of health until it is gone. Sickness reminds us of our frailty and dependence on divine help. Left Weldon at 1 A.M. Reached Petersburg in time for connection to Richmond. Preserved by a kind heavenly father. Put up at the Linwood House. Head some better, thanks to God for his great loving kindness. Read Bible. Oh for the spirit of wisdom. Called on Newton Lewis. Paid him for borrowed money, left my watch with him. Locked up my trunks.

Thursday, October 23, 1862

Rose early, went to depot, took the Central Cars for Staunton. Happy to meet with my good friend Mr. J. A. Spilman on train to Gordonsville. Met Col. Bratton[3] at Charlottesville. Reached Staunton. John Stringfellow and I stopped at private house. Headache some better. Staunton is an unpleasant place. Read a chapter in the N.T. It is difficult to attend properly upon the reading of God's word when I am traveling. And am disposed to make too many excuses.

Friday, October 24, 1862

God has permitted me to spend another day. My health is better than yesterday. Stringfellow and I found conveyance to Winchester in an ambulance, price $10.00. Very dusty. Met a great many soldiers coming from Winchester. Stopped at Mt. Crawford at a good house. Very cool. Health good. Thanks to God for his goodness to me.

Saturday, October 25, 1862

Rose early; white frost, very cold. Set out after getting a good breakfast for our destination; had a pleasant day. Found difficulty in getting lodging at night. Passed through Harrisonburg, New Market and Mt. Jackson. Stopped in a little town, Hawkins Town, at a poor lady's house. Thankful to get any kind of shelter but there is no place like home.

Sunday, October 26, 1862

Rose early. Cloudy and rainy, quite cool, thought of home and the Sanctuary where my fathers worshipped. I spent the day without reading God's word. This is a *sin*. May God forgive me and enable me to be a consistant Christian. Travelled all day; heavy rain but I was comfortable. Passed through Woodstock and Strasburg. Stopped with Mr. Rads in Middletown. He was very kind to us all. I am free from all pain. Great is God's mercy to me. I am far from home but it is near to my heart and in my mind night and day.

Monday, October 27, 1862

Another week has passed since I left home. Rose early. Cool and windy. Bought two pair of socks, $1.00. Set out for Winchester, arrived at noon. My passage and my trunks from Staunton cost me $21.00. Winchester is crowded with soldiers sick and warworn. Jno. Stringfellow and I started for the Reg. I took my trunks. He left me with my baggages 6 miles from Winchester on Martinsburg Rd. I built a fire and expected to spend the night alone with[out] shelter or supper. But I carried my trunks to another fire some 300 yds distant and fortunately found Mr. Jackson[4], a member of Orr's Regiment. He had a good tent and he gave me shelter from the cold and frost. Capt McAlilley, J. Lt Lipsey came out to take me to their camp. I delivered the clothing &c to them but remained with my friend.

Tuesday, October 28, 1862

Rose very early. Ground was covered with hoar frost. Went over to 23rd S.C. V. but Oh how changed since I left it below Richmond near Laurel Hill Church. Mr. Baird is no more! "He sleeps his last sleep; he has fought his last battle." Eat breakfast with Capt. Atkinson[5] but felt very sad indeed. There is no attraction to me it seems. Went to Greggs brigade, found it marching. Followed on and overtook Orr's Reg. at Bunker Hill. Glad to meet with my good friends John and Robert Hemphill, Win. L. and others. Eat dinner with Robert. Slept with Jno and Robert, fared very well. Gave Win and Robert their clothes. I should be very thankful for all the blessings conferred on me. But I often forget my Creator.

Wednesday, October 29, 1862

Rose before daylight. Slept between Robert and John, quite warm. Eat breakfast with the boys, "old veterans"; their fare is very simple but they are in good health and good spirits. Sorry to leave them on a long march, probably to Berryville. Dined with Capt. Atkinson in Co.of 23 S.C.V., felt very sad all the time. I missed Mr Baird and I think the company does too. Called a while in the 17th. S.C.V. Returned to Winchester. Walked six miles. Very tired at night. Slept on the floor.

Thursday, October 30, 1862

Another day has passed. I am one day nearer my journey's end; life is wasting away. May I improve every moment as it flies. Met Dr. Gaston on Street and Dr. Babcock. Made inquiries about taking corpse to Staunton and succeeded. Took up the body of Jas. Douglass. Called on Dr. Babcock, found him sick. Saw six Irishmen fight like dogs. This is the effect of liquor. My health is good, thanks to God for his continual goodness. I long to get home again, the dearest spot on earth to me.

Friday, October 31, 1862

Blessed beyond my merits. Health good. Packed up the remains of Jas. Douglass and set out for home once more. Not sorry to leave Winchester. One Mr. Henry took me to Woodstock in a wagon, charged me $25.00. Stopped at the National Hotel. Dined in Middletown with Mr. Boads. Saw the battleground of Kernstown[6] where Jackson and Ashby gained a glorious victory over our enemies. Had a splendid view of the mountains. They look like a vast carpet spread out to the sun. They are a monument of God's wisdom and greatness and power.

Saturday, November 1, 1862

Rose before sunrise. Searched all Woodstock for a conveyance to Staunton. Mr. Grebell agreed to take me for $40.00. Breakfasted and started for Staunton, passed through Mt. Jackson where I met with Thompson, an old college friend. Passed New Market, eat supper and reached Harrisonburg, put up at hotel. Wrote diary and read Bible, the only guide and comfort in this world of tribulation. Many are the afflictions of the righteous but God is their strength. Thou has been my dwelling place in all generations, our fathers trusted in Thee and were delivered.

Sunday, November 2, 1862

Another holy Sabbath has passed away but I have spent the day in travelling from Harrisonburg to Staunton. Oh that I could have spent the day in the exercise of God's worship! May His grace be sufficient for me! Eat breakfast in Mt. Crawford at the house of Mr. Pinkle, received a likeness for Mr. Hope. Reached Staunton at 4 P.M. Met Thos. McFadden and Ralph Nunnery at depot.

Stopped at Mrs. Brandenburg's, read Bible and engaged in prayer but my devotions are cold and languid.

Monday, November 3, 1862

Rose early. Eat breakfast and went to Depot; put remains on Cars and left for Richmond on morning train. Had a tedious ride. Met Robert Haddon at Gordonsville. Read Despatch and two tracts. Reached Richmond at 6 P.M. Met Dr. Jas. Gaston. Received letter from Sister Sarah. Stopped at Linwood House. Read Bible and retired. Thanks to God for his mercies.

Tuesday, November 4, 1862

Preserved to see the light of another day. Rose early. Engaged in secret prayer. Walked up to 3rd and Carey Streets to see Mr. Gannon, the undertaker. Got him to make two coffins for the bodies of Lt. Latimer[7] and Ellis.[8] Took up the bodies, packed them, went to S.C. depot; dined and left for Petersburg, made connection for Weldon. Happy to set sail for my dear home again. God has been my fortress and hightower. Met Col. R. Yeadon at Weldon; travelled with him to Raleigh. I took a bottle of whiskey from a mere youth who was drinking on the train. Paid him two dols. and threw the bottle out the window. God save the youth of the land from drunkenness!

Wednesday, November 5, 1862

No accident happened during the night. God has watched over me both in the house and by the way. Why need I be afraid when he takes care of the smallest insect that floats in the air. Not even a sparrow can fall, etc. Reached Raleigh in time for train to Charlotte. Put corpse aboard and set out in company with Col. Yeadon, Thos. McFadden & others. Had a tedious ride, dined at Company shops. Sent dispatch home. Rain in the evening. Reached Charlotte but too late for Cars to Columbia. Put up at the Mansion House in Charlotte. Slept with an Ala. soldier.

Thursday, November 6, 1862

God's loving kindness is everlasting. I not only deserve no favors but deserve the severest punishments. Yet God is waiting to be gracious. Another day has dawned and I enjoy richest blessing at the hand of God. Set out for home at 9 A.M. Reached Chester, met Isaiah and William and many friends. Sister sent my dinner down to the R.R. by Becky. I went on to Col. Stopped at Congaree. Subscribed for Col. Yeadon's paper, "The Charleston Courier", for one month. Read Bible and engaged in prayer, oh for the spirit of prayer and supplication.

Friday, November 7, 1862

Under the protecting hand of God I again rise to see the light of another day and am able to go on my journey. Again set sail for Due West, my second home. Reached Donalds at 3 P.M. Met the bereaved widow and mother. Rode with Mr. Robt. Ellis to Due West. Called at my old home (Mr. Grier's), left my baggage and went to the funeral in the graveyard near Mr. Jos. Ellis. Returned to Mr. Grier's. Happy to meet with my kind friends once more. I feel at home, yet I miss my good friend Livy! Josiah went over to stay with Mrs. Hemphill. Mr. H. being absent. I slept in my old college room. Those happy days are gone.

Saturday, November 8, 1862

Another week has passed away. My life is still spared but it is not because I deserve to live but because of God's long-suffering and kindness to me. Rose early. Went in to worship – read Bible and engaged in secret prayer. Talked with the children. Called on Mrs. Hemphill. Had a good time with Belle. Calvin and I went out to Col. D. O. Hawthorn to see about getting some wool carded. Calvin went after butter. I settled with Messrs. Ellis for corpse. Took tea with Mr. Bonner. Happy to see Miss Morse and hear her play. She is a fine lady and an excellent performer on the piano. Returned to Mr. Grier's. Talked with Joe. Read &c, retired to rest, sensible of God's watchful care over me.

Sunday, November 9, 1862

"How lovely is thy dwelling place, O Lord of Hosts to me &c." Today I have been permitted to join in the worship of God my Savior in Due West where I've often joined with his people in days gone by never to return. Dr. Grier preached from Mat. 5.47. Attended prayer meeting in the evening. Mr. G. conducted. I sung for him and led in prayer. Oh, that the the Spirit would take up His abode in my heart. Read Bible, engaged in prayer. Wrote diary and retired to rest. There is a rest for the people of God.

Monday, November 10, 1862

Rose early. Blessed with health. Read Bible and engaged in prayer. Called on Mrs. Hemphill and Bella. Had a pleasant time. Called on Lizzie Young. I sympathize with her in the loss of her good mother. Wrote letter to Isaiah. Went to Female College to hear Miss Morse and her pupils sing and play, but our pleasant meeting was broken up by the sad news of Win Lindsay's misfortune in losing his arm in a fight.[9] Took tea with Dr. Miller and sat until bedtime. Mr. Bonner called to see me about going to see Win. I returned to my room, talked with Joe Moffatt until 11.

Tuesday, November 11, 1862

Rose early. Wrote letter to Isaiah by Mr. Bonner. Walked up town with my good friend, W. L. Pressly. Read Hebrew with Joe Moffatt. Went to Col. Hawthorn's for wool (carded). Took supper with Mr. Hemphill. Returned to Mr. Grier's, received bundle of clothing from Mrs. Cohen. Wrote a note to Belle Grier. Learned "Gallant Girl" &c.

Wednesday, November 12, 1862

Providence is smiling on me every day of my life. Rose early. Engaged in prayer. Packed up my baggage. Called on Mr. Hemphill and family, told them goodbye. Took leave of my dear friends Mr. Grier and family. Joe Moffatt took me to depot in time for Cars. Stopped in Newberry with Dr. McMorris. Had a delightful time with Misses Nannie and Erin. They sang and played for me some beautiful songs! "Music fills my soul with sadness" &c. Sorry that Dr. McMorris was not at home.

Thursday, November 13, 1862

Rose early. Crowned with blessings. Engaged in secret devotion. Took a walk with Caldwell. Eat breakfast. Dr. McMorris returned home, glad to see him. Miss Nannie and I took a ride on horseback through and around Newberry. Had a delightful ride indeed.

She is a noble young lady. Dined; Miss Nannie sang "Music fills my soul with sadness" and I bid her and all the family farewell and took the train for Columbia. I wrote my name in Miss Nannie's album. Reached Col. in time for Cars to Chester. Called at Mr. Alexander's shop. Rec'd $2740 for Bro. William. Reached home at 10 P.M. Met Isaiah at Depot.

Friday, November 14, 1862

Time is rolling on and bringing me nearer and nearer to my journey's end. When shall I rest from these scenes of toil, sorrow and disappointment? "Lord not my will but thine be done." Conducted worship, read Bible &c. Called on Mrs. Gaston and Mrs. Hemphill. Took Grier with me. Went to Mr. Elliott's; Mrs. Elliott gave me a nice box of ottar of rose geranium. Wrote diary. Father is down on the coast making salt.

Saturday, November 15, 1862

Another week has come to an end. How short it seems — life is but a dream. Rose early. God's loving kindness is everlasting. Went to Union with Sister Sarah and children. J.H. Peoples preached. Had the pleasure of speaking to Miss Kate Caldwell. Also my friend Moffatt Grier. Dined with Mrs. Moffatt. Moffatt and I rode to Rich Hills. Returned to Mrs. Moffatt's. I went to Sister Mary's. Called Mr. McDonald. Read the riches of Bunyan. Conducted worship and retired to rest. Oh for grace to improve God's mercies.

Sunday, November 16, 1862

The Christian Sabbath has dawned again upon this wicked, troublesome world. Oh that it would bring peace and tranquility. Conducted worship but my devotions are lukewarm. Flora and I went to see Jos. Martin lying wounded and very sick. Went to church. Peoples preached in the morning; Mr. McDonald administered the Sacrament. I made some remarks at the second table— the first time I ever addressed the table of my Lord and Master. My words were few and altogether unprepared before hand. Returned home late at night.

Monday, November 17, 1862

By the blessing of God I was permitted to enjoy the light of another day. Health and peace of mind, what rare and precious blessings! Wrote letters to Belle and Laura Grier about the flowers, also to Messrs. Bonner and D. O. Hawthorn. Put handle to box of flowers. Dined and took train for Columbia. Went to G&CRR. Met J.R. Wilson with boxes for Orr's Reg.; took them to C & S.C. depot, supper at Janey's. Happy to see Rev. Brice and went with him to the Shiver house and took lodging with him. Engaged in secret prayer and retired to rest. But we talked a long time.

Tuesday, November 18, 1862

It is a difficult thing for me to feel that I deserve no favors at the hand of God. Self-righteousness has a strong hold in the human heart. By the grace of God I am what I am. Reached home today in safety. Sent clothing for Orr's Reg. on to Charlotte. The Reserve Corps left Chester today for camp. Great crowd at Depot to witness their departure. Oh the sacred ties perhaps broken today. Many hearts are sad and full of grief to see their loved ones taken from their dear homes perhaps to return no more.

Wednesday, November 19, 1862

I left my dear home today for the Army. Rose early, blessed with good health. Conducted worship, went to shop and depot to pack boxes of clothing to the 6th S.C.V. Took train for Charlotte. I always feel sad to leave home. Met with Miss Brown (Sister of Miss Laura Kerr) on train. Left Charlotte on evening train. Had a pleasant trip, cars were not crowded. May God grant me a safe journey and permit me to return to my dear old home.

Thursday, November 20, 1862

In the kind providence of God I have reached Richmond. Made a very successful trip, with all my baggage consisting of 11 boxes and two trunks. Stopped at Linwood house. Slept with J. W. Butler from Cedar Springs Abb. S.C. Wrote diary, read Bible and retired; thankful for the preservation of my life and health.

Friday, November 21, 1862

I am still a recipient of unmerited blessings. Amidst the uncertainty of life and health, I enjoy both. May I not be ungrateful to my Creator and Preserver. Rose early, eat breakfast, went to depot on Broad Street to get Mr. Baird's trunk but failed. Received letter from Mr. B. Jorden, White Hall, S.C. Slept in S.C. Depot. Met Robert Haddon on street. He told me that Win Lindsay was doing badly, very little hope of recovery.

Saturday, November 22, 1862

One week nearer my journey's end, time is carrying me on. Rose late. God's mercy never fails, His love is everlasting. Remained in S.C. Depot all day. Glad to meet Dr. Branch. Eat supper at Spotswood[10], good oysters. Wrote letter to Miss Morse, Due West. Slept in S.C. Depot. Very lonely. It is bad for me to be alone. Satan has intercourse with my heart which is evil and that continually. May God's grace be sufficient for me in the hour of temptation.

Sunday, November 23, 1862

In great mercy God has preserved my life to behold the light of another Christian Sabbath. Rose late in S.C. depot. Eat snack, went to PO; met New Lewis. Went to see Major McClure, found him at Med Col(lege)[11] convalescent; his wife asked me to remember him in my prayers. Met Dr. Branch, Les Brayerd McClure, Lewis and I went to hear Dr. Hoge. He preached an excellent sermon from Jno 8:32. Dined at American Hotel. Went to S.C. depot. Read Bible and tracts. Had a long chat with Dr. Branch about R. W. Barnwell. Went to Dr. Moore's church. Heard a good sermon from Isaiah. Oh that I was engaged in preaching the unsearchable riches of Christ.

Monday, November 24, 1862

God's [mercies] are manifold and never fail. While many are lying on beds of sickness, many are driven from their homes, I enjoy good health and the untold comforts of home. Called on Major McClure, found him improving. Eat supper at Spotswood; wrote letter to Bella Hemphill, a good friend. Slept in S.C. depot. Put up a stove in the depot; felt very comfortable. Sat up until 12 o'clock. Thanks to God for continued mercies.

Tuesday, November 25, 1862

Rose late, enjoying the smiles of a benignant Providence. Visited the battlefield of Gaines Mills with Robert Haddon. First went to one Mr. Otter who loaned us a horse, we rode double and time about. Then to Camp Norton where Orr's Reg. was encamped before the battle. Went by the field hospital, then to the spot where Dr. Clinkscales was killed; then where Pointset Lindsay; then where Livy Grier. My recollection of the places was perfect and vivid. I never shall forget that sad time! I thought of my friends who fell in the shock of battle. Saw the bones of the enemy bleaching, rooted up by hogs. Brought off the under jaw of one of the 95 N V.

Wednesday, November 26, 1862

My health is good. I am blessed far beyond my dessert. Rose late this morning. Met Mr. Bonner and J. O. Lindsay with the remains of Winfield.[12] Another friend has passed away. The friends of youth are passing like autumn leaves. And I too am a day's march nearer home.

> "Here in the body pent
> Absent from Heaven I roam
> Yet nightly pitch my moving tent
> A day's march nearer home."

Dined at the American Hotel with Mr. Bonner and Lindsay. Went to Petersburg depot, got remains on train. Took a sad leave of my good friend. May God bless the widow and the orphan. Finished letter to R. C. Grier.

Thursday, November 27, 1862

Good is the Lord to all his creatures, His mercy never ends. I remained all day in S.C. depot. Wrote letter to Mr. B. Jordan. Sat up until midnight. When shall I learn to be more economical? I spend money for that which satisfieth not. Chas. Fudge and Mr. Gaston called to see about getting transportation. I made arrangements to go to the 6th S.C. My heart is deceitful above all things and desperately wicked. Who can know it but thou O God alone. May I not fail to read his word daily and not only be a hearer of the word but a doer. May the spirit of truth abide with me forever.

Friday, November 28, 1862

Rose in good health as usual, yet I am unthankful and evil. Eat breakfast at Restaurant and supper at the Spotswood, relished the oysters very much. Took goods to the Fredericksburg R.R. Depot. Called on Maj. McClure, found him. May God be merciful to him. Met Big Neely with him. Attended prayer meeting at Dr. Moore's church. I called on the Dr. to get the loan of a manuscript sermon he preached last Sabbath night in his church. Wrote letter to Sister Sarah.

Saturday, November 29, 1862

Rose very early to take the Fredericksburg cars for Jenken's brigade to take clothing to the 6th S.C. Felt quite sleepy. Messrs. Fudge and Gaston went with me. We reached Point of Landing at noon. Met Wm McClure. I walked to Camp of the 6th Reg., dined with Captain Agure[13], then went to Kershaw's brigade and returned to R.R. to rec. goods for various Regs. Glad to meet the soldiers who are suffering for the cause of freedom and independence. God grant that we as a nation by their valor and strength be able to drive the foul invaders from our sacred homes. I opened the boxes of clothing for the veterans. Eat supper with Capt. Agure and slept very comfortably in his tent.

Sunday, November 30, 1862

Rose late in Camp of 6th, S.C. The Sabbath is scarcely known in camp. This is one of the calamities of war. Eat breakfast with Captain Agure. Called on Captain Strait &c. Then rode Paul Bonner's horse to Kershaw's Brigade to distribute clothing I brought out to Captain Hudgen's Co. Returned to 6th. Distributed clothing to various persons in Jenkins' Brig. Slept with Alex Wylie. While some are attending to the spiritual wants of the soldiers others are supplying them the comforts of this life. But it might be said of me as our Savior said to Peter, "Come follow me and I will make you fishers of men", that is, I will put you at better employment.

Monday, December 1, 1862

Another month has commenced its round. Time is stealing away notwithstanding the bustle and tussle of war and all of its attendant evils. Many will pass from time to eternity before 30 days are ended; many will reach that happy home in heaven and some will know the pains of eter' death. If God should see fit to remove me from time to eternity, I hope and pray He will take me to that Rest He has prepared for those who love His appearing. Eat breakfast first with Alex Wylie then Col. Bratton urged me come eat with him. Called on all my friends in 6th Reg. then left with Messrs, Fudge and Gaston for the R.R. and reached Richmond. Slept in S.C. Depot. Oh what a wicked heart I have. Supper at Spotswood. Rec'd letter from R. C. Sharp.

Tuesday, December 2, 1862

Slept late but sat up late last night. Eat breakfast at Restaurant. Went to Bradford's on Franklin for overcoats for Buckhead Guards, found 5, took them to the S.C. Depot. Met Rev. J. O. Lindsay; he and I went to depot on corner of 4th and Cary to hunt Col Lindsay's clothing. I received transportation for 16 packages to Gregg Brig., took them to Fredericksburg Depot. Got a passport, eat supper at Spotswood. Called on Robert Haddon at Mrs. Babers on Main Street. Met Mr. Seawright, talked until bedtime. Heard some good music. But "Music fills my Soul with sadness, yet I fondly love its strain". Went to Linwood for lodging. Wrote diary and retired to rest enjoying the blessings of Heaven. Oh that men would praise the Lord for his goodness &c.

Wednesday, December 3, 1862

God in great mercy has prolonged my days thus far. His mercy never fails. Rose early, went to Fredericksburg R.R., took Cars with Messrs. Fudge and Gaston for the Army. Reached Hamilton's Crossing at 11 A.M. Met Wm McClure. Walked to 6th Reg, dined with Capt. Agurs. Returned to Cars on horseback. Rec'd my box &c. Returned to 6th Reg., distributed all my bundles to their proper owners. Slept with Capt. Agurs.

Thursday, December 4, 1862

Rose before daylight. Slept very comfortably in *my ditch* which was dug by Orr's Reg. last spring. Had no breakfast except the crumbs of the depot agent's table. Met R. N. Anderson, waited patiently for a wagon. It came at last and I set out for Orr's Reg. with my goods. Found everything all right and my friends well, delivered all my clothing to the boys. Glad to meet with my dear friends, Jno. and Robert Hemphill. I miss my friend Win. Lindsay, he has passed away, he sleeps his last sleep, he has fought his last battle. Eat supper with John and Robert and slept between them.

Friday, December 5, 1862

Quite cool this morning. Rose early, talked with the boys. Commenced raining, then sleeting, and finally set in to snowing. Very cold. Eat a splendid dinner with Jno., Robert and Calvin G.[14] They made a nice pie out of the dried fruit I brought them. Helped the mess to carry wood in the snow. The snow and the Camp reminded me of "Valley Forge" of the Revolution of '76. The snow continued to fall until 10 at night. I will never forget the 5th of December 1862.

Saturday, December 6, 1862

Rose early. Thanks to God that I slept as much as I did last night. I still have many comforts, notwithstanding the cold and exposure. Many soldiers have no shoes and very little clothing to protect them from the keen chilly winds of a snowy December. God grant that such scenes of suffering and privation may soon come to an end. Eat a hearty breakfast with the boys. Set out in company with Mr. Wright for the R.R. in a wagon. Had a cold ride. Reached Guineas[15] in time for train. Reached Richmond at 5 1/2 P.M. Eat supper at Linwood and slept in S.C. Depot. Met Perry Hawthorn and McAdams at Linwood.

Sunday, December 7, 1862

I am glad to see the Sabbath return again. Amidst the turbulence and disquietude of this world, the Sabbath brings a sweet relief to the weary soul. Went to First Presbyterian, heard a good sermon from Dr. Moore at 11 A.M. and also at night. Called on Major McClure, found him improving. Dined at American. Slept in S.C. depot. Read the Bible and *The Words of Jesus,* an excellent little book by J. R. McDuff.

Monday, December 8, 1862

Blessed with health, thanks to my Creator for his preserving care and goodness. Rose early, eat breakfast at Restaurant. Met Perry Hawthorn, hired a wagon. Went to Belvin's for a box then to the York R. R. for charcoal and went to Laurel Hill Church; took up the remains of Moses Smith[16] and returned to Richmond in time for the evening train. Met Rev. J. O Lindsay, eat dinner and supper at Res. Wrote letter to Capt. Miller.[17] Wrote diary. Bought the "Mind of Jesus" by J. R. McDuff.

Tuesday, December 9, 1862

Man is blessed above all other creatures, yet he is the most ungrateful. "The ox knoweth his owner &c but my people doth not consider, saith the Lord." Received letter from my good friend Joe Moffatt. Conveyed my boxes of clothing to Fredericksburg R.R. Depot. Secured transportation. Wrote diary. Slept in S.C. depot. Fixed up a lunch for tomorrow and retired to rest.

Wednesday, December 10, 1862

Rose before daylight, packed up and went to the Fredericksburg R.R. depot. Took Cars for Guineas. Reached the station at 11 A.M. Met Parker, delivered his bundle, had a lonely day. Slept with a Mississippi soldier. Had short rations, bought a raccoon for my breakfast. Retired to rest in a wagon after skinning the coon.

Thursday, December 11, 1862[18]

Aroused by the roar of artillery at Fredericksburg about 3 A.M. The sound was a prelude to battle, Oh that nations would beat their swords into plowshares &c and learn war no more. Waited at Guineas Sta. until train arrived, then went to Orr's Reg., had a tiresome walk — carried a heavy bag and my coon for the John Hemphill's mess. Glad to meet my friends in camp. John and Robert Hemphill are among my best friends on earth.

Colonel George McDuffie Miller began as Captain of Company G of Orr's Rifles later rose to commmand the regiment.

Friday, December 12, 1862

Roused early by the rolling of the drum, the call to battle. The Regiment formed and marched towards Fredericksburg by Hamilton's Crossing.[19] Saw the Regiment load their guns and go into position in the woods on the brow of the hill just to the left of the R.R. Heard the artillery open about 5 A.M. I rode Capt. Miller's horse back to Camp and slept with Robt. Hemphill.

Saturday, December 13, 1862

Rose before daylight. Returned to the Regiment on line of battle. Remained there with the boys awhile. Met Rev. Monroe Anderson. He and I went above the lines to the right. Had a splendid view of the enemy advancing to meet our army.[20] Mr. A. and I engaged in prayer for soldiers about to go into battle. About 2 P.M. Orr's Regiment was surprised by the enemy but it was at last driven back. Some of our brave men fell, martyrs to the cause of freedom. Gen. Gregg was mortally wounded.[21] I helped to put him in the ambulance. George Chiles was wounded in the shoulder; Lieut. Higgins[22] was killed. I waited on the wounded all evening. Made Chiles a bed of straw and returned to the Camp, thankful to God for his mercy.

Sunday, December 14, 1862

The holy Sabbath has returned, but Oh what a contrast between the day and the employment of the day. Behold two vast armies arrayed against each other ready for the work of destruction and blood[shed]. Returned to hospital, found Chiles doing well but many have passed from time to eternity. Gen. Gregg with all his military glory has gone to meet his final judge who is no respecter of persons. Earthly honor and position will not shield any from the shafts of death. I started to the 6th S.C. but became tired and returned to Gregg's.

Monday, December 15, 1862

Life and health are continued to me. May God's grace be sufficient for me. Rose early in camp; eat breakfast, returned to the hospital, found Chiles still lying on the ground. Rode Capt. Miller's horse up to the 6th S.C., took a view of Fredericksburg and the Yankee army from the surrounding hills. Thanks to God for his goodness in delivering us as a people from the invader's cruelty.

Tuesday, December 16, 1862

Time is rolling on and many changes are taking place. Rose early in camp, roused by a heavy wind and rain. Robert H. and I were sleeping in a little fly tent but had to leave it. Eat breakfast, rode Major Norton's [horse][23] to see Geo. Chiles at Mr. Ballock's near the R.R. summit. Then started to the brigade but met it coming back to camp.

Wednesday, December 17, 1862

Rose early, blessed with health. O that I might be able to promote God's glory by living a life of holiness and devotion to the truth. Read Bible, took Chiles to R.R., put him on Cars. And spent the day in putting the wounded Yankees on the Cars. Left for Richmond at 6 P.M., rode in ambulance car. Reached Richmond at 2 A.M. in the morning. Took Chiles to Keen & Baldwin hospital.[24] I saw a soldier die soon after entering the hospital. Went down to S.C. depot. Woke up Glasgow and went to bed.

Thursday, December 18, 1862

God in much mercy has spared my life during the darkness of the night. The day has dawned and passed away and what have I done to advance the glory of God? Went to see George Chiles at hospital. Called on Rev. Anderson at Linwood, also Maj. McClure, found him improving in health. Sent dispatches to Dr. Branch and Geo. Chiles' father. Wrote letter to Sister, commenced one to Joe Moffatt. Received one from Sister Sarah. Met Rev. J.O. Lindsay on street. Slept and took my meals in S.C. depot. Bo't one lb. butter, paid 10 dols, my part of cooking stove.

Friday, December 19, 1862

In the good providence of God I am still enjoying life and health without which life itself is a burden. Rose early, eat breakfast, finished letter to Joe Moffatt. Went with Rev. Lindsay to see Jno. M. Pruit in the Roister Hospital.[25] Returned and called on Geo. Chiles. Sat a while. Called on Major McClure, found him better; took him a bottle of sherry wine. Dr. Moore and wife called on the Major while I was there. They are very social and friendly. I called at Linwood to see Rev. Anderson and Lindsay, the latter went to Transportation office. I went to Broad Street.

Saturday, December 20, 1862

Rose very early. Took the Cars for Fredericksburg with clothing for Kershaw's Brig. Had a safe trip to Hamilton's Crossing, waited for my goods which arrived after daylight. I slept very comfortably, invited a Georgia and N.C. soldier to sleep with me. They caused my oilcloth and blanket to be burned. They stuck their feet into the fire while sleeping. But kindness will have its reward at some future time, if not in the present. Very cold night.

Sunday, December 21, 1862

Permitted to see the day dawn and pass away. Eat a very light breakfast. Waited for the wagons to come after my boxes but they did not come. Spent the Sabbath in watching my goods. Oh that

I could enjoy the blessings of the Christian Sabbath. May I soon return to my master's work.

Monday, December 22, 1862

Slept well last night on a pile of tents. Weather very much moderated. Glad to see it warm. Wagons came for the boxes which I delivered to the QM of the 2nd S.C. V. Set out for Orr's Reg. towards Port Royal which I found about sunset. Glad to meet my dear friends again.

Tuesday, December 23, 1862

Slept with John and Robert last night. Thanks to God for friends and a shelter from the cold. Wagons returned from Guineas with the 4 boxes of clothing which I distributed to the destitute soldiers from Abb[eville] in Gregg's Brigade and surplus to the needy in Orr's Regiment. Tired at night. John and Robert Hemphill and Calvin Galloway received their clothing at last. I was glad it was not lost. The mess received a tent which was large enough for two; namely, Jno. H. and Jno. Chiles. We had butter and potatoes for dinner and supper. They came from Due West.

Wednesday, December 24, 1862

Time is rolling on "waiting for no man". How much of my time has run to waste? May I be enabled to live to the glory of God henceforth. Rose early in good health. Eat breakfast with John and Robert and left Camp for R.R. Reached Richmond at dark. Stopped at S.C. depot. Wrote diary. Read Bible &c. Retired to rest.

Thursday, December 25, 1862

The 25th of December has come again; how has the year passed away? Many friends are sleeping in their graves. Thanks to God for one more year. May the next be a year of peace! Rose early. Went to P.O., received letter from J. McClure, called on Geo. Chiles in morning and took him some rice pudding and eggnog which I assisted to make on the 3rd floor in S.C. depot. Had a fine dinner. May I not abuse God's mercies. This is Sister Sarah's birthday. What a change has come over her heart and home since her last birthday. May God's grace be sufficient for her.

Friday, December 26, 1862

God in his great mercy is giving me life and health, food and rai- ment in abundance. "Bless the Lord O my soul and forget not all His benefits." Rose early, assisted in preparing breakfast. Went to P. O.; received nothing. Called on Chiles, took him some apples. Called on Major McClure. Weather quite warm. Brought knapsacks of the Orr's Regiment from Fredericksburg depot to S.C. depot. Played piano in a music store. Mr. G. Poor brought his violin down. I was glad to see it. Read chapter in the Bible. Engaged in prayer and retired.

Saturday, December 27, 1862

This is the last Saturday of 1862. Life is like a shadow. I am one year nearer my eternal home. I am guilty of a great burden of sins committed during the past year. God has not dealt with me as I have sinned. Oh may I not abuse his forbearance! Assisted in getting breakfast. To P.O., received letter from Dr. Branch. Put away knapsacks. Called on Chiles. Took him some apples. Bought five pounds of lard and a pipe for Captain Miller and tobacco for Chiles. Wrote letters to old Mr. Chiles and Robert Hemphill. Called on Major McClure. "By the grace of God I am what I am."

Sabbath, December 28, 1862

I have no claims on the mercies of God yet He is crowning me with His loving kindness and tender mercies. Called on Ma- jor McClure, Branard and N. Lewis. I went to Dr. Hoge's church, heard a good sermon. Dr. H. was absent to Europe.[26] Took Mrs. McClure to Dr. More's church, was introduced to Dr. M's mother-in-law.

Monday, December 29, 1862

Rose in good health. I am dependent on God for all I enjoy. The year is nearly gone, I have committed a multitude of sins, and yet I cannot count the mercies bestowed on me. Went to P.O. &c. Called on George Chiles, found him improving. I am very anx- ious to go home to see my dear friends.

Tuesday, December 30, 1862

Nothing is important to record today. Still blessed with health. Amidst the disease which prevails in the City I go unharmed. A merciful Providence is watching over me, guarding off the shafts of death.

Wednesday, December 31, 1862

This day the year closes. God has brought me to its close. His eyes have been upon me for good from the beginning to the end. I can say, "Hitherto has the Lord helped me". "Praise the Lord O My Soul." Tomorrow I will begin a new year. May I set out afresh and may I be kept from all evil and keep close to my Savior.

Farewell 1862, one year nearer heaven, my home.

Notes

[1] Refer to Isaiah 48:10b.

[2] 1 Peter 4:18.

[3] Colonel John Bratton, commmanding the 6th South Carolina Infantry.

[4] There are at least four members of Orr's Rifles with the last name Jackson.

[5] Captain J. F. Atkinson, commanding Company F, 23rd South Carolina Infantry.

[6] The battle of Kernstown was fought on March 23, 1862, and resulted in a tactical defeat for "Stonewall" Jackson. Strategically, Jackson was able to keep Union troops in the Shenandoah Valley away from McClellan's army then besieging Richmond.

[7] Benjamin Milton Latimer, died in Richmond, August 1862 of wounds received at Gaines Mill.

[8] William F. Ellis or William J. Ellis, both of Company G, Orr's Rifles both died of disease in Richmond in the summer of 1862.

[9] A small skirmish occurred on November 2, 1862 at Castleman's Ferry on the Shenandoah River near Snicker's Gap. Gregg's Brigade lost only three wounded, one of which was Private Winfield Lindsay, aged 23.

[10] The Spotswood Hotel, one of the most famous hotels in Richmond.

[11] The Medical College of Virginia Hospital, holding up to 68 patients.

[12] Winfield Lindsay died on November 20, 1862 of his wounds received at Castleman's Ferry.

[13] Captain John L. Agure, Company A, Calhoun Guards 6th South Carolina Infantry.

[14] Calvin Galloway, Company G, Orr's Rifles.

[15] Guinea's Station, the northern most supply point on the railroad line to Richmond.

[16] J. Moses Smith, Company G, Orr's Rifles, died of disease in Richmond, August 1862.

[17] Captain George McDuffie Miller, commanding Company G, Orr's Rifles.

[18] On this day the Union Army of the Potomac, now commanded by Ambrose Burnside, crossed the Rappahannock River to engage Lee's Army of Northern Virginia at Frederricksburg.

[19] A.P. Hill's division marched to join the main body of Lee's army at Fredericksburg. The division held the high wooded ground south of the town.

[20] Burnside's army attacked the Confederate army in two separate assaults around Fredericksburg, both of which were repulsed.

[21] Gregg was killed while trying to keep Orr's Rifles from firing on the Union attackers, whom he mistook for his own men. Orr's Rifles lost 21 killed and 149 wounded in the battle.

[22] Lieutenant W. W. Higgins, Company G. Orr's Rifles.

[23] Major Joseph J. Norton, Orr's Rifles, who was wounded and lost an arm in the battle of Fredericksburg.

[24] General Hospital Number 6, formerly the dry goods business of Keen, Baldwin, and Company. The Hospital was located on Main Street and held approximatley 100 patients.

[25] The Royster Hospital, or First Alabama Hospital, was formerly the Royster Brothers and Company Tobacco factory and was located on 25th Street.

[26] Moses Drury Hoge, a noted Presbyterian preacher — In 1862 he ran the blocade to England and returned with a cargo of 10,000 Bibles, 50,000 Testaments and 250,000 misc. publications. p. 366, *I Rode with Stonewall* by Henry Kyd Douglas, U.N.C. Press.

Chapter 9

"GOD REMEMBERS MERCY"

As the year of 1863 comes into being, the Confederacy seemed ready to fulfill it's promise as a new nation. After early reverses of the previous year, the war was carried North into Kentucky and Maryland, only brought back to Virginia and Tennessee by the end of the year. The spirits of General Robert E. Lee's army were lifted with the victory at Fredericksburg, and despite reverses in the West, the South seemed ready to continue the war until independence was won.

For Simpson, the year opened with the backbreaking work of tending to the sick and wounded soldiers in the crowded hospitals in Virginia, the bereaved families at home, and caring for the soldiers still in the ranks in the freezing cold of winter. Under such labor, the mental fatigue of observing so much suffering would have been tremendous, and in times of need, Simpson would turn to God in his prayers for the strength to continue his work of mercy.

Thursday, January 1st, 1863

A new scene of time begins today. I am one year older, and one year nearer the grave. Many are the changes since this 12 months ago. Alas! how many of my dearest and best friends have passed away! God has afflicted the nations and caused them to feel the power of His anger. But thanks to the Governor of the world for his great and signal blessings to us as a nation. He has not only delivered us from our enemies but has enabled us to drive them before our victorious armies. Many homes have been sad and desolate by the cruel enemy. But God will provide for the widow, the orphan and the needy, who put their trust in him. Zion has been made to mourn the loss of her children. God is their refuge in the day of trouble. I commenced the year in good health, may God grant me grace and strength to spend the year in promoting his glory and the welfare of all his creatures. Teach me O God so to number my days that I may apply my heart to wisdom.

Called on Maj. McClure, met Mr. Robt Sites with Geo. Chiles. Wrote letter to Sister Sarah. Mr. Glasgow & I cooked dinner &c in Maj Poor's absence. May God continue to bless me.

Friday, January 2, 1863

The year has opened fair and beautiful; may God crown it with his goodness. He has given success to our armies in the west. Went with Mr. Sites to the Dill farm and took up the body of Thos Jordan & sent it home by Mr. Sites. Sent a telegram. Called on my sick & wounded friends.

Saturday, January 3, 1863

Blessed with good health. Rose early, took Fredericks' R R for Hanover.[1] Stood on platform for 10 miles, very cold. Delivered my boxes. Met Rev. Barnwell and returned to Richmond. Safely through another week, God has brought me on my way, Alleluia!

Sunday, January 4, 1863

The Sabbath has dawned again but I have wasted much of its precious hours in bed. Oh! that I were a faithful servant of Christ. I pray for strength to improve my time. Called on my sick & wounded friends. Heard Dr. Moore preach the funeral of 3 members of the Washington Artil.[2] Heard Dr. Burrows at night.

Monday, January 5, 1863

Set out for home today with Maj McClure. God has spared his life; may he repent and be converted. Went over to Chimborazo[3] in morn' to see Dr. Babcock; rec'd 100 dols & letter from him for his wife. Left Richmond in even'; reached Petersburg & tarried for the night. Had prayer in Mrs McC' room. Wrote letter to Glasgow.

Tuesday, January 6, 1863

Rose early; invoked God's blessing during the day. Permitted to pursue our journey home. Maj McC' became very sick in the cars at Petersburg. Had a prosperous journey to Weldon & Raleigh. Very much pressed at Raleigh; cars about to leave us. But I succeeded in getting everything aboard.

Wednesday, January 7, 1863

God has granted me a prosperous journey. I reached home to-day with Maj McClure. Found all my friends enjoying God's blessings. Glad to meet my friends at home once more. Very tired. Took a nap in evening. Conducted worship; wrote letter to Dr. LaBorde & wrote diary.

Thursday, January 8, 1863

Rose in good health. Once more I breathe my native air. What a grateful creature I should be! Put on a linen shirt: had my hair trimmed. Called on Maj McClure who is doing well. He made me a nice present in a pair of boots and a pair of dog skin gloves. Miss Ida Melton called on Sister Sarah. I met Miss Mag Alexander at Mrs. McClure's. Spent a pleasant evening at Mrs. Melton's with Misses Mag & Ada. Miss Mag played some beautiful songs; I thought of those by gone hours. Settled with Mr. Harris &c. Mr. Harris gave up his notes for half price.

Friday, January 9, 1863

In great mercy God is prolonging my unprofitable life. Did nothing worthy of record. Worked with my hat and coat. Went up town. Sent letter (to) Dr. LaBorde. Rain to-day, very muddy.

Saturday, January 10, 1863

The week has come to a close; all its deeds are recorded and I must give an account in the Day of Judgment. Conducted worship in the morn. Read Bible &c. Went down to Elim's to work on my hat; finished it. Called on Mrs. Gaston & Miss Eliza also Maj. McClure. Went over to Mrs. Melton's – had a fine time with the ladies. Sang some beautiful songs.

Sunday, January 11, 1863

The Christian rejoices to see the Sabbath. It gives an opportunity to commune with God our Father and Savior. Oh, that the spirit would keep my heart from every evil thought. Went to Union, heard Mr. McDonald from Dan. 3. Took Emaline to Church. Went by Uncle John Fennell's, dined at Joe Wylie's, borrowed a pocket handkerchief from Mrs. Wylie. Returned home at dusk. Read Bible and retired on the lounge.

Monday, January 12, 1863

Rose at 1 o'clock this morning; took the cars for Columbia. Had a safe journey. Stopped at Nickerson's. Met Ruf Pratt and Capt Haddon. Called on C. D. Melton at Gov' office. He introduced me to Dr. LaBorde and Rev. Martin. I bought Hadley's *Sacred Mountains*. Called on Miss Virgie Melton at Dr. Reynold's; had a pleasant visit. Saw Miss Alice McFadden. Took night train for Chester. Brought a valise for Mrs Melton. Reached home in safety at 10.

Tuesday, January 13, 1863

Permitted to see the light of another day. Assembled the family round the family altar and worshipped the God of our father. The loving kindness of the Lord fills &c. Called on Mr. Harris & Mrs. McClure to tell them that I was not going to Va to-morrow. Called on Mrs. Melton; no one home but Miss Eliza &c. Eat supper at Wm's. Elihu & boys came up. Sarah has a severe headache.

Wednesday, January 14, 1863

How rapidly time flies! One month of 1863 is half gone. Oh that I could chain the hours as they pass. Thankful to say my health is good, far beyond merit. Conducted worship &c. Went down to depot. Read *Last Days of Pompeii*, until 12 o'cl P.M. Rev. Rob. Lathan's[4] sisters spent the night with us.

Thursday, January 15, 1863

Although this is a world of Sin and trouble I enjoy many good things: Life, health, home and kind friends — Priceless blessings. Conducted worship. Read Bible &c. Worked on Spinning Jenny. Played violin & piano. Read *Last Days of Pompeii*.

Friday, January 16, 1863

God's mercies never fail, the loving kindness of the Lord is everlasting. In excellent health. Conducted worship &c. Oh for a new heart! Read Bible. Played piano & violin. Read *Last Days of*

Pompeii. Took tea with Mrs. Hemphill. Called on Miss Mag Alexander; returned home at 11 1/2 P.M.

Saturday, January 17, 1863

Another week with all its sorrows, its trials, and its joy is gone forever. I am permitted to sing of mercy and unnumbered blessings. Read Bible, assisted Isaiah to read Horace. Read Bulwer. Went uptown; bought thread &c. Saw militia drill.

Sunday, January 18, 1863

I do not love the Sabbath as I should. My heart is too much concerned about temporal things. Oh for grace & strength to resist the evil one. Read Bible. Went to Church; heard Rev. White.[5] Read "*The Mind of Jesus*". Retired at 10.

Monday, January 19, 1863

Rose early, blessed with health of body and mind. Oh how grateful I should be to God the Fountain of all good. Went to depot. Sent letter to Joe Moffatt. Happy to meet my good friend R. R. Hemphill. Went with him to Mrs. Gaston's. Saw R.W. Brice; met Mrs. Gaston (on) street. She kissed Robt. We then called at Mr. Hemphill's & dined. Talked with the family. Walked to Mr. Hemphill's office. Returned to H's for tea. Robt. came over with me. We sat up till the train came. He and father went down to get her. Father went to Charleston.

Tuesday, January 20, 1863

Rose later than usual. Read Bible; assisted Isaiah in getting his Greek lesson. Went to Depot; attended to some boxes. Went up town. Called at Mr. Abbright's; then to West for cap front. Dressed; went to Maj. McClure's & dined. Fixed Spinning Jenny. Took tea at Mrs. Brawley's. Sat until bed time; had some good music; played violin & returned home at 10. Wrote diary; read Scripture; retired to rest.

Wednesday, January 21, 1863

God has blessed me with good health; a good home; kind friends. Thanks to God for his great mercy. Wrote diary. Read Bible.

Rec'd letter from Rev. Martin & replied. Went up town. Sister Sarah made me a nice cap. Mrs. Melton gave me the cloth. Read *Last Days of Pompeii*.

Thursday, January 22, 1863

I have many mercies to record. In a time where disease & war are carrying thousands to the grave I am spared. Conducted worship. Went up town &c. Packed up my trunk. Called on Mrs. Melton who gave me Mrs. Alexander's silk dress to sell in Richmond. Sorry to leave home; bid the loved ones goodbye; took the cars for Richmond. Delayed at Charlotte. Called on Miss Laura Kerr. She gave me two songs: "Then You'll remember Me" and "Lorena".

Friday, January 23, 1863

Left Charlotte this morning at 3 o'clock; put all my baggage on the train. Set out in good health. Met with a detention on the way to Raleigh. The baggage car broke down and ran off the track & crossed over a high bridge. Thanks to God for his deliverance from destruction.

Saturday, January 24, 1863

Reached Ral(eigh) this morning about 2 o'clock. Very grateful that my life has been preserved amidst the dangers to which one is exposed travelling. Reached Weldon at 10 A.M. Delayed until morning train. Had no sleep. Oh, for a grateful heart!

Sunday, January 25, 1863

The Sabbath has dawned again upon a wicked world. I left Weldon at 3 A.M. for Petersburg. Christians desire to spend the Sabbath in reading the Scriptures and communing with God. Heard the church bells chiming for the first time. Oh what joyful sounds! Reached Richmond at 7 P.M. God granted me a safe journey; met with Wm Walker, the author of Southern Harmony.

Monday, January 26, 1863

Rose late, but in good health. Eat breakfast; read Bible. Went to P. O. rec'd letters from Rev. J. I. Bonner, Miss Morse, Joe Moffatt

& Moffatt Grier and Rev. W.R. Hemphill & Robt. H. Glad to hear from my friends. Rec'd transportation & book boxes to Fed R Dpt.

Tuesday, January 27, 1863

Rose early. Crowned with mercies. Took cars for Hamilton's Crossing; reached the 6th S.C. at 11; found all in good health and fine spirits. Heavy rain but the Soldiers have good tents with chimneys. Dined with Romere. Slept with Sir Stringfellow.[6]

Wednesday, January 28, 1863

Permitted to see a new day. God's mercies never fail. Took breakfast with Stringfellow. Went over to the 2nd Reg; also the 5th. Took the cars for Richmond. The ground is white with snow and it is still falling. Sung with Mr. Walker.[7] Reached Richmond in safety at 6 P.M.

Thursday, January 29, 1863

Rose late but in good health. Sent letter north for Miss Morse. Went to 2n Auditors office. The conscript officer stopped me on street. Played violin and read newspaper. Called on my friend Chiles; he is doing well. Thanks to God.

Friday , January 30, 1863

Blessed with excellent health. I am unable to number the mercies bestowed on me. "By the grace of God I am what I am." Rec'd letter from home containing one from Joe Moffatt & J.R. Wilson. Called on Geo. Chiles; took some religious papers for him to read and to others in No. 8.[8]

Saturday, January 31, 1863

Another week closes today. My life with all its comforts is still continued. Thanks to God for his goodness. Walked to Peters' R R Depot. To transportation office, then to Va Central R. Depot. Brought Soldiers from "*Soldiers home*"[9] to supply their wants. Rec'd power of attorney from Sister. Sung with Mr. Walker; read, engaged in prayer.

Sunday, February 1, 1863

Time is moving rapidly, weeks seem as days. The holy day of rest has come and gone. May God forgive the sins of this day; my heart is evil and that continually. Oh for a fresh supply of grace. Went to Pres(byterian) C(hurch); read Bible &c; called on my friend. Rain at night.

Monday, February 2, 1863

I still enjoy rich temporal blessings – life, health, food and raiment, these all come from God the Giver of all good. Rose early, took cars on the Cen' Va. for Gordonsville, thence to Culpepper with boxes for 1st S.C. Cav. Had a safe journey. Stopped at Mr. Shorts. Wrote letter to my good friend.

Tuesday, February 3, 1863

Rose early in good health; slept with a stranger. Weather very cold & snowy. Waited for the freight train; met Joe Westbrook, Flenniken. Was glad also to meet my good friend Callie Lindsay. Came to Gordonsville on freight, very cold. Read Bible &c.

Wednesday, February 4, 1863

Rose in good health; slept very cold last night. Took the 6 o'clock morning train for Richmond. Read Bible & Bulwers *Disowned*. Reached Richmond at 11 A.M. Called on Chiles, found not doing so well. Went to P.O. Talked with Glasgow &c. Called on Newton Lewis; received my watch from . . . .

Thursday, February 5, 1863

Thanks to God for his goodness. He is crowning me with loving kindness. Glasgow went to the army with supplies. I wrote a letter to Miss Mollie Martin for my friend Chiles, also to his father. Called on Chiles, read letters to him. Went to soldiers home.

Friday, February 6, 1863

Time passes away almost like a dream. Life is short. Oh that I might spend my life in promoting the glory of God, who is so kind to me. Met Lieut. Charles. Went to Peters' Depot at night, met

Robt Hemphill and saved him from Sergt Crows home. We went up to Spotswood at night to see Lt. Charles.

Saturday, February 7, 1863

Rose late. Eat breakfast. Robt H. gave us some butter. We went to see if Crow would give him transportation but he refused. Went over to Manchester. Then to transportation. Robt got transpor' and also a passport to Guineas. We visited Va St Library. Went into Pizini's Saloon on Broad Street.[10] Robt treated, Bought sigars. Called on Chiles who is doing some better.

Sunday, February 8, 1863

The holy Sabbath has returned with all its blessings to man and beast. Rose early, went to Fred. R.R. Depot with Robt Hemphill who left for the army. I returned to bed, had a good sleep. Went to Dr. Moore's church, heard Boggs, chap(lain) of 6th S.C.V. preach. Met Robt. Poag. Called on Chiles, found him doing some better.

Monday, February 9, 1863

Health is good, excepting sore tongue and throat. Went to Rockets[11] with Robt Poag, took boat for Drewry Bluff.[12] Visited all the fortifications. Went on board the *Richmond*[13] commanded by Capt. Pegram. Returned to the city; highly pleased with my excursion. Called on Chiles.

Tuesday, February 10, 1863

Beautiful day, mild as spring. Read Bible but I must confess that I do not search the Scriptures as I should. Wrote letters to Mr. Chiles, Jno. R. Wilson, R.C. Sharp and Mrs. W. W. Higgins. Went to P.O., to the soldiers home — sat up with Chiles to vent his wound. Played piano, learnd Lorena [song].

Wednesday, February 11, 1863

No one properly estimates health until he is sick. Thanks to God for his goodness to me! Sat up all last night with Chiles who is improving. Went to Hos. No. 18,[14] distributed papers and talked with sick and wounded S.C.V. Took a nap after breakfast. Fixed my boot etc.

Thursday, February 12, 1863

God is daily loading me with his benefits. May He enable me to improve his blessing. Went to P.O. Went to Hos N 18 looking after the wants of S C soldiers. Met Mr. Wright and his son. Bought pair Boots for Grier, price 6 dollars. Sat up last night took a nap in evening.

Friday, February 13, 1863

Sat up with my friend George Chiles. He is improving I pray God may spare his life and restore him speedily to health and friends. Met my friend O. A. Wylie on furlough home. Went to Soldiers home in evening.

Saturday, February 14, 1963

Another week has passed away. The year is creeping slowly by. Retired to rest at 5-1/2; my friend rested well last night. I slept until 10 AM. Went out to Hos No. 1, found four S.C. soldiers.[15] Met Dr. Jas Gaston at Depot. Went to sleep at 6 P.M. Went to No. 6[16] to sit up with Chiles. Mr. Pickle came tonight with supplies.

Sunday, February 15, 1863

Retired to rest this morning. Sat up all last night with my friend Chiles. Slept too late for public worship. Alas, how I waste the precious hours of the Sabbath. Read Bible, engaged in secret prayer. Took a cup of coffee at Restaurant.

Monday, February 16, 1863

I begin another week crowned with rich temporal blessings. While thousands are confined to bed I enjoy good health. Retired to rest at 5 . Slept until 10. Went to Hos No. 1, rec'd letter from Moffatt Grier. Wrote letter to Mr. Bonner while sitting up with Chiles before day this morning.

Tuesday, February 17, 1863

Felt very sleepy this morning, retired at 6 A M, slept until 9 ; eat breakfast. Went to P.O. Called on Chiles, bought him a pie. Met Mr. Romere. Helped in arranging boxes. Wrote letters to Jno.

Chiles and Thos. Chiles. Mr. Markley treated (me) to some nice cake. Mr. Price and I played checks. Sang Lorena for him.

Wednesday, February 18, 1863

My health is good, but get very little rest. Do not go to bed until 6 A M, sit up all night with my friend Chiles. Very cool, damp weather. Wrote letter to Moffatt Grier; commenced one to Joe Moffatt. Read Bible, but my mind is too much engaged with earthly things.

Thursday, February 19, 1863

Still cloudy, very damp. Oh for the merry sunshine once more. Retired this morning at 6. Rose at 9 went to hospital, then to the Medical Director. Got a transfer for Chiles to the Samaritan Hospital.[17] Put him in an ambulance. He sat up all the way. Found a more comfortable place. I dressed his wound and washed him and put on clean clothes. I went to bed at 11. The 6th S.C. Reg. passed through Richmond today.[18]

Friday, February 20, 1863

The sky is clear and the sun once more gladens the earth with its rays. Arose refreshed from a good night's rest. God's mercy never fails. Went to Depot, breakfasted, returned to Hos', dressed Chiles wound and sent for a barber to trim his hair. Sat and talked with a Mr. F. Sanders. Meet Lt. Cousan at S.C. Depot. Wrote letter to Thos. Chiles.

Saturday, February 21, 1863

Rose early in good health, thanks to God for all his goodness to me. Eat breakfast, dressed the wound then to the S.C. Depot; packed some boxes. Hammond and I went to Camp Windor,[19] I met with some old friends. Talk(ed) with a dying soldier Clinton from Union. Read some Psalms to him and engaged in prayer. Returned to Depot. Wrote letter to R.R. Hemphill. Bought him some articles. Played violin and drafts with Hammond. Very cold, snow began to fall at night. Sent dispatch to Mr. Thos. Chiles.

Sunday, February 22, 1863

The Sabbath has returned with a heavy snow on the ground, and it continued to fall the most of the day. Rose early, dressed the wound, went to Depot. Read Bible &c But I did spend the day very profitably. Thought too much on the world. Mr. Walker and Markley took tea with us.

Monday, February 23, 1863

Sent 340 dollars home by Geo Melton. Rose early, blessed with health far beyond my merits, "Oh that men would praise the Lord for his goodness &c. " Dressed wound, went to Depot. Played violin with Hammond. Clear all day, sunshine. Went to Soldiers home &c.[20] Geo. Chiles rec'd a box and two letters from home.

Tuesday, February 24, 1863

Blessed with good health. Had myself vaccinated by Dr. Little. Dressed Chiles' wound, wrote letter to his father. Wrote to Sister Sarah. Streets very muddy, snow is melting very fast. Nothing of interest to record. Received letter from John Chiles. Wrote to Capt. Miller.

Wednesday, February 25, 1863

Time is rolling on, life is wasting away little by little; it will soon be gone. Oh how diligent I should be in preparing for the world to come. Went to soldiers home, saw Furguson and Patton from Neelys Creek. Commenced reading "Lily and the Bee". Dressed the wound night and morning.

Thursday, February 26, 1863

Rose early and in good health, arm sore from vaccination with a slight headache. Dressed the wound which is doing well. Came to Depot. Heard of Rev. H. T. Sloan being in the City. Returned to Hospital and was happy to meet with a dear friend. We went to the Senate chamber to see Col. Orr, quite warm and rain all day. Mr. Sloan and I talked a long time with Chiles. He brought me a letter from Mr. Thos. Chiles. Went to Soldiers home. Saw some of Orr's Reg[iment].

Friday, February 27, 1863

The month is nearly gone. My life and health have been preserved. Thanks to God for goodness. Dressed the wound. Went to Depot, met Rev. Sloan on Street. Chiles received letter from H. Gray. Went to Peters' Depot. Read "Lily and the Bee". Messers Price and Pickle returned from army. Returned to Hospital; found Mr. Sloan &c. Bought a pair of tuning forks, price 5 dollars.

Saturday, February 28, 1863

Another small segment of time is gone never to return. Rose in good health; walked over to Chimborazo. Saw J. E. Johnson, Thos. Wylie and others. Returned to Depot with headache. Dressed Chiles. Read Bible and retired to rest.

Sunday, March 1, 1863

The morning was cool and wet. Came to Depot for breakfast; returned to hospital, dressed the wound and went to hear Dr. Moore. Heard a good Sermon. Dined, read Psalms &c. Went to church. Dr. M at night, thence to hospital; dressed Chiles wound.

Monday, March 2, 1863

Delightful day, mild and pleasant as May. Oh for peace once more. Eat breakfast at depot. Returned to hospital, dressed the wound. Had a conversation with R. W. Barnwell about getting a Chaplain's place. Have a very sore nose. Read "Lily and the Bee".

Tuesday, March 3, 1863

Another beautiful day. "Spring is on her way." Felt weak and very badly, nose very sore with a boil in the inside. Dressed wound, went to Peters' depot. Finished "Lily and the Bee". Met Mr. H. T. Sloan at Linwood. Glad to see him. Slept at S.C. Depot.

Wednesday, March 4, 1863

"Oh that men would praise the Lord for his goodness &c". He gives me richly all things to enjoy. Rose early. Dressed wound. Boy, Cyrus, was severely injured in the Depot. Hammond and I cooked supper. I returned to hospital, read "The Two Lights".

Thursday, March 5, 1863

I am still a recipient of God's mercies. Dressed wound, read Bible. Returned to Depot. Received letters from Sister Sarah, Rev. C. B. Betts and one Mr. Graham. Wrote to Lester S. Green. Poor returned from army. Met Sergt. Pratt from Due West.

Friday, March 6, 1863

Rose early, and in good health. I thank Thee O Lord for thy mercies. Dressed wound. Went to Fredericksburg; attended to shipping supplies to the army. Dined at 3 P.M. Worked with baggage of Col. Orr's Regiment. Talked with Chiles at night &c.

Saturday, March 7, 1863

Another week has passed away. Time will soon be gone with all its troubles. I am unable to count the mercies I enjoy: Life, health, friends, and hope, all are mine. Dressed wound, changed treatment from charcoal to flour. Read The Two Lights. Received letter from Sister Sarah.

Sundays March 8, 1863

Blessed day, the best of all the week. Rose early to take the cars for Guineas but failed to get off. Was out in a heavy rain. Heard Dr. Moore in the morning. Read and studied the Psalms. Bright sunshine all day. Returned to hospital. Met Lt. Pratt[21] and Wilson[22] from Due West. They called on Chiles.

Monday, March 9, 1863

Rose early, took the cars for Guineas. Had a safe journey in company with Lt. Pratt and Wilson. Met Capt. Haskell[23] and Mr. Price at the station. Delivered my baggage to them and returned to Richmond. Read The Two Lights on the train. Returned to hospital. Met Hammond at Depot. Read "The Fallen" a poem in the Southern Illustrated news. Talked with Chiles.

Tuesday, March 10, 1863

Oh that men would praise the Lord for his goodness and for wonderful works to the children of men. Rose early, breakfast at the hospital, dressed wound, returned to S.C. Depot; played drafts with Hammond. Met J. C. Maxwell on street. Snow and sleet in the morning; rain in evening.

Wednesday, March 11, 1863

How rapidly time passes away. March is nearly half gone. Rose early in good health. Dressed wound. Wrote letters to Mr. Chiles and Sister Sarah; played violin. Met my classmate J. C. Maxwell. Played drafts. Went to Dr. Moore's church. Walked with Mrs. Mayo to her home.

Thursday, March 12, 1863

Life, health, and hope are still extended unto me. Rose early, went to depot for breakfast; returned to hospital and dresssed Chiles' wound. Read "The Two Lights". Sent off letters. Called on Mr. Walker, borrowed singing book from him.

Friday, March 13, 1863

Man's days are like a weaver's shuttle. No time should be spent in idle thoughts and conversation. But alas I abuse God's mercies. Dressed the wound. Went to breakfast. Went to see the place where a mournful accident occurred, 40 or 50 ladies killed and wounded by the explosion at the laboratory.[24] Ladies called on Chiles; I was introduced to them.

Saturday, March 14, 1863

God's love is everlasting. How precious is thy grace Oh Lord of hosts. Another week is numbered with the past. Read Bible. May the Spirit of God quicken my dead heart. Had a conversation with Dr. Lafan. Played violin &c Talked with a Soldier Mr. Hanson on a death bed; sat up with him until 12 at night.

Sunday, March 15, 1863

The holy Sabbath brings untold blessings to man and beasts. Read Bible; went to Church, heard Dr. Moore. I communed with the Presbyterians for the first time. I felt like joining the people of God in celebrating his wondrous love. His text was Ruth 1.16-17. Had an oyster dinner. Heavy rain at night.

Monday, March 16, 1863

The month is half gone. Oh that I could improve each moment as it passes. Read Bible &c. Dressed wound; went to S.C. Depot; talked with Mr. Pickle. Played drafts with Douthet, played violin. Changed my board from Depot to the Samaritan Hospital. Saw a fire engine work at night. Got a passport for Gordonsville.

Tuesday, March 17, 1863

Rose early, and in good health. Thanks to God for his providential care over me. Took the cars for Gordonsville to look for S. P. McGaw. Found his name registered, sent to Lynchburg. Stopped at hotel. Looked at the Soldiers' graves at Gordonsville.

Wednesday, March 18, 1863

Slept soundly, rose refreshed. "Oh, that men would praise the Lord &c." Bought two fur hats, $15.00 a piece. Took the cars for Lynchburg at 12, passed through Charlottesville, reached Lynch' safely, went to Fergusons hospital. Found that McGaw died on the 10th of Dec. '62.

Thursday, March 19, 1863

Rose before sunrise. Had a good night. Slept in the Ferguson hospital. Went down to the Norvell house for Breakfast. Wrote letter to Rev. Wm Hemphill. Sent a telegram to Rev. H. T. Sloan. Eat dinner at Norvell, 2 dolls, a meal. Took cars at 5 P.M. for Richmond. Heavy snow.

Friday, March 20, 1863

Reached the Samaritan Hospital at 4 A.M. Slept until 8, breakfast and took a nap. Went down to S.C. Depot, rec'd letters from Lt. O. A. Wylie and Lt. Pratt. Went to Surge' Gen' for Landers papers. He & I called on Mrs. Mae Watkins & family; took tea. Enjoyed ourselves very well. Played piano &c.

Saturday, March 21, 1863

God's love is everlasting; He is good to the unthankful and the evil. Read Bible &c, went to P. O. & S.C. Depot. Loaned Lorena (song) to Miss Ida Watkins. Sat up all night with Mr. Hanson. Sung with Mrs. Mayo. Wrote diary. Oh for peace.

Sunday, March 22, 1863

Went to bed this morning at 6. Thought Mr. Hanson would die before the morning would dawn. I took a sleep after breakfast. Mr. H. died at 11 A.M. Felt dull and sleepy all day. Read nothing but the Bible, and not much of it !!

Monday, March 23, 1863

Death has entered the Samaritan Hospital and carried off a victim. May the living take warning. Dr. Moore conducted the funeral services. I went to the burial. Mrs. Watkins called in evening. Read Greek Testament; played drafts with Chiles. Conducted worship and sung a hymn for the first time.

Tuesday, March 24, 1863

Rose late but in good health. Chiles is improving. He and I read a Chapt. in Greek Testament. I went to Surg. Gen., to P.O. and S.C. Depot. Wrote letter to Sister Sarah. Fixed clock in hospital. Sung at night with Mrs. Mayo. Exchanged pocket books with Mr. Monday but he backed out.

Wednesday, March 25, 1863

Life is passing and will soon be ended, with all its troubles and sorrows. Received letter from Sister S and Jno Hemphill. Bought a gold clasp from Monday. Went to S.C. Depot. Played violin, talked with Mrs. Brice and Mr. Pickle. Called on Mrs. Watkins; found no one at home. Walked with Mattie and Ellen Watkins on Capitol Square. Went to Lecture at Dr. Moore's church. Talked with Chiles and retired to rest after reading the Bible.

Thursday, March 26, 1863

Another day has ended. Nothing of interest to record. Life and health are continued. Worked on clock. Dined. Took a nap. Went to P.O., received letter from Robt Hemphill. To the S.C. Depot, talked with Price and Pickle. Read "La Moure" Talked with Chiles. Read Bible, engaged in prayer.

Friday, March 27, 1863

In the midst of deserving wrath God remembers mercy. Rose late. Went to P.O. Thence to Depot. Called on Bot Poag. Went to Dr. Moore's church in morning. To 2nd Pres. Eat supper. This day was observed as a day of humiliation, fasting & prayer. Captain Miller called on us at night.

Saturday, March 28, 1863

Time passes by almost unnoticed. We are all soon to go the way of all living. God is loading me with his goodness. Rain and cool. Did not go out. Wrote diary; felt very sleepy. Read Bible. Oh for the Spirit of wisdom.

Sunday, March 29, 1863

The gospel is the wisdom of God &c. Oh that I were more zealous in proclaiming the good news to a dying world. Went to P.O. Heard Dr. Reed in 1st Pres(byterian) Church. Heard Dr. Junkin in 2nd Pres. Church. Went to Dr. Moore's Church at night (preached) from Song of Solomon 2:15, "Take the foxes, the little foxes that spoil the vines." Mrs. Dr. Hoge and Mrs. Dr. Brown called to see Chiles.

Monday, March 30, 1863

March is drawing to a close. Thanks to God for his mercies to me and to my country. He is the God of nations. May He ere long deliver us from our persecuting foes. Read Bible. Mrs. Watkins called on us. I called on her at night. Played piano &c. Rec'd Due West Telescope.

Tuesday, March 31, 1863

Another month begins today. I pray that God would spare my unprofitable life. Bless our army and give us victory and peace. Read Bible &c. Called on Col. Orr in reference to getting a chaplaincy for John Hemphill. Mrs. Watkins called.

Notes

[1] Hanover Junction, approximately 25 miles north of Richmond, where the Virginia Central Railroad joins the Richmond, Fredericksburg, and Potomac Railroad.

[2] The Washington Artillery of Lousiana was one of the elite artillery units in the Army of Northern Virginia. The three soldiers were killed in the battle of Fredericksburg, December 13, 1862.

[3] The Chimborazo Military Hospital was perhaps the largest hospital in the world during the Civil War. The hospital was located on a bluff overlooking the James River.

[4] Robert Lathan was a minister in Yorkville, S.C., who graduated from Erskine College in 1855 and the Seminary there in 1858.

[5] Archibald Whyte, a prominant and well respected minister from York County, S.C., who also served several terms in the state legislature.

[6] J. J. Stringfellow, Company F, 6th South Carolina Infantry

[7] Wm Walker, author of "Southern Harmony".

[8] St Charles Hospital.

[9] Confederate Hospital on Henry and Clay Streets.

[10] Pizzini's Palace of Sweets was well known for it's confectionary delights.

[11] Rocketts Landing was the main dock for the city of Richmond for James River traffic.

[12] The fort located at Drewry's Bluff marked the outer Richmond defense line on the James River, and blocked Union gunboats from attacking the city.

[13] The C.S.S. Richmond was a Ironclad vessel built for the defense of the Confederate capitol.

[14] General Hospital Number 18, established in 1861 and caring for at least 260 patients. Located on 22d Street, between Main and Franklin Streets.

[15] General Hospital Number 1, or the Alms House Hospital. Opened in June 1861, the city poor house became a haven for wounded and sick Confederate soldiers.

[16] General Hospital Number 6, or the former Keen, Baldwin, and Company dry goods store located on Main Street held about 85 patients.

[17] Samaritan Hospital was a private hospital with a capacity of 90 patients. Located on Clay Street.

[18] The regiment along with the other units of Hood's and Pickett's Divsions were moving toward Suffolk, Virginia under command of Lieutenant General James Longstreet. The move was to counter any Union attack up the James River.

[19] Winder General Hospital was a 98 building complex housing over 3,000 patients.

[20] A small hospital housing about 40 patients. Located on corner of Clay and Henry Streets.

[21] Lieutant James Pratt, Company G, Orr's Rifles.

[22] James S. Wilson, who left Erskine College to join Company B, 7th South Carolina Infantry in 1861. He was discharged in 1862 with rheumatism and before completely recovered joined Company G, Orr's Rifles in March 1863.

[23] Captain William T. Haskell, of Abbeville S.C., commanding the Sharpshooter Battalion of McGowan's Brigade.

[24] A building in the cartridge manufacturing plant on Brown's Island exploded, killing 40 women and injuring 20 more. The shortage of manpower in the South forced women into war manufacturing.

Chapter 10

"MOTHER WEPT TO SEE HER SON HOME AGAIN"

As spring neared, everyone in Virginia and for that matter everyone in the South knew that battle was not far away. With the good weather and improved roads, the Union armies would soon be on the move to renew the struggle to conquer the Confederacy. For Simpson and almost everyone in the South, there was hope that through the battles of 1863 there would come resolution to the war, that from suffering would come the reality of Southern Independence. The hopes of the South were focused on Virginia, where Robert E. Lee's army would again take the measure of the Union strength.

In the coming months, Simpson would be in the center of the events in Virginia, as the battle of Chancellorsville raged around him. He would be close to the dying "Stonewall" Jackson, and see the movement of Confederate troops north toward a small town in Pennsylvania called Gettysburg. Yet, despite the drama in the clash of nations, the need to be home in South Carolina was foremost in his mind. Throughout the bloodshed and suffering of battle, Simpson's thoughts turned foremost to home.

Wednesday, April 1, 1863

Rose early. Bought shad for boys in camp, gave $25.00 for five. Went down to Medical Director's Office. Witnessed a mob rob a Store on Cary & Main Streets.[1] It was an awful sight. Walked home with Mrs. Watkins. Went over to Chimborazo, saw Dr. Babcock and Dunlevy.

Thursday, April 2, 1863

Time is rolling on. Life and health are continued. Went down to the Med' Director's Office. The low women of Richmond assembled and robbed Several Stores. I never Saw Such a Sad Spectical.[2] Felt bad at night; Chiles and I played drafts &c.

Friday, April 3, 1863

Rose early. Went down to P.O., and S.C. Depot. The women collected again but were dispersed by the military authorities. Took Chiles to Med. Dir' to be examined. Got a transfer to Col[umbia]. S.C. Went to S.C. Depot, packed up our clothing, took leave of the Samaritan Hospital and set out for Petersburg Depot. Called at Mrs. Watkins. Reached Weldon after midnight. Chiles stood the travelling well and so did Smith a N.C.V. from the Samaritan.

Saturday, April 4, 1863

God favored us with a Safe journey. Reached Raleigh about 4 PM. I succeeded in getting my patients on the train for Charlotte. Had 2 seats for each one. They rested very well, slept very little. Left Smith at Harrisburg about daylight.

Sunday, April 5, 1863

Chiles and I arrived in Charlotte at 6 A.M. Put up at Kerr's, eat breakfast and went to bed and slept until 5 P.M. Felt very tired. C endured the trip very well. I called on Mrs. Kerr. Read Telescope. Retired at 8 P. in good health.

Monday, April 6, 1863

Rose late, but blessed with the richest temporal blessing, life and health. Took the cars at 8 A.M. for Col(umbia). Reached Chester at 12 M. Glad to meet Mother and Sister and all the family with a good dinner. Arrived in Col[umbia], put up at Wayside Hos.[3] Met Gen. Braley and Mr. Kennedy. Eat Supper at Nickerson.

Tuesday, April 7, 1863

Rose early. Dressed Chiles' wound, took him before the Med. Board and rec'd a furlough. Went to Nickerson Hotel. Met Dr. Gray, C's brother-in-law. Mr. Hemphill took me "to the Leg' Hall, heard speeches on the Distillation bill which passed the House. Talk with Dr. Gray and Capt. Bradley.

Wednesday, April 8, 1863

Morning dawned beautifully; took train at 7 . Reached New Market at 2 P.M.; met a carriage and arrived at Gen. A.P. Bradley's at 5. Geo. Chiles' mother wept to see her son home again. Stopped at B's then to T. Chiles. Met Miss Gray and others.

Thursday, April 9, 1863

Rose early and in good health. Met Jno. Chiles' wife, talked with family until 10-1/2, then went to R.R. and ran up to Due West. Glad to see my dear friends again. Talked with Mr. Grier and family. Met Mr. Bonner and Miss Morse at Gate. Gave Belle Grier a photograph.

Friday, April 10, 1863

Blessed with usual good health. Breakfast, took a walk. Conversed and left for Chester. Sorry to part with my friends so soon. Reached Chester 12 at night. Happy to get home again; retired at 2 o'c. Latt' to see the war.

Saturday, April 11, 1863

Oh that men praised the Lord for his Gracious gift. I am an ungrateful creature. Went down to Union. Heard McDonald. Went to Sister Mary's in evening & Isaiah was with me.

Sunday, April 12, 1863

How the privileges of the Sabbath have come and gone. Father and mother came down. I went to Bro. Elihu's. Mr. Brice assisted Mr. McDonald in his communion services. How lovely are thy Tabernacles Oh Lord of Host to me. I conducted worship.

Monday, April 13, 1863

Rose early, eat breakfast; John Calvin took me and Grier to Lewis T.O. Met Messrs Rosborough and Joe Wylie at T. O. Came to Chester on train. Glad to get home. Met Mr Rev. Hunter on the train. Called on Mrs. Melton. Saw Miss Mag Alexander. Wrote letter to Mrs. Mayo at Samaritan, Richmond.

Tuesday, April 14, 1863

God's love is everlasting and His mercies fail not. Commenced a Sermon on Jno 3. 19; wrote very little. Oh for more grace and wisdom. Called on Mrs. Melton. Sung with the Misses Alexander. Very cool and rainy all evening and night.

Wednesday, April 15, 1863

I am still the receiver of unmerited blessings. Conducted worship night and morning. Wrote on Sermon with some success. Mr. Jno Poag called to see me. Played violin, piano &c. Read papers, Called to see Bro. William.

Thursday, April 16, 1863

Oh for more grace to preach the everlasting gospel. Conducted worship morning and evening. Wrote Sermon. Talked with Miss Mag Alexander. Elihu came up. Mrs. Nail, Mrs. Dunlevy called to see me. Played violin. Took a smoke before going to bed.

Friday, April 17, 1863

Time seems to fly more rapidly when we are busily engaged. Man strives for worldly honors: "Vanity, all is vanity". Finished Sermon. Miss Mag Alexander asked me to go fishing but I had no time. Took tea with William, Grier eat with me.

Saturday, April 18, 1863

Health is still continued. God be praised for his goodness. Studied sermon to be prepared if called on to preach. Took the cars for Rock Hill in company with Rev. Hunter and wife. Rev. Boyce and Rev. Brice on our way to Pres[bytery]. Stopped at D.C. Roddy's and spent the night. Brice and I slept together.

Sunday, April 19, 1863

The holy Sabbath is a blessing to the human race. But the day is often desecrated and spent in sin and folly. Conducted worship, D Roddy took us to Tirzah. Glad to see the Brethern once more. Rev. Boyce preached. I sung for Lathan. Betts and I went to Mr. Jno Barron's.

Monday, April 20, 1863

Weather clear and warm, very pleasant. Conducted worship. Played piano for the ladies, took a walk. Went to Church. Lead the singing; Mr. Brice preached. The pres(bytery) called on me for excuse for absence at last meeting, was sustained. Pres called on me to make a statement of my labor in the Hospitals. Went with Lathan to Mr. Steel's. Conducted worship.

Tuesday, April 21, 1863

Rose in good health. God's mercy is everlasting. Took a walk with Lathan, Betts and Steel. Looked at his fine hogs &c. Went to church. Pres(bytery) appointed me as "Hospital Missionary". Spent an hour in devotional exercises. Pres adj(ourned). I went to Rock Hill, dined in Ebenezer with Mr. Killian, played piano for his daughters and they played for me. Stopped at Mr. D Roddy's until train came; took cars with Betts and Boyce. Mr. Boyce stopped in Chester and spent night with father.

Wednesday, April 22, 1863

Rose late. Mr. Boyce conducted worship. Talked a while. Mr. B and I called on Mrs. Gaston. Worked with my bees, added another box and removed. Read papers. Played violin and piano. Called on Miss Virgy Melton. Had a pleasant visit; Oh for peace once more.

Thursday, April 23, 1863

Sun rose clear and warm. Conducted worship; read Bible and called on Mrs. Gaston; was introduced to Mrs. Dr. Jas Gaston. Called on Mrs. Hemphill and Miss Anna Wylie, looked at her bees. Delivered fifty dollars to Mr. Babcock. Fixed my bees. Took tea with Mr. Maj E C McClure. Maj McClure gave me an exemption. Talked with Mrs. McC and Mr. Harries. Returned home and packed up to leave for Richmond. Mother and Sister sat up until I left at 12 at night. Isaiah went to Depot. Took leave of my dear loved ones at home.

Lucius Gaston Home, York St, Chester, South Carolina.

Friday, April 24, 1863

Reached Charlotte at 5 A.M. Met Mr. Howze and Mrs. Dr. Jas Gaston and Mrs. Dr. B. Gaston. Mr. Howze put the ladies in cars for the army. I had a pleasant time on the cars. Little "Bernard" (son of Mrs. B.G.) was good company and a beautiful boy. Reached Raleigh at 11 P.M.; had a safe trip.

Saturday, April 25, 1863

Reached Weldon at 8 A. M. Procured passports and transportation. Left for Petersburg at 9 A.M. Took a nap but Little Bernard woke me up. Reached Petersburg at 3 P.M. called at S.C. Hos(pital); delivered bundle to Mr. McMaster. Reached Richmond in safety at 6 P.M. Put up at Arlington House. Wrote letter to Sister Sarah.

Sunday, April 26, 1863

Rose early, left Arlington House for Fredericksburg. Succeeded in running the blockade with the Mistress Gaston. Reached

212

Hamilton's Crossing at 10. Met Drs Jas & Brown Gaston: delivered their wives to them. I returned to Guineas and walked to Camp Gregg. Glad to meet my friends in Orr's Reg[iment] and the 12th & 13th.[4] Met my dear friend Rev. McElwee in the 12th., R.R. Hemphill walked over with me.

Monday, April 27, 1863

Rose late, felt tired from my walk from Guineas. Took a walk with R.R. Hemphill over to the 37th N. C.[5] to see Sergt Torrence, brother of Mrs. Dr. B. Gaston: returned by the 13th S.C. Saw Al S. Douglas. Talked with Bro. McElwee: prevailed on him to preach at night in Orr's Reg. I sung for him &c.

Tuesday, April 28, 1863

The month is rapidly passing away God is displaying his great loving kindness towards me, an unworthy creature. Went over to the 12th S.C. Met Bro. McElwee, talked with him and his brother and (had) mess. Enjoyed Jno and Robt's "box from home"; slept with Jno & Robt Hemphill.

Wednesday, April 29, 1863

Rose early. Eat breakfast; Jno. Hemphill & I started for Hamilton's Xing to get Lieut Higgins' body. Heard heavy guns before leaving camp. Saw the Yankees crossing the Rappahannock.[6] Jno H. went back to camp. I went to Mr. Guests[7] to see the Mrs. Gaston and spent the night.

Thursday, April 30, 1863

Rose early. Slept in Mr. Guest's parlor. Heard that the Yankees were crossing in a strong force.[8] The Messrs. Gaston prepared to leave for Ashland. I took them to Guineas; too late for the train. We went to Mr. Chandler's[9] and spent the night. Great excitement — wagons came back by hundreds.[10]

Friday, May 1, 1863

Blessed with good health. Rose late, went down to Depot. Heard wild rumors about the Yankees. Put the Ladies on the Cars but failed to get part of their baggage on the train. They went on, I remained with the baggage. Met Bro. McElwee, took baggage up to Mr. Chandler's and spent the night. Heard firing.[11]

Saturday, May 2, 1863

Mr. McElwee and I slept late, took a walk. Heard heavy firing. Took the cars for Hamilton Crossing. Bro. McE. and I started for the McGowans Brigade; failed to find it.[12] Slept in a Stable. Met Dr. Jas Gaston on the plank road. We drove the Yankees back 2 miles.

Sunday, May 3, 1863

Could not sleep last night on account of the roaring of musketry and artillery. Beautiful morning: but Oh what awful fire works for the holy Sabbath! Bro. McElwee and I engaged in prayer for the success of our arms. Set out to hunt our friends. I found some of Orr's Reg[iment] S.C. wounded & killed on the field.[13] Bro. McElwee and I walked over the dreadful battlefield of Chancellorsville.[14] Saw men shot and mangled in every way. Went to the field hospital. Met Bob Haddon who informed me of our wounded. Found Jas Wilson killed on the field and buried his body.[15]

Monday, May 4, 1863

Slept with Robt. Hemphill last night who was slightly wounded. Went to D.H. Hills hospital,[16] found Mittie Witherspoon of the 30th N.C. mortally wounded.[17] Met Jno Witherspoon in the breastworks on the plank road. Started to Hamilton's Crossing to send dispatches &c; came in range of the Yankees on the plank road. Was between two fires on the plank road. Aimed to get to Mr. Guest's but the Yankees were there.[18] Returned (to) Kershaws hospital[19] and spent the night with Tom Brown.[20]

Tuesday, May 5, 1863

Heavy rain today. All the field hospitals were flooded; the wounded were in a bad condition; ground wet and muddy. Bro McElwee and I had a good tent but did not sleep very much. I read and prayed with Mittie Witherspoon, told him there was no hope of life and asked him concerning his prospect for the future. He expressed a hope of eternal life through the Lord Jesus Christ. May God be merciful and pardon his sins.

Wednesday, May 6, 1863

Still blessed with health, God's mercy never fails. Still raining. I went down to see the Orr 's Reg., found them in rifle pits but under marching orders. Heard the Yankees had recrossed.[21] Bro. McElwee left me, sorry to see him leave for Orange. I slept alone. Went up to A P Hills hospital before night.

Thursday, May 7, 1863

Still cloudy and damp. Talked with Mittie about the Salvation of his soul. He told me that he trusted in the Lord Jesus Christ as his Savior and in a few minutes died. I closed his eyes and left for Hamilton's Xing, Left Mr. Black to bury Mittie. I reached the Crossing just in time for the ambulance train.[22] Stopped at Guineas and spent the night with Chandler. Heard that Gen. Jackson was worse.[23] They would not allow me to go into his room.

Chandler House, Guineas Station, Virginia, house where General Stonewall Jackson died.

215

Friday, May 8, 1863

Rose late but very much refreshed. Read Bible and engaged in prayer. Went down to Depot. Met a friend, Dav Saunders of Ala. I went to Hamiltons. Sent dispatches to Mr. Hemphill and others, and to Dr. Boyce. Met Lt McLauchlin and Arthur Wardlaw.[24] Fixed them up comfortably in a tent; worked with the wounded nearly all night.

Saturday, May 9, 1863

Time is rolling away rapidly, life is short. Oh that I could improve every moment as it flies. Put Lieut McLauchlin and Wardlaw on the cars and left for Richmond in a box car. Took Wardlaw to the Samaritan Hospital, dressed his wound and retired very tired. I met Mrs. Watkins at Hospital.

Sunday, May 10, 1863

Rose late but in usual health; dressed Arthur Wardlaw's wound. Read Bible, went to Dr. Moore's church. Met Newton Lewis and Robt Poag. Felt dull, took a nap. Read some. Found Alfred Wardlaw on train, took him to Mrs. Watkins'. Dressed wound. Mrs. Watkins called to see Wardlaw. Oh for peace.'

Monday, May 11, 1863

Rose early and in good health. Oh that men would praise the Lord for his goodness &c. Went to see Alf Wardlaw at Mrs. Watkins. Dr. Logan removed him to the Poor House Hos.[25] I sent dispatches to his father and to Arthur. W. J. Wardlaw reached Richmond this morning; called at Samaritan.

Tuesday, May 12, 1863

Very warm and oppressive. Oh for a cool shower to refresh the poor wounded soldier. Dressed the wounds. Read the Bible to the wounded. Met Rev. Gillyard from Greenville, S.C. Read Newspapers. May God spare the lives of our Soldiers.

Wednesday, May 13, 1863

Time is rapidly rolling away, thousands go to their long home every day; am I prepared to go? Am I redeeming the time? Dressed wound, called to see Lt Cothrans.[26] Met Dr. Wardlaw from Abb(eville) S.C. to see his son. Conducted worship. A cool and refreshing shower fell in the afternoon late.

Thursday, May 14, 1863

Rose very late. Sat up all last night with the wounded. Went to Chimborazo. Visited the wounded, distributing religious papers. Called on Dr. Babcock. Went to Poor House Hos: Wardlaw's still living. Took him to Dr. Bolton's on Grace Street. A number of Ladies called to see the wounded at the Samaritan. Rec'd a letter from Sister Sarah.

Friday, May 15, 1863

Rose very late, eat breakfast at 10 A.M. Lay down this morning at 5. Mr. W.H. Smith died this morning at 2 o'clock, a young man, I dressed the body. The Father of the deceased was present and was sore grieved. I endeavored to sleep but could not. Wrote letters to Robt Hemphill and Jno Witherspoon and one to the Due West Telescope.

Saturday, May 16, 1863

The earth is full of the loving kindness of the Lord. Felt dull, called on Mrs. Watkin's. Maj and Dr. Wardlaw called at Samaritan. I made arrangements about coffins to take to Fredericksburg for Higgins', Wilson's and Witherspoon's remains. Sat up with the wounded. Oh for peace!

Sunday, May 17, 1863

Rose late, slept 3 hours last night. Took a nap after breakfast. Dressed Wardlaw's wound. Went over to Chimborazo; distributed *Telescopes*. Heard General Jackson's funeral by Dr. Moore. It was a good sermon from . . . and was heard by an immense audience.[27] Retired at 11 o'clock.

Monday, May 18, 1863

Rose early, blessed with good health. Eat breakfast early, went to S.C. depot, then to Fred[ericksburg] R R; took the train for Hamilton's. There I met Jno Hemphill, Maj Wardlaw and R H Wardlaw and set out for Chancellorsville. Took up Witherspoon's and Wilson's remains about sun down. Met some Yankees on the battle field hunting the bodies of their friends. Slept on the ground near the battlefield.

Tuesday, May 19, 1863

Rose early, eat a little snack and set out for the R.R. Took up Lieut. Higgins' body, carried it and the others to Richmond, reached City at 5 P M. Stopped at Samaritan, found that my friend Wardlaw had gone home. Washed and retired, very tired.

Wednesday, May 20, 1863

God's loving kindness is my only security from suffering and death. Went over to Chimborazo. Rec'd 10 trunks from S.C. Depot. Packed the bodies in charcoal dust. Put them on train; failed to get on Col Nails' remains, the train left too soon. I reached Weldon 3 o'clock A.M. Eat supper in Petersburg.

Thursday, May 21, 1863

God has in great mercy permitted me to travel towards home thus far in safety. Left Weldon at 5 A M, breakfast . Reached Raleigh and left at 12. Dinner Shops, God's eyes are upon all those who fear him. Succeeded in getting on all the corpse.

Friday, May 22, 1863

Reached Charlotte at 6 A.M. Breakfast at Kerrs Hotel. Met Bro. Sloan and wife. The whole family are in great distress in consequence of the death of W. J. Kerr,[28] killed at Chancellorsville. Reached Chester at 12, met Sister Sarah with a good dinner and a nice coat and pants. Glad to see home once more. Went on to Col[umbia], stopped at Nickerson's, met Jno. Bryson in gold buttons. Put on my new coat and called on Miss Virgie Melton.

Saturday, May 23, 1863

Another week has passed into eternity. I have been kept on the shore of time by the mercy of God, may I be prepared to launch forth when called upon. Left Col. at 7. Met with Mrs. Dr. Wardlaw and daughter on train; happy to form their acquaintance. Left Lieut. Higgins' body at Hodges Depot. Went on to Donalds with Jas Wilson's body, and delivered it to his bereaved parents. I went to Mr. Jno R. Wilson's house with remains. Joe Moffatt and I came to Mr. Grier's for supper and returned to Jno R Wilson's.

Sunday, May 24, 1863

The quiet Sabbath has returned, I hail the morn with Joy and gladness. Breakfast, took a walk, conducted worship. Brought Bella Hemphill to Due West. Moffatt Grier and I went to funeral at Long Cane.[29] Dr. Turner preached. We returned home in even. to Due West.

Monday, May 25, 1863

I am happy to meet my friends in Due West once more. But some are on beds of sickness, viz, Mr. Bonner, Jno H. Wideman, both very sick. Talked to Mr. Grier and family; called on Mrs. H. Belle Grier played for me. I conducted worship. Slept up stairs. Called on Boyd at Fed Nances.

Tuesday, May 26, 1863

A very pleasant time at the Female College. Miss Morse gave me some good music. Walked home with Lizzie Young. Dined with Mrs. Hemphill. Belle Grier treats me very coldly and disrespectfully. Fixed Mrs. H's sewing machine. Sat up with Mr. Bonner.

Wednesday, May 27, 1863

Time rolls away rapidly although the war hangs heavily upon us. Very gloomy news from Vicksburg.[30] May God deliver us. Joe M. and I dined with Mr. Young. Went to Female College; "Won by the sweet omnipotence of Song". Joe M. and I took tea with Mrs. Lee, called on Mr. Bonner and Mr. Wideman.

Thursday, May 28, 1863

A day long to be remembered by me. Demanded a return of my ring and likeness from Miss Belle Grier; she refuses to give them up and refuses to see me in parlor with her Mother. Called on Mrs. Gallaway and Mrs. Droker. Called on Mr. Bonner with Dr. Grier. Slept with Moffatt. Mrs. Grier and all the family treat me with great kindness.

Friday, May 29, 1863

Rose early, packed up trunk preparatory to leaving Due West. Belle Grier and the boarders came to room to bid me good bye. I went over to Mrs. Hemphill's; told all goodbye. Took leave of my dear friends Mr. & Mrs. Grier and family. Moffatt and I set out for Abbeville C.H. in a buggy. Had a pleasant ride, Asked Moffatt to explain Belle's conduct towards me. Moffatt had his papers fixed up and returned home. I stopped at Col. Perrins[31] to see Arthur Wardlaw. Had a pleasant time with Miss Sallie McBryde.

Saturday, May 30, 1863

Rose late, conducted worship last night and this morning for Mrs. Col. Perrin. Enjoyed Miss Sallie McBryde's company and Mrs. Perrin's. Called on Judge Wardlaw and General McGowan,[32] was introduced to Judge W's daughters. They played for me and I for them. Called on Lt. Cothran at Col. T. C. Perrins. Dined with Mrs. Col. Perrin. Called on Mrs. Dr. Wardlaw, assisted in getting her unfortunate son out of the cars and into the house. A sad scene when his mother met him. Mr. Sloan sent up for me in a buggy. Reached his house at sunset; glad to meet my friends.

Sunday, May 31, 1863

Rose a little after Sunrise. Walked over to Dr. Devlin's after breakfast to see Mrs. McGaw and Bro. J.E. Pressly. Mr. Sloan requested me to preach for him. Studied sermon. Went to Long Cane, preached in evening from Jno. 3.19. J.E. Pressly preached in the morning. I met a great many of my old pupils in music; they have changed very much since I used to sing at Long Cane. I came to Mr. Thos. Chiles with Capt. Bradley. Spent night with my old friend George. Wrote letter to Moffatt Grier.

Monday, June 1, 1863

Rose quite early, blessed with good health. Eat breakfast. Sat and talked with Mrs. Chiles and Miss Fannie Gray. Told her all about my love scrape with Belle Grier and how she treated me. Went up to Dr. Devlins, dined with him and Mrs. McGaw. Mr. and Mrs. Sloan and Mr. Pressly also dined with them. Had a pleasant day. Returned to Mr. Chiles, then went to Esqu Ad Wideman to see Miss Sallie and Miss Statia. Miss Sallie played for me, spent a very pleasant evening. Conducted worship and retired.

Tuesday, June 2, 1863

The month has set in beautifully with refreshing showers from heaven. Conducted worship this morning. Miss Sallie played for me again. I bid Miss Statia goodbye. Walked with Miss Sallie to her school room; fixed her piano, tuned it and fixed 9 keys. Dined with Mr. Robt Sites. Spent a very pleasant day with Mrs. Sites; told her how Belle Grier had treated me and what I thought of her. Returned to Mrs. Chiles. Rode up to Capt Bradley's and spent the night. Told Thos C. Bradley all about my love difficulty. Conducted worship for Capt. B.

Wednesday, June 3, 1863

Heavy rain early this morning. Rose before sun up. Conducted family worship, breakfasted, took a walk with Thos. Bradley. Had fine fun in driving Capt. Bradley's bees; they stung everything and everybody but I drove them into a chest and took some nice honey. Returned to Mr. Chiles after dinner. Met Mrs. Jno. Chiles, chatted about the war, the girls, and matters in general. Succeeded in getting George in the notion of going to see his sweetheart. Told him all about my difficulty with Belle Grier.

Thursday, June 4, 1863

Rose a little after three o'clock in order to get to the R.R. in time for the cars for Alston. Eat breakfast before day light and bid adieu to my dear friends in Abbeville. Thos. Bradley went with us to New Market. Arrived in time, met my trunk from Due West. Received letter, types &c from Belle Grier. Showed them to Geo. Chiles on the train. Stopped at Alston. Met my friend and rival

Jno. Martin who took us to his house and treated us very kindly of course.[33] His father had to visit a sick sister. Miss Mollie did not play for me, but I played for her &c.

Friday, June 5, 1863

Rose late this morning, eat breakfast, took a walk, chatted and played a little. Then took piano all apart and fixed two keys. Dined and took leave of dear friends; teased Jno. Martin about Belle Grier; challenged him for a duel in sport. Jno sent me to his aunt's house where I met Dr. Boyce. Mr. Martin's aunt died this morning. Mr. Boyce took me to his house. Met Mrs. Boyce with tears in her eyes; she weeps for her dear son Mittie whose remains I brought from Chancellorsville. Met Miss Galloway. Conducted worship and retired.

Saturday, June 6, 1863

Time is rolling away very rapidly. Life is but a shadow which quickly passes. Rose early, eat breakfast. Mr. Boyce gave me $40.00 as a gift for bringing home Mittie's remains; gave her his bible; she could not suppress her tears! Bid the afflicted family adieu perhaps not to meet again in this vale of tears. Dr. Boyce sent me to the R.R. I reached home at noon; found Sister Sarah quite sick. Glad to get home again.

Sunday, June 7, 1863

Permitted to spend another Sabbath at home with dear father & mother. Sister Mary is up waiting on Sister. Sent for Uncle Jno Fennell. Miss Alexander called. Read Bible but my mind was on other things. Oh for peace once more.

Monday, June 8, 1863

Rose in good health, conducted worship. Sister is better. May God spare her life & restore her to health again. Worked with bees, took some nice honey. Took some from Miss Anna Wylie's hive, her bees stung me and every one on the place. Called on Miss Mag Alexander at Mrs. Melton's. They found my head full of bee sting. Sat up with Sister. Jno Calvin B. came up. He and father started to Charleston for salt. Miss Anna gave me a nice bouquet. Called on Mrs. Hemphill.

Tuesday, June 9, 1863

Rose late, eat breakfast late. Sent Miss Belle Hemphill a piece of honey. Fixed Miss Anna Wylie's bee palace. Called on Mrs. McLure, took tea with her. Sister is still improving. Oh for peace! May God grant me abundant grace. Bought valise from Bob West $20.00.

Wednesday, June 10, 1863

God's mercy is still extended to me. I deserve nothing at his hand. Went up town, packed up my trunk & valise. Bees swarmed, left them with Isaiah. Eat dinner, bid adieu to mother & Sister & brother; took cars for N. C. Met Mrs. Boyce on train. She stopped me at Charlie Bell's to see Cap Jno Witherspoon who had just arrived from army very sick. Met Mrs. Hassie Witherspoon for the first time since she was married. Conducted worship and retired. Wrote a letter to Moffatt Grier and to Mrs. Ellen Caldwell.

Thursday, June 11, 1863

Jno Witherspoon is still very sick. Conducted worship; talked with Mrs. Boyce and Witherspoon. Charlie Bell took me to the Pump on C & S C R R. Took cars for Davidson Col. Met Mrs. Stringfellow (Student), Mr. Halpen furnished me with a horse I rode out to Coddle Creek; stopped at Bro Jno E. Pressly. Happy to meet my old friend Miss Phemie Hawthorne and Miss Mattie McGaw.

Friday, June 12, 1863

Rose early. Eat breakfast, took a walk with Bro. P. He is not in good health. Conversed on the times &c. Walked down to Mr. Bell's. Went up to Mrs. Witherspoons and spent the evening with Misses Phemie & Mattie. We took a walk through the grave yard at Coddle Creek Church. It was a sad solemn walk. I preached my first trial sermon in Coddle Creek Church. Conducted worship for Miss Phemie.

Saturday, June 13, 1863

Rose very early, eat breakfast by candle light. Bid adieu to Miss Mattie. Miss Phemie & I set out for Davidson Col., arrived in time for the cars. Had a pleasant ride with Miss Phemie to Charlie

Bell's. Found Jno Witherspoon better. Dined with Mrs. B. Took cars for Richmond. Rec'd a letter from Mrs. Caldwell at Harrisburg. Met Mr. E. Elliot and Capt McAlly at Charlotte on their way to Jenkins Brigade.

Sunday, June 14, 1863

I regret to record in this diary that I am travelling on the Sabbath. But consider it a work of necessity. Reached Weldon in the evening. Met Col. Bratton of the 6th S.C. and some of his men. Capt Crawford fell from a window in the hotel last night and was badly injured by the fall. May the gospel be blessed wherever it has been preached today.

Monday, June 15, 1863

God has given me a Safe journey to Richmond again. Stopped at the Samaritan hospital. Happy to meet Mrs. Mayo and friends. Many of the patients have been sent away; some to other hospitals, some to their Regiments, and alas some to the tomb.' Many soldiers have died since I left here. May God have mercy upon us as a people. Rec'd letter from Joe Moffatt.

Tuesday, June 16, 1863

Rose early; Blessed with health. I am a fortunate creature: thousands are on beds of suffering. Took cars for Hamilton's crossing. Met Rev. Anderson & David Simpson who informed me that the troops had left for Culpepper.[34] I returned to Richmond.

Wednesday, June 17, 1863

Took the Va C R R cars – reached Gordonsville at 12, delayed for 3 or 4 hours. Took cars for Culpepper, arrived in safety. Learned that McGowan's Brig had not passed through.[35] Slept in an open field under a waggon of Orrs Reg'. Oh for friends far away.

Thursday, June 18, 1863

Slept very well last on a soldier's bed. Penders Division began to pass through early, McGowan's Brig. about 10 A M. Happy to see my friends once more. The troops marched 3 miles and camped. Jack & Jno & I carried a box and some clothing to Co G & B.[36] It was very hot & dusty. Men were fainting on the march. Refreshing rain in the evening. Slept with Jno & R Hemphill. Talked with my dear friends.

Friday, June 19, 1863

Rose before day; aroused by the sound of the rolling drum. Eat a soldier's breakfast. Reg' took up the time of march at 5 A M, road muddy but the air was cool. March 2 miles with my friends. Sorry to part with them; perhaps I never will see them again. May God shield and protect them from all danger. Walked 5 miles to Culpepper in time for the cars for Richmond. Met Mrs. Rachel Billingstine Apperson on the train. She was glad to see me from Due West, her old home. Called on Rob Poag.

Saturday June 20, 1863

I am still enjoying God's favors. Washed and dressed up. Called on Rev. Anderson & Col Harrison at Linwood.[37] Rec'd a trunk of provision of Capt Jno Witherspoon at Exp Off'. Called on Mrs. Watkins, was introduced to Miss Moseley of Greenwood, S.C. Went over to Howard Grove to see Raney.

Sunday, June 21, 1863

The holy Sabbath has come again. Went to hear Dr. Jeter in 3rd Bap. Took a nap. Went over to Chimborazo to visit the sick. Met by chance with Bros. W.B. Pressly & Lathan; talked awhile with each other. I returned to Samaritan. Went to Church 1st Pres[byterian]; heard Dr. Moore preach a sermon to the young ladies.

Monday, June 22, 1863

Rose quite early. The earth is full of the love of God. Went over to Chimborazo, became acquainted with Mrs. Cassels, matron of 4th Div.[38] Returned via Howard Grove,[39] saw Ramey. Met Bro. Pressly at N C Depot. Sat and conversed. Oh for more grace.

Tuesday June 23, 1863

Still enjoying God's protecting care. Rec'd letter from Moffatt Grier. Walked over to Chimborazo. Called at N.C. Depot; found

Bro. W.B. Pressly. I went down to Rockets with him. Saw him leave on a gunboat. Met Lathan & Dr. Barron on Street. Lathan is going home tomorrow. Walked home with Mrs. Mayo.

Wednesday, June 24, 1863

Rose late but in good health. Thanks to God for his goodness. Conducted worship this morning. Walked over to Chimborazo. Saw Mrs. Cassels and Dr. Babcock & Dunlevy. Returned via 'Howard Grove'. Called at Treasure Dep' to see Miss E Christian. She was not in but I saw Mrs. Christian who told me where to find Miss Emely. Wrote letters to Sister Sarah & Rev. Sloan. Heard Gov. Letcher make a speech to the citizens of Rich(mond). Mrs. Dr. Brown called to see me.

Thursday, June 25, 1863

Life & health still continued, unmerited favors from God. Conducted worship in morning. Went over to Howard Grove Hos. Called on Miss Emely Christian at Mrs. Binfords, had a very pleasant visit. Wrote letter to Moffatt Grier. She was a friend and a sister to him while a prisoner. Called on Robt Poag, Mrs. Brown. Rec'd letter from Mr. Hemphill, Bro. Pressly & slept at a boarding house &.

Friday, June 26, 1863

The mercies of God are bestowed with a liberal hand and without regard to merit or respect of person. Took train for Fredericksburg, with a coffin to get remains of Segt R M Caldwell. Rode in a cart from Crossing to town; hired conveyance to Chancellorsville. Stopped at one Mrs Alsops, hired another cart to go to the battle. Reached it about sun down. Stopped at one Mr. Hawkins[40] near the Wilderness Church.[41] Sung with his daughters after worship.

Saturday, June 27, 1863

Rose late. Took up remains, with the assistance of Mr. Hawkins. Found R M Caldwell's body well identified, packed it & went to Hamilton. Found arms & legs at field hospital still unburied. Cars failed to come up. Yankee raiders cut the bridges on Va Central.[42]

Went to Mr. Morgan to spend the night, conducted worship. Wrote letter to Joe Moffatt.

Sunday, June 28, 1863

Another Sabbath has come cloudy and gloomy. Eat breakfast, went to Crossing, heard that no train would be up; took a walk up R R. Read bible, finished letter [to] Joe Moffatt. Spent night at one Alsops near Crossing. I am a great sinner.

Monday, June 29, 1863

Rose late at Mr. Alsop's, went down to Crossing, learned with joy that a train would be up. Waited with patience until its arrival, put corpse on board & reached Richmond at 5 P M. Met W B Pressly at Depot. Went to Gannons with the remains. Went to Samaritan hospital. Thankful to return in safety.

Tuesday, June 30, 1863

By the kindness of God I am living and enjoying good health. Walked over to Howards Grove. Saw Ranney, but the Surg would not grant him a furlough. Met Wm Brawley in I. N. Lewis office. Hired a waggon for 40 dols to take corpse to Petersburg, the bridge being broken there was no train. Brawley took a seat with me as far as Chester[43] on the R R. We [had] a ride with a Scotchman, long to be remembered. Reached Chester at 10 PM.

Notes

[1] This incident was the origin of the infamous "Bread Riots" which occurred the next day. The winter of 1862-3 coupled with spiraling inflation meant difficult times for the poor of the city, who on this day robbed store in downtown Richmond.

[2] The mob robbed many stores of their goods, and refused to stop the rampage despite the appeals of the Mayor, Governor, and even President Davis. Only the threat of force dispersed the crowd. The riot did force food reforms in the city for the rest of the war.

[3] The Wayside Hospital was a large hospital established in 1862 at the Columbia railroad junction.

[4] The 12th and 13th South Carolina Infantry Regiments composed Brigadier Samuel McGowan's Brigade, along with Orr's Rifles, the 1st and 14th South Carolina Infantry Regiments.

[5] The 37th North Carolina Infantry belonged to Lane's North Carolina Brigade, in the same division as McGowan's Brigade, that of A.P. Hill.

[6] The Union army under General Joseph Hooker had divided itself, one wing crossing the Rapidan above Fredericksburg and the other under the observation of Simpson was crossing in support just below Fredericksburg. This was the opening of the Chancellorsville Campaign.

[7] The house of George Guest located two miles west of Fredericksburg just south of the Orange Turnpike.

[8] The Union force across the Rapidan now was preparing to move east along the turnpike to Fredericksburg.

[9] Thomas C. Chandler's Fairfield, located on a small hill overlooking Guiney's Station.

[10] As General Lee prepared to give battle to the Union army on May 1, he moved his supply trains to the railroad should he need to withdraw from Fredericksburg.

[11] Lee met the Union force along the turnpike west of Fredericksburg, forcing Joe Hooker to withdraw back into the Wilderness around the Chancellorsville intersection.

[12] McGowan's Brigade on this day was making a flank march around the Union army. The South Carolinians did not arrive in time to join in the battle, which resulted in the demolition of the Union 11th Corps.

[13] In the early morning hours of May 3, A.P. Hill's Division, including Orr's Rifles, assaulted the Union positions at Fairview, just across the turnpike from the Chancellor House. The regiment was driven back in a bloody repulse, losing 20 killed, 91 wounded, and three missing, the largest loss of McGowan's Brigade.

[14] By noon of May 3, Lee captured the Chancellorsville intersection and had driven Hooker's army back to a position anchored on the Rappahannock River.

[15] James Wilson, Company G, Orr's Rifles, who had only recently joined the unit not having fully recovered from illness. His tombstone reads in part, "He fell pierced in the left breast with a minie ball and died without a struggle."

[16] D.H. Hill's Division of Lee's Army, now commanded by General Robert Rodes.

[17] The 30th North Carolina was a part of Stephen D. Ramseur's Brigade, which captured Fairview on May 3.

[18] General Sedgwick's 6th Corps advanced from Fredericksburg to assist the Union forces at Chancellorsville, but driven back across the river after dark, completing the Confederate victory at Chancellorsville.

[19] The hospital of Brigadier General Joseph B. Kershaw's South Carolina Brigade.

[20] Thomas C. Brown, graduate of Erskine College, hospital steward, 3rd South Carolina Infantry.

[21] Hooker finally withdrew his army north of Chancellorsville across the Rappahannock, confirming the Confederate victory. Union losses totaled 17,000 while the Confederates lost 13,000 men.

[22] Guiney's Station became the forward hospital area for the Army of Northern Virginia following the Chancellorsville battle.

[23] Lieutenat General Thomas J. "Stonewall" Jackson was wounded by his own men during the evening of May 2. On May 4, he was moved to an outbuilding of the Chandler house, away from the noise and commotion of the main house.

[24] Private Arthur Wardlaw, Company B, Orr's Rifles, killed in the Battle of the Wilderness, May 1864.

[25] General Hospital Number 1.

[26] Lieutenant James S. Cothran, Company B, Orr's Rifles, shot through wrist at Chancellorsville.

[27] On May 10, Jackson died at the small house at Guiney's Station; on May 17, his funeral was heard by an immense crowd in Richmond. Jos. A. Waddell, *Annals of Augusta County with Reminiscences*, p. 309, "Monday, May 11, 1863. A report of General Jackson's death .... It is like 'the mourning at Hadadrimmon, in the valley of Megiddo,' when King Josiah was slain."

[28] Captain W. M. Kerr, Brigadier General James H. Lane's Brigade.

[29] The funeral of James Wilson at Long Cane Cemetery, Abbeville South Carolina, killed at age 21.

[30] The Union army under General U.S. Grant had at this time laid siege to the Confederate army holding Vicksburg, the key to holding the Mississippi River.

[31] T.C. Perrin, father of Colonel James M. Perrin, Orr's Rifles, killed at Chancellorsville, May 3, 1863.

[32] General Samuel McGowan, wounded while leading his brigade at Chancellorsville, May 3, 1863.

[33] Mr. Martin was competing with John Simpson for the affections of Belle Grier. Martin later marries Belle Grier.

[34] The Army of Northern Virginia was now moving north to initiate the Gettysburg Campaign. McGowan's Brigade was one of the last units to move, beginning their march on June 15.

[35] On this day, McGowan's Brigade was just a few miles away from Culpepper, marching from Fredericksburg.

[36] These two companies were formed from the Abbeville District, South Carolina,

[37] Monroe Anderson, Minister and Colonel Frank E. Harrison, Orr's Rifles. Harrison did not go with the regiment to Pennsylvania, due to health problems.

[38] The hospital, being so large was divided into at least 5 divisions to hold over 3,000 patients.

[39] Howard's Grove Hospital was a 62 building complex on the north side of the city, with a capacity of almost 2,000 patients.

[40] Mr. Alexander Hawkins, whose farm lay in the direct path of Jackson's flank assault on May 2.

[41] The Wilderness Church was a Baptist house of worship, of wooden construction, and was the center of Union resistance by General O.O. Howard's 11th Corps. After Confederate capture, the church was used as a forward aid station.

[42] Union cavalry from Yorktown attacked the railroad bridge over the South Anna River, testing the Confederate strength around Richmond while Lee's army moved into Pennsylvania.

[43] Chester Station on the railroad lay almost midway between Richmond and Petersburg.

Chapter 11

"GOD'S MERCY ENDURETH FOREVER"

The reality of the war set in for Simpson in the summer of 1863. Despite the promise and excitement of the Confederate Army's movement into Pennsylvania, he went in the opposite direction, back to South Carolina bearing the body of a dead soldier. Simpson had seen enough pain and suffering resulting from the war, with no clear end in sight. He resigned himself to bearing his work as best he could, and trusting in God's wisdom to end the fighting. As each month went by, more of his friends and family were wounded, killed, or captured, leaving a great sorrow in the heart of John Simpson.

Wednesday, July 1, 1863[1]

The day dawned beautifully. Brawley & I parted. He went to see his sweetheart and I set out for home. Sent the Scotchman on with corpse. I took cars for Petersburg arrived in time for train to Weldon at 10 A M. I refused to pay the Scotchman his price, because he did not reach Petersburg in time for last night's train, paid him only 35 d. Heavy rain on the way to Weldon.

Thursday, July 2, 1863

God's care and protection are still extended to me. Rode all night, did not sleep much. Reached Charlotte in time for cars to Chester at 6 o'clock P.M. Left Corpse at Harrisburg. Met the bereaved widow & mother. May God sustain & comfort them. Reached home at 11 P.M. Slept on the portico.

Friday, July 3, 1863[2]

Happy to meet my dear friends & loved ones at Home. Rose late somewhat tired. Sister Sarah & the children were on Fishing

Creek. Looked at my bees, went up town, called at bank. Mr Harris paid expenses on his bro-in-law's remains and made me a present of 45 dol; had my hair trimmed. Saw Misses Belle Hemphill & Mary Brawley on Street. Called on Mrs. Melton at night; was introduced to Miss Mattie Clawson and others. Sorry to leave them, took cars for Due West at 11.

Saturday, July 4, 1863 [3]

Reach Columbia at 5 A.M. in co[mpany] with Miss Lizzie Moffatt & Jno Flenniken. Took cars for Donaldsville. Happy to meet with Misses Mary Bonner & Maggie Jones from Ala en route for Due West. Met Mr. Bonner & others at Depot. Jno Mathis took me to Due West. Heard with Sorrow of the illness of my dear friend Miss Jennie Sites. Stopped at Mr. Grier's, glad to see my friends; called on Mr. Hemphill.

Sunday, July 5, 1863

How lovely is the Sabbath at home where the church bell is heard; I love to hear its deep solemn tones. Read Bible. Took a walk. Went to church, was invited to lead in singing. Heard Rev. Sloan of Tenn. preach a sermon to the grad' class in female col[lege]. Went to Prayer meeting in evening; lead in singing and once in prayer. Answered the Shorter Catechism to Mr. Grier. Called to see Miss Jennie Sites, found her very low. Sat up until 11 o'clock; she knew me.

Monday, July 6, 1863

God's mercy never fails. While many are on beds of sickness & pain, I am in good health. Went to examination in Female Col.; heard the Juniors in Geom.; they did admirably. Dined with Mrs. Hemphill. Returned to Col[lege], met with all the girls, heard them practice for concert. Happy to meet with the fair sex and hear them sing. Happy to meet my dear friend Chiles. Met him in Mr. Bonner's yard; eat supper with him at the Hotel. Met Miss Mollie Martin, Miss Ellen Dendy. Was introduced to Miss Nola Polhill. Went [to] Exhibition at Male Col[lege] with Miss Ellen Dendy. Talked with Phemie & others.

Tuesday, July 7, 1863

Slept last night with my friend Chiles at hotel, but we were waked up at 3 A M to see poor Jennie Sites die. We hastened to Mr. Bonner's to see her. I felt her pulse grow weaker & weaker. I closed her eyes in death at 10 ; 30 or 40 school girls were around her bed. May they prepare to meet their God. Spent the night with Lindsay.

Wednesday, July 8, 1863

Had a good night's rest; rose early to go to the funeral of my dear friend Miss Jennie Sites. Rode with Capt P H Bradley & Mr. Talbert. Reached.Cedar Springs at 1 P M. Funeral at 2, assisted Mr. Sloan in the religious exercises. Miss Morse & I returned to Due West [in] heavy rain; had a pleasant ride with Miss Morse. Reached Due West at 9 P M. Went up to church concert, was half through. Went home with Jane Grier and spent night at Mr. Grier's.

Thursday, July 9, 1863

This is a world of change and of parting – rose early, went down to Mr. Bonner's to bid my lady friends farewell. Sorry to see them leave, but such is life. Spent most of the day at Mr. Grier's; talked with Mrs. Grier. Called on Mrs. H. & Belle Hemphill. Took honey for Mr. H at night. Slept upstairs alone. Went into Moffatt's room a long time.

Friday, July 10, 1863

Rose early, prepared to leave Due West. Mr. Grier gave me some buds from his early peach. Took a seat in Mrs. Lindsay's carriage with Misses Sites, Morse & Lathrop to Depot after bidding my dear friends adieu. Had a pleasant ride with the ladies to Depot. Miss Lathrop left us at Cokesbury. Miss Morse & I stopped at Greenwood, met Rev. Sloan & Mr. Sites who took us in his carriage to Gen Bradley's where all dined. Happy to see Miss Fannie B up and improving from her fatigue in traveling and waiting on Miss Jennie. Called on Geo. Chiles and Miss Fannie Gray. Met Miss Erin McMorris; took tea with Chiles. Spent night with Gen Bradley.

Saturday, July 11, 1863

Rose early, conducted worship for Gen Bradley. Sat and talked while he made me a bouquet, and I bid Miss Fannie & all the family goodbye and went to New Market. Called at Mrs. Dendys to see ladies Misses M Martin & E Dendy. Met Miss Nannie McMorris and had a pleasant ride with her as far as Chappell's. I reached Col[umbia] in time for train to Chester at which place 1 arrived at midnight. Happy & thankful to get home again; found all well.

Sunday, July 12, 1863

The quiet peaceful Sabbath has come once more. Oh what a blessing to man. Conducted worship, eat breakfast and went to church at Union, took Grier with me. Heard Mr. McDonald; sung for him. Went to Sister Mary's. Mark tried to run away in buggy; frightened by thunder & umbrella. Heavy rain.

Monday, July 13, 1863

Permitted by a kind & merciful God to see another day pass yet I have often sinned against that Being who gives me all good things 1 enjoy. Elihu called to see me. Called at Mr. McDonald's and Mrs. Moffatt's; had a long talk with my best friend. She is now feeble and I fear she will not live long. She is a true disciple of Jesus and a noble Christian. I told my disappointment with Miss _____. She sympathized with me and wished I had been treated otherwise. I told her it was all in the hands of God who doeth all things well. We parted in tears. I returned home. Fixed Mr. Grier's sheep shears.

Tuesday, July 14, 1863

Still in good health — God does not consult merits. Called on Miss Mattie Clawson at Mr. Alexanders. Walked with her to depot. She gave me an oleander. Mr. Brice called to see my bees. Budded peaches which I brought from Due West. Fixed Mr. Grier's sheep shears. Called on ladies at Mrs. Melton's; had a pleasant time.

Wednesday, July 15, 1863

Very warm, read Bible &c. Took window out of milk house, and moved two hives of bees into the milk house. Called on Miss Anna Wylie, not at home; called on Mrs. Hemphill, met Miss Mary Brawley & her Mother. Called on Mrs. Gaston. Took tea with Mrs. Melton. Brenicke and Isaiah played on violin (for) ladies. I played guitar. Had good music. I enjoyed myself finely. Wrote letter to Mr. Grier today and gathered up some strips of glass for him.

Thursday, July 16, 1863

Rose early, felt dull with a severe headache. Conducted worship for the last time until I return home again. Bees doing well. Packed up, eat a good dinner and called at Mrs. Melton's to tell ladies goodbye. Sorry to leave home – train behind time. Returned to house for haversack. Reached Charlotte in time for train, had a severe pain in head all day.

Friday, July 17, 1863

Reached Raleigh too late for morning train to Weldon. Lay over in Raleigh. Dined at Hotel. Bought paper &c. Read *"Prince of the House of David"*. Eat supper and took train for Weldon. Left W for Petersburg in evening. Felt much better; God's loving kindness is everlasting.

Saturday, July 18, 1863

God has watched over me in the house and by the way. Travelled all day on R R cars from Weldon to Richmond. Felt sad and lonely all day. Slept on train, reached the city at 7 P M. Stopped at Samaritan Hos', met Bro. J. E. Pressly. Happy to return to my field of labor among the hospitals. Oh that this cruel war was over.

Sunday, July 19, 1863

The holy Sabbath with its untold blessing to man has returned. May the gospel be blessed over all the world. Pressly & I attended Dr. Moore's church in morning. Went to Howard Grove, had preaching at 5. I returned to Samaritan & went to church with Mrs. Mayo.

Monday, July 20, 1863

Still crowned with mercies. Rose late. Called on Miss Ida Watkins who left this evening for S.C. – to Second Auditors office then to Adj Gen office to get papers fixed about Mr. Baird's dues. Stopped at S C Depot, glad to meet Grier Poor & Mr Markley. Went to Howard Grove for dinner with Mr Pressly and friends in hospital – visited the wounded – returned to Samaritan – Newton Lewis brought me a telegram from John C. Simpson about David being wounded – Wrote letters (to) Mrs Walker and to Co A 9th S.C. & Co D 1st S.C. Cav'.

Tuesdays July 21, 1863

Providence is very kind to me. Conducted worship at Samaritan Hos[pital]. Went to P O, rec'd Telescope of 17th. Sent a bundle by express to Capt Jno G Witherspoon; went over to Howard G. Pressly & I went to Chimborazo. I dined with Dr. Babcock. Called on Mrs. Cassel. Took dinner with Dr. Babcock. Left Chimborazo, went to 2nd Auditor's and to QM; received money due Mr. Baird's Estate. Took Pressly to Tredegar works.[4] Saw a cannon moulded &c. Returned to Samaritan and spent night. Bro P conducted worship.

Wednesday, July 22, 1863

Rose early in good health, "God's mercy endureth forever". Bid Bro P. adieu & took train to Staunton to hunt for wounded & sick S.C. V's.[5] Reached S at 8 P M, put up at Mrs. Brandenburg's. Saw Gen Imboden on train.[6] Retired at 9 . Oh for peace again.

Thursday, July 23, 1863

Rose early, went to hospitals to examine registers, found very few S C V's. Met Price, Esqr & Rev Stewart. Rev S & I went to the Asylum, 1 met 2: Cochran[7] & Milford[8] from Co G Orrs Reg,; heard sad news most of Co G were captured.[9] Hospitals are crowded. Soldiers transferred rapidly to Richmond; moved my baggage over to depot with Price & Stewart.

Friday, July 24, 1863

Oh that these scenes of suffering and distress were over. See men from all parts of the land looking for Sons & brothers. Visited hospitals today, wounded are doing well. Sent telegram to John C. Simpson about David. Rev Riley of Laurens came up today. God gives me health & strength day by day. Wrote letter to Capt P H Bradley & to Sister. Wrote a letter for a soldier to his wife Mrs Alewine, Loundersville, S.C.

Saturday, July 25, 1863

"The loving kindness of the Lord doth fill the earth." Bro R failed to get on train for Gordonsville. I visited hospital in morning – took a sleep in evening. Wrote diary. Read papers. Dined at Mr. Arnold's with Price & Bro. R.

Sunday, July 26, 1863

Sabbath has returned, but there is no peace and rest for the weary Soldier. Oh God lift up us the light of thy countenance once more. Bro. Riley left for army by private conveyance. I went to Bap Church, heard D Broddus. Visited hospitals in evening. Read Bible & Barnes on Acts.

Monday, July 27, 1863

Another week's work has set in. Felt dull, took a sleep. Heard that Thos Polhill was killed at Gettysburg, another friend gone. Commenced letter to Miss Nola P. Felt sad and lonely. Went to hospitals, talked with sick and wounded.

Tuesday, July 28, 1863

Time is rapidly passing away, another month will soon be gone. When I review my life it gives me sorrow: I have spent a life of sin and folly.' Read Bible, visited Hospitals. Wrote five letters for sick & wounded soldiers. Heavy rain. In good health.

Wednesday, July 29, 1863

Time and tide wait for no man. Life will soon be gone and what have I done.' May I be more diligent in time to come. Price left this morn for Richmond and I am alone. Visited hospitals, read the Bible & prayed with the wounded. Wrote two letters for the wounded to inform their friends of their condition. Commenced letter to Due West Telescope. Retired at 11. Oh how I long for peace.

Thursday, July 30, 1863

I have again to record the loving kindness of God, though many are in great pain I am in good health. Read Bible. Visited hospitals. Read and prayed with Soldiers. Wrote two letters for a Ga. & a N C Soldier. Took a sleep in evening. May the Spirit of God rest upon me.

Friday, July 31, 1863

Tonight another month is numbered in the eternal past. What have I done to advance the glory of my Maker. I come far short of my duty. Visited the Sick and wounded. Dined at Mr. Arnold's. Had prayer in room with wounded Soldiers & read Bible and studied German. Health good. Closed the eyes of Soldier O P Ransom[10] from Edgefield, S.C., packed the body to be sent home to his mother.

Saturday, August 1, 1863

August began very warm. May God bestow abundant showers of rain upon the fields, to cause them to yield abundantly. Visited the Soldiers in their loneliness – Read the Bible & prayed with them. Was introduced to Rev. Warden of Culpeper. Met with Mr. Fitcher agent of tract So at Petersburg, Va. Wrote letter to Telescope. Received a letter from Sister Sarah, welcome letter.

Sunday, August 2, 1863

The first Sabbath of August has passed away. May God forgive the sins of the most holy day. Read Bible to Soldiers & prayed with them. Went to Presby' church in morning. Eat breakfast & dinner at Arnold's, supper at Hospital with Rev. Hauser, Chap[lain] 48th Ga.

Monday, August 3, 1863

Today I am 29 years old! how rapidly my days pass away! Commemorated the day by writing a letter to my dear father. Eat supper at Hospital. Visited sick & wounded. May God restore them all to health again. Wrote two letters for Soldiers. Sat up late, had a slight headache.

Tuesday, August 4, 1863

Mercies still continued. God's loving kindness is everlasting. Read Bible. Wrote letters for Soldiers and spent the day in endeavoring to comfort The Suffering Soldier. May God preserve their lives, Amen.

Wednesday, August 5, 1863

Very warm, eat breakfast at hotel. Put Mr. Alewine of the 14th S. C., And. Lea of 1st S. C. Cav and a Ga Soldier on train and brot' them to Richmond. Stopped at Samaritan hospital; rec'd a letter from Sister Sarah & Mr. Hemphill.

Thursday, August 6, 1863

Rose early & in good health; felt dull, took a nap. Went to S.C. Soldiers home. Happy to meet with Mrs. McMaster, dined with her, talked about Chester & old times. Slept at Samaritan, conducted worship at night. Went [to] Maj. Ould's office.

Friday, August 7, 1863

Time is rolling away like a swift stream. Went down to Seabrooks Hospital,[11] thence to Robertson's hospital[12] to see Alewine, Lea, and Walker. Took dinner with Mrs. McMaster. Called at S.C. Depot. Wrote letter to Mrs. Hemphill, Due West. Very warm.

Saturday, August 8, 1863

Rose early, conducted worship. Read Bible. Wrote letter to Sister. Went out to Camp Jackson hospital to see friends;[13] happy to meet Rice Ellis,[14] Prent & others. Dined at S.C. Sol home. Spent night at Samaritan. Wrote letter to Telescope. Worked with a wounded Miss[issippi] Soldier.

Sunday, August 9, 1863

Another blessed Sabbath has returned. Read Bible. Went to P.O. Rec'd letters from Joe Moffatt & one Mr. Wells of Abbeville, S.C. Went to S.C. Soldier's home; took a sleep. Dined with Mr. McMaster. Went to Jackson hospital, talked with wounded & spent night.

Monday, August 10, 1863

Rose early, expecting to go to Petersburg, but too late for cars. Came to Samaritan for breakfast. Dined with Mr. McMaster. Took a good nap. Weather exceedingly warm; Oh for rain. Could scarcely sleep. Called on Robt Poag & Newton Lewis. Spent night at Samaritan.

Tuesday, August 11, 1863

Left Samaritan for Petersburg train, arrived in time. Went to Petersburg. Called at S.C. hospital to see paroled prisoners. Went to Jenkin's brig; happy to meet with the old 6th S.C. again. Dined with Lt. McDaniel; attempted to return to Richmond but too late for cars. Returned to camp, spent night with Lt McDaniel. Went to Preaching. Heard Baptist prayers & preaching. Pleasant night in camp with my friends; very warm.

Wednesday, August 12, 1863

Rose at daylight, took train for Richmond; arrived at 7 A.M., went to Samaritan hospital for breakfast. Called at S.C. Soldiers home; dined with Mrs. McMaster, . . . Camp Jackson to see friends. Ellis and others doing well. Oh for peace. Still trust in God!

Thursday, August 13, 1863

Delightful and abundant rains. Thanks to God for his constant blessings upon our land. Failed to get to Camp Jackson. Sent for N C Pres Church Intel', Ch Ad, S. Pres. Confed Pap S Lut S.W. Bap Holston Jour' to give to Soldiers.[15] Got a passport for Chancellorsville. Good health.

Friday, August 14, 1863

Time is passing rapidly. Went out to Camp Jackson. Distributed papers to the Soldiers, who were glad to get them. Rice, Ellis & Melford are doing well. Went to Howard Grove, found Stevenson very low but improving.

Saturday, August 15, 1863

Rose very early, left Mr. Hawkins before breakfast. Returned to the hospital burying ground to get the board at Mattison's Grave.

Reached Hamilton's Xing in time for train to Richmond at 11 AM; arrived in city at 3 P M. Went to S.C. Soldiers home & dined.

Sunday, August 16, 1863

Rose late, read Bible. Walked to S C Soldiers home, talked with Mrs. McMaster. Went to hear Dr. Moore in morning; Camp Jackson in evening, distributed some religious papers. Returned to city; heard Dr. Moore again. Took dinner & supper at S C Sol Home. Rec'd Telescope. Went over to Camp Jackson to see T. A. Stevenson, found him very low but he was thought to be some better. Mr. McMaster went with me to Camp Jackson.

Monday, August 17, 1863

The time is stealing by; August will soon be numbered with the eternal past. Health is good. God's mercies endure forever,[16] great is his loving kindness towards me. Went to hospital, Saw Ellis, Pruit & others, they all are doing well. Wrote letter to Stevenson's father. Worked with my Yankee hand from Chancellorsville.

Tuesday, August 18, 1863

Still enjoying God's favor. My life and health are continued. To Camp Jackson to see the wounded. Returned to Samaritan Hos'. Mrs. Mayo & Miss Martha went to Petersburg on a visit. Mr. Sleight & I went with them to Cars. Went to S.C. Soldiers Home. Ellis went before the board but did not get a furlough.

Wednesday, August 19, 1863

God is bestowing unmerited blessings upon me from day to day. Rec'd letter from Bella Hemphill stating that Jno & Robt were in Baltimore Jail.[17] Went out to Howard Grove. Stevenson is improving. May God preserve his life. Rec'd Telescope. Dined & supped at S.C. Soldiers Home.

Thursday, August 20, 1863

Nothing of interest to record today. Oh God, so teach me to number my days &c. Read Bible, but my mind is too much engaged in worldly things. Went to Camp Jackson, found the wounded all improving; may their souls be renewed and strengthened for every duty. Called on Mrs. Dr. Brown, rec'd papers from her, gave her ten dollars.

Friday, August 21, 1863

Rec'd letter from my good friend Mr. Hemphill in Due West, contain mistake letters to John & R Lend to go by truce boat.[18] Called on Mrs Dr. Brown. Rec'd papers from . . . Went to Chancellorsville after body of Mattison,[19] Co G Orr's Reg – fast day.

Saturday, August 22, 1863

Spent the day as usual. Visited hospitals &c. Called on Mrs. Dr. Brown, rec'd papers from her. Called on Mrs. Dr. Hoge who loaned me a rocking chair for Stevenson. Went over to H. Grove, and returned to Dr. Hoge's for chair. Felt very tired.

Sunday, August 23, 1863

Rose in good health, thanks to God for his great loving kindness. Read Bible. Went to hear Dr. Moore, on the last word in N[ew] T[estament]. To Camp Jackson in even, distributed papers &c. Heard Dr. Moore at night on "Oh that I like a dove had wings".[Ps 55:6, by Ed.]

Monday, August 24, 1863

Pleasant day. Visited sick & wounded, all doing well. May God preserve their lives and by his Spirit convert their Souls. Oh that I were more zealous in the work of saving souls. Mr. Stevenson's father arrived to day. Rec 'd letter from W R Hemphill and one from Rev Aldrich – Ed of Southern Lutheran.

Tuesday, August 25, 1863

Good news from home to day, rec 'd letter from Sister Sarah. Went out to Camp Jackson & Rice Ellis, got a furlough. To Howard's Grove, found Stevenson still improving – to Chimborazo, saw Dr. Babcock. Rec'd Tele[scope], So. Presby., Southern Lutheran for soldiers. Felt very tired, played violin after tea at S.C. S H. Mrs. Watkins sent a bundle to me.

Wednesday, August 26, 1863

Rose early at Samaritan hospital. Called on Mrs. Watkins. To P.O., rec'd letter from R R Hemphill, a paroled prisoner at Petersburg.[20] To Camp Jackson, distributed 300 papers. To City, dined at S.C.Sol.H. Returned to Camp Jackson for Rice Ellis. Took him and Mattison's body to Petersburg Depot. Left for Petersburg in company with Robt Poag. Stopped at S.C. Hospital. Was happy to meet Robt H., Jno Chiles[21] just out of the prison in Baltimore. Sent dispatches home. Talked with my friends until late.

Thursday, August 27, 1863

Rose early. Wrote letter to Mrs. Mayo. Eat watermelons with Robt H & Neal Johnson. Put Ellis, and remains on cars & left for Weldon, arrived in time for cars to Ral[eigh]. Sent dispatch home. Made con[nection] at Ral[eigh]. Slept well on cars. Thankful for a safe journey so far.

Friday, August 28, 1863

Travelled all day, met with no misfortune. Reached Charlotte at 5 P M. Called at Kerr's Hotel. Saw Miss Laura. Took Supper. Left for Chester, arrived there at 11 P.M. Met Isaiah, with lunch & clothing. Went to Col[umbia]. God's mercy is very precious.

Saturday, August 29, 1863

Reached Col[umbia] at five this morning. Met Mim Ellis at his camp, went with us to Greenville Depot. Reached Donald's at 3 P.M. Delivered the remains of Mattison to the bereaved family. Went to Due West with Mr. Hemphill. Stopped at Mr. Grier's, happy to see my dear friends. Took tea with Mr. H & family. Slept in my old room alone. Thought of my college friends, all gone! Some killed in battle; felt sad & lonely. Read Dr. Furonan's sermon to Liz & Moffatt's class. – Conducted worship.

Sunday, August 30, 1863

Rose early, took a walk down the lane, a familiar road! Often have I walked it with friends who are gone to the grave. Heard Mr. Grier preach; sung for him. Dined with Mr. Bonner. To prayer meeting. Said Shorter Cat[echism] with Mr. Grier & children, Mrs. G. asking. Mr. Grier & I went down to Mrs. Ellis' to see Rice & Turner. Late returning. Slept in my old room, I love it I love it.

Monday, August 31, 1863

Blessed with good health. Packed up, went over to Mr. H's to bid them good bye. Sorry to leave my dear friends Mr. & Mrs. Grier & little girls dear to me. Rode to depot with Cal & Bell H. Met Miss Nola Polhill & Miss Sallie McBryde on train. I stopped at New Market. Found a horse to ride to Mr. Chiles. Met Mrs. Chiles at Mrs. McClellan's, dined. Stopped at Gen Bradley's, eat grapes, went down to Mr. Chiles. Glad to meet my dear friends Geo. Chiles & the family. Spent night with them. They had some trouble with the negroes. Gen. Bradley lost his horse & buggy.

Tuesday, September 1, 1863

God is crowning me with his loving kindness. Rose early, eat breakfast. Left for depot, called Gen. B's. Made connection with train at N. Market. Met Mr. Bonner & Miss Maggie Jones on train going to Ala[bama], had a pleasant ride with her to Columbia. Sorry to leave her. Made connection with Charlotte train for Chester. Met Bro. Stewart at depot. Took cars for Chester.

Wednesday, September 2, 1863

Reached Col[umbia] this morning, returned on down-train to get carpet sack left at depot; found it and returned on up-train, reached Chester at noon. Found all well, called on Mrs. Melton, had a fine time. Conducted worship.

Thursday, September 3, 1863

Home sweet home. Oh that this cruel war was over. Packed up my trunk, went up town called at Mrs. Gaston's, found her absent. Called at Mrs. Hemphill's. Went to P.O., met Miss Gaston with her sister Mrs. Dr. B. G. on the street. Played violin. Called on Miss Virgie & Miss Alexander. Enjoyed myself very much. Father left for Col. at 10 P.M. I took the cars for Richmond at 1 A.M.

Friday, September 4, 1863

Reached Charlotte at 5 this morning. Changed Cars for Raleigh. Formed acquaintance of Mrs. Dr. Hoyt & Mother. Enjoyed lunch with them. Reached Ral at 11 P M. Had a safe journey! Read Signs of the Times by Dr. Cummings.

Saturday, September 5, 1863

Time is rolling away. Oh that the war would soon end. But my trust is [in] God who doeth all things well. Had a safe trip to Richmond, arrived at 6 P M. Stopped at Soldier's Home. Called Samaritan hospital. Glad to meet friends. Met R R Hemphill & Johnson in Petersburg.

Sunday, September 6, 1863

The quiet Sabbath has returned with its untold blessings to man. Went to Church to hear Dr. Moore but heard a stranger preach a good sermon. Went to Howard Grove to see Stevenson; found him convalescent. Heard Marshall of Vicksburg in the Broad Street Methodist Church.

Monday, September 7, 1863

Rose early in good health. Went to Samaritan H. Thence to Camp Jackson, found Pruit very bad, foot still sloughing. Distributed papers to the Soldiers. Returned to City, called at S.C. Depot. Met Bro Stewart at Soldiers home. Packed boxes for army.

Tuesday, September 8, 1863

Rose at 5. Set out for V.C. R R Depot, took cars for Gordonsville, thence to Orange C H. Reached it at 4 P M. Walked to Orr's Reg. 1 1/2 miles.[22] Glad to see my old friends but many were prisoners and in soldiers graves in Pa. Conducted prayer meeting in Orr's Regiment.

Wednesday, September 9, 1863

Aroused by Reveller. Slept well in Capt Pratt's tent.[23] Col. Miller gave me a horse to ride to Dr. Gaston's quarters, but he had gone home on furlough. Brought coffee back, but eat the pies & I divided with Col. Harrison[24] & Miller. Studied some in evening, preached to the Reg. at night.[25] Had a good and attentive audience. Found good quarters in Cap Pratt's tent.

Thursday, September 10, 1863

God is daily loading me with his kindness. Went to Orange CH from camp, met W P Price; took cars with Soldiers for Richmond. Read a small work on Prayer. Stopped at S C S Home. Came down on train with Gens Longstreet & Hood.[26]

Friday, September 11, 1863

Went to Camp Jackson, distributed about 200 papers to soldiers. Found Pruit better. Went to Howard Grove to see Stevenson, found him still improving. Called at Samaritan Hospital. Played violin. Talked with Bro. Stewart. Bought some. . . .

Saturday, September 12, 1863[27]

Rose early this morning, took train to Petersburg, met no train for Weldon. Called at S C Hos. Saw Dave Wilson. Sam McDill Troops moving to Chattanooga, met Pickle, took tea with him. Thanked guards on train and got in at a window; had a free passage in a saloon to Weldon. Met Cousin D Simpson just from Prison in N Y.

Sunday, September 13, 1863

Reached Weldon at 3 this morning, changed cars for Raleigh; met my old friend Wm Hood on train, just from prison in N.Y. but he did not know me. Reached Raleigh in time for train to Charlotte. O for peace! A Sabbath at home.

Monday, September 14, 1863

Reached Charlotte at 8 A M, had a safe journey. Tried to get on a soldier train but the Col put me off after the train started. I jumped on the last coach with Gens Hood, Jenkins & Wofford.[28] Met a large crowd at Chester to greet and refresh the soldiers of the 13th Miss.[29] Great excitement at Chester, the 6th S C is looked for tomorrow. Found all well at home.

Tuesday, September 15, 1863

Rose late but in good health. Went to depot. Met Miss Kate Caldwell & Miss Kate Caruthers. Walked up town with them. Called on Mr. Harris. Mr. Price came down on train. Soldiers passing all day. Called on Mrs. Melton.

Wednesday, September 16, 1863

God is rich in mercy towards me. Conducted family worship night & morning. Went down to depot. Great crowd to see 6th S.C. pass. I had a pleasant time with ladies. Misses Caldwell & Caruthers &c. Heavy rain, Reg came at 5 P M, left at 7. Jno Fridge spent night at home. Father's Sugar mill broke.

Thursday, September 17, 1863

Rose early, conducted worship. Went to town, had my watch fixed. Packed up in a hurry, left unexpectedly on down train for Synod. Took seat in box car with Soldiers of 6th Reg. Axle of tender broke, box cars broke & smashed in but no one killed. John Fudge[30] jumped out & car fell on him but did not kill him; another had an arm broken. Thanks to God for preserving my life. Slept with Larry Caldwell & John Stringfellow.[31]

Friday, September 18, 1863

God's almighty arm has been around me. Rose early, took S.C. train with Mr. McDonald, Brice, McLaughlin, Chalmers &c, and Joe Pedan & Jno Stringfellow, had safe journey to Augusta. Slept with Brice at S States hotel; arrived at 1 A M.

Saturday, September 19, 1863

Rose early, paid 3 dols for breakfast. Took Waynesboro R R car. Had a safe journey over a splendid road. Reached Louisville about 2 P M, dined at Mr. Bothwell's. Met Turner, did not know him. Met my friend Jas Lowry at his father's, glad to see him but he did not know me. Took a walk through town. Saw Miss Nola Polhill & Lizzie Quigg. Called on Mr. Philips. Met Grier D D, Rev Jno Miller who gave me a pair of nice gloves, a present from my friend Maggie Jones of Ala.

Sunday, September 20, 1863

Sat up late last night, & rose late his morning; conducted worship. Called at Mr. Bothwell, Mr. Turner & I rode in a buggy to Ebenezer. Good horses & a fine wide road. Sung with Wm Lowry & Joe Lowry. Rode to Louisville with Miss Nola Polhill. Joe Moffatt & I spent night with Mrs. Cain. Sat up late.

Monday, September 21, 1863

Rose early, commenced my report to Synod but did not finish it. Went to church with Miss Nola, too late to hear all of Mr. Brice's sermon, retiring Mod[erator]. Assisted in Singing. Glad to meet my friend Jim Lowry & other brethren, returned to Louisville with Miss Nola & Joe Moffatt. Heard an excellent sermon from Dr. Wilson of Augusta.[32] Spent night with Jim Lowry at Wm Lowry's; talked about old times in Due West.

Tuesday, September 22, 1863

Rose in good health, thanks to God for his goodness. Rode to church with Miss Nola in time for service. My report was read. Went to Mr. Robt Stone's, had a pleasant time and some nice watermelons. Dr. Wilson made some good remarks; Miller of Ala replied. Called on Miss Sue Brown, Robt Hemphill's friend.

Wednesday, September 23, 1863

Rose early, conducted worship. Rode to Church with Miss Robinson, a beautiful lady, Sister-in-law to Mr. Stone. Had a debate on union question. Synod adjourned. Sad to part with the brethren. Mr. Bonner being sick asked me to stay with him until able to go home. Rode to Louisville with Miss Nola. Took tea & went to Mr. Philips where Mr. Bonner was lying sick.

Thursday, September 24, 1863

Oh that my heart was right in the sight of God. Felt sad & lonely, all the brethern are gone, perhaps to meet no more. Mr. Bonner is very sick at Mr. Philips': I remained to nurse him. Called on Miss Nola. Philips is good company.

Friday, September 25, 1863

Time is flying rapidly away, Oh that I would spend my days aright! Conducted [worship] at night. Bro B is still sick; I fear he will have a long spell of fever. Mrs. Polhill & Mrs. Cain called to see him. Sent him some luxuries.

Saturday, September 26, 1863

Where are the friends of my youth? Time has carried them away. Another week is past and gone. Oh the past! it ne'er returns. Went to P. O. Read papers. Bro. B is some better. May God spare his life & restore him to his family.

Sunday, September 27, 1863

Went (to) Bethel today, heard Joe Lowry preach. Dined with Jim Lowry's mother. Jim took me to Mr. Philips' in evening. Heard Joe L. preach in Louisville at night. Mr. B is still improving. Mrs. Polhill called to see him. Another Sabbath gone.

Monday, September 28, 1863

Had a delightful time today fishing in the Ogeechee with Mr. Philips & Jim Lowry. We caught 25 perches. Found Mr. Bonner sitting up when we returned. Went up to P O. Called at Mrs Cain's for tea. Jim Lowry came out from Mr. P's after tea; we had a moonlight walk to Judge Brown's with Sue & Nola. Returned to Mr. Philips'; had a pleasant talk.

Tuesday, September 29, 1863

Clear and pleasant day. Left Bro. Philips' to day with Mr. Bonner. Called at Mrs. Cain's who sent us to Depot. Took 2 trunks for Mrs. Polhill. Bid adieu to Jim Lowry, Miss Nola & Louisville. Reached Augusta at 6 P M. Took Supper at Southern S Hotel; took train for Col(umbia) at 7. Stood up 17 mi.

Wednesday, September 30, 1863

Mr. Bonner & I had a safe journey to Col S.C. but too late for train to Donaldsville G.R.R. Stopped at Janneys. Met with Mr. Hemphill Esqre of Chester. Went to Legislative hall with Col Fair, of Ala. Thanks to God for his care over us.

Notes

[1] The opening day of the Battle of Gettysburg, Pennsylvania.

[2] The final day of the Battle of Gettysburg, in which the Confederate army is repulsed, and Lee's invasion of the North is turned back.

[3] The fall of Vicksburg to Union forces under General U.S. Grant, opening the Mississippi River to the North.

[4] The Tredagar Iron Works in Richmond were one of the biggest supplier of arms to the Confederacy.

[5] The wounded and sick from Gettysburg arrived in Staunton, along with the Union prisoners on July 20.

[6] Brigadier General John D. Imboden commanded the Confederate cavalry brigade bringing the wounded and prisoners from Gettysburg.

[7] Private J. W. Cochran, Company G, Orr's Rifles.

[8] Private George W. Milford, Private, Company G, Orr's Rifles, wounded in leg at Falling Waters, July 1863.

[9] The company was on skirmish duty covering the retreat of the Confederate Army over the Potomac River at Falling Waters, Maryland, and was almost entirely captured in the fighting.

[10] Sergeant Phaides Orion Ransom, Company G, 1st South Carolina, died of wounds received at Gettysburg.

[11] General Hospital Number 9, or Seabrooks Hospital, held over 900 patients. The location near the Virginia Central Railroad was a prime factor in the use of the hospital.

[12] A small hospital located in the house of Judge John Robertson, holding only 22 patients. The hospital was run by the famous Sally Tompkins, under whose care a patient was rarely lost. Such good care made the Robertson the only private hospital to operate in Richmond from 1863 to the end of the war.

[13] The Jackson Hospital opened in June 1863 and held almost 2,000 patients, all from South Carolina, North Carolina, Georgia, and Louisiana.

[14] Private A. Rice Ellis, wounded in the hip at Falling Waters, Maryland, July 1863. Gangrene set into his wound, but Ellis eventually recovered.

[15] These papers and journals were all religious tracts to be distributed as reading material for the soldiers.

[16] Psalm 118:1

[17] Both were captured at Falling Waters, and were taken to Fort McHenry as prisoners of war.

[18] Letters to prisoners of war were required to pass the lines by way of a boat of truce.

[19] Private James M. Mattison, Company G, Orr's Rifles, killed in action at Chancellorsville, May 3, 1863.

[20] Hemphill's uncle, a United States Senator from Texas, used his influence to make certain of early exchange.

[21] Corporal J. H. Childs was captured at Falling Waters with the rest of the company.

[22] In the days following Gettysburg, Orr's Rifles with the rest of the Army of Northern Virginia, took position behind the Rapidan River north of Orange to resist any Union advance. The Federal army, under command of Major General George G. Meade, followed Lee cautiously.

[23] Captain James Pratt, commanding Company G, Orr's Rifles.

[24] Colonel Frank E. Harrison, commanding Orr's Rifles. Miller and Harrison shared quarters at this time.

[25] The regiment at this time held a prayer meeting every night.

[26] Generals James Longstreet and John B. Hood, commanding the Confederate First Corps and a division of the First Corps. Longstreet's Corps was being transfered by rail to North Georgia, to repulse the Union advance from Chattanooga, Tennessee.

[27] On this day, Simpson is caught up in the great movement of Longstreet's soldiers on their way to North Georgia.

[28] Hood and his two Brigadier Generals, Micah Jenkins of South Carolina and William T. Wofford of Georgia.

[29] The 13th Mississippi Infantry of General Lafayette McLaw's Division, Longstreet's Corps.

[30] Private John Fudge, Company A, 6th South Carolina.

[31] John J. Stringfellow, Company F, 6th South Carolina Infantry.

[32] The Rev. Joseph Ruggles Wilson, pastor of First Presbyterian Church of Atlanta, Ga., went to Louisville, Ga., to preach at the Associate Reformed Presbyterian Synod. He was father of Woodrow Wilson and one of the leaders in the split of the Presbyterian Church, U.S., from the PCUSA, (from the Smithsonian Guide, Historic America, p. 164).

Chapter 12

"*Where are the Friends of My Youth?*"

As the cool days of Autumn came to South Carolina, Simpson was called to return to his work of supporting his friends in the units on the front lines. This time, his travels would take him to new areas of the Confederacy, following the movement of the 6th South Carolina Infantry as part of Lieutenant General James Longstreet's movement into East Tennessee. There, Simpson would be caught in the daily activities of the campaign, and be cut off from his sanctuary in South Carolina by Union advances. Now the fortunes of the Confederacy were ever more on the wane, with Simpson caught in the approaching Union tide of victories.

Thursday, October 1, 1863

Rose early this morning; took train for Donalds in company with Col Fair. Met with Joe Moffatt, Bell Grier, & Pat Sharp at Hodges. Reached Due West in due time. Stopped at Mr. Grier's, my old home in Due West.

Friday, October 2, 1863

In my old familiar room but where are the friends of my youth? Many are in their graves. Livy Grier is missed and others. Robert H is home on furlough, Joe Moffatt & Moffatt Grier are here. We all spent evening with Mr. H. Fixed Mr. Grier's clock. Dined with Mr. Bonner. Fixed his piano and played some, played on Belle Grier's Melodean; Moffatt & Robt sung with me. I remember the past when I taught the girls to sing [and] play.

Saturday, October 3, 1863

Took leave of my dear Due West friends this morning. Robt Hemphill took me to the depot. Stopped at New Market, met Gen

Bradley, Geo Chiles. Manuel had a buggy for me. Called at Gen B to see Miss Fannie, found her looking *beautifully*. Met Misses Dendy and Conner at Gen B's. Miss Fannie played for me and I played for her. Geo C came up. I went down home with him. Had a pleasant time with Miss Fannie Gray.

Sunday, October 4, 1863

God is good in all his dealings to man yet man often rebels against God. Conducted worship. Went to Long Cane church on horse. Heard Jim Lowry preach. Sung for him. Glad to see my old friends at Long Cane. The ladies looking well. Miss Sallie Widman's sweet heart was killed at Gettysburg. Went home with Jno Chiles for dinner. Lizzie is a nice little girl of 12 summers.

Monday, October 5, 1863

Rose quite early. Mrs. Chiles gave me a present of 10 candles. Took leave of my dear friends. Called at Gen Bradley's and went to R R at New Market. Met with Miss Marie Wardlaw on train, had quite a pleasant time: enjoyed a lunch with her & Miss Belcher. Up train baggage cars burned at Littleton. Met with Bro Murphy going to N.C. Bought 166 dols worth of clothing for Joe Moffatt. Met with Mrs. Baron on train. Reached home at midnight safely.

Tuesday, October 6, 1863

Rose late, glad to get home again and to find all well. Assisted in making molasses. Played piano, learned "Minstrels returned from the war". Worked with my skin to fix my gloves with, had a severe pain in head, eat no supper. God is angry with me. May I be able to say "Thy will be done".

Wednesday, October 7, 1863

Did but little today worth recording. Time rolls away rapidly; read Bible & attempted to pray in secret but my heart is too much on the world. Assisted in making molasses. Played piano. Called at Bro. William's to see his bees. Wrote letter to Moffatt Grier.

Thursday, October 8, 1863

Assisted in making Molasses; read Bible & oh for more grace. "My heart is desperately wicked". Went up town to get my watch cleaned. Called on Mrs. Melton; Miss Virgy was not at home. Played piano. Blessed with good health. Oh wretched man that I am!

Friday, October 9, 1863

Still in health. God's mercy is everlasting. Read Bible & engaged in prayer. Assisted in making Sirup. Very tired, went to sing with my old class at night. Pleasant yet sad, some are gone! killed in battle. Oh for peace.

Saturday, October 10, 1863

Another week has passed away: many souls have passed from time to Eternity. God is still bearing with me. Endeavored to read His word & commune with Him. Played violin & piano. Assisted in making molasses. Took tea with Mrs. Hemphill. Belle played for me, I played *"Minstrel returned from the war"*

Sunday, October 11, 1863

The Blessed Sabbath has come again & I have been permitted to enjoy its blessings at Home in the place where my fathers worship. Sister Sarah & Grier & I went to Union. Mr. McDonald preached. Went by Cousin Thomas Simpson's with a dispatch from him in hospital in Augusta, Ga. I started for Augusta with his wife at night.

Monday, October 12, 1863   Augusta, Georgia

Left Col S. C. this morning, reached Augusta at 4 P M in safety — found Cousin Thos. S in the old Small Pox hospital after considerable hunting. His wound is very bad with gangreene. Had prayers at night. Oh for patience in well doing.

Tuesday, October 13, 1863

Health good – God is good to the evil – dressed T. Simpson's wound. Took him to 3rd Ga Hos'. Sent telegram home. Sent "When this cruel war is over" to Belle H of Chester. Witnessed the amputation of a foot this even. Oh for Peace! Peace!

Wednesday, October 14, 1863

Time is flying – Rose early – assisted in dressing wounds. Walked up town; visited the Hospitals. Called on the leg maker – bought envelope and a collar. Wrote letter to father. Cousin Thomas' wound is improving. Read Old Telescopes of 58 & 59 – they bring to mind the past.

Thursday, October 15, 1863   - Atlanta

Health good. Wrote letter to Cousin Elizabeth Simpson. Bought 2 flannel shirts, 25 dols each. Saw some wounded Yankees at Hospital; took evening train to Atlanta for a new field of labor.

Friday, October 16, 1863

Reached Atlanta this morning. A Stranger in a Strange City. Met Mr. Bigham on his way home with remains of nephew – talked to the bereaved widow – met W P Price on street – visited the Fair Ground Hos.

Saturday, October 17, 1863

Another (day) has passed away, how rapidly the hours fly. My pulse tells me how fast I am dying. Wrote letter to Sister. Visited F M Inst. J T Collins is improving. Distributed tracts &c. God's mercy never fails. Oh that men would praise the Lord for his goodness. Bought "Life of Emmet." Eat with W P Price.

Sunday, October 18, 1863

Beautiful Sabbath, Oh how calmly. Read Bible & engaged in prayer. Distributed tracts and papers to Soldiers in Hos. Heard Chaplain of Post make some remarks to Soldiers at Med Col. My heart is stirred up to the importance of my work.

Monday, October 19, 1863

Happy to meet with friends today: Bros Quigg, Lindsay & Stewart. Q. & Son on way home; Lindsay remains for a time. Found Bob F McCaslan my friend at Med Col Hos, glad to see. Oh for grace to perform my duties well; not to be ashamed of Christ.

Tuesdays October 20, 1863

Tired to night; went thro' Fair Ground Hospital hunting up S.C. Troops. Visited F M Inst. & Med College. Talked to a wounded Miss. Soldier about his soul 's salvation; found him full of hope, prayed with him until midnight – another victim of the cruel war. Wrote letter to father. Went to Depot with stores.

Wednesday, October 21, 1863

God is loading me with his benefits. Yet I am a vile sinner living in rebellion against God & his love. Took a nap before dinner; wrote sermon. Met C Rader Stringfellow & others going to their Reg. Went to Gate City Hospital – to Female Inst Hos. Then to Med. Col. Lt R F McCaslan's wife came to see him; he went to hotel. I met his Mother.

Thursday, October 22, 1863

Done nothing today worthy of record. Visited the Hospitals as usual. Sick and wounded are dying rapidly. With what zeal should I show for their souls' salvation? One Woodall of Miss. had an artery to break loose and bled freely. O God be merciful to all the wounded.

Friday, October 23, 1863

God is good – it is very consoling to know we are in the hands of a merciful God. Distributed tracts and papers to Soldiers. Oh that I was not ashamed of Christ. The Surgeon will not allow me to sleep and eat at Hospital. Went to Hospital in a heavy rain.

Saturday, October 24, 1863

Rose early – took train to Griffin to look after S.C. Soldiers. Arrived at 5 A M. Visited all the Hospitals, found 10 or 12 needy, gave them something for soul and body. Returned to Atlanta on evening train. Spent $2 for dinner. Went to hos. , found all some better. Bought a dozen oranges for sick & wounded in hospital at $6.

Sunday, October 25, 1863

Read Bible – went to Presby Church; heard old Dr. Wilson. Read Scriptures, started to Hos' but met Bro Lindsay at Depot – talked a while – to P.O. Rec'd a letter from Cousin Thos. Simpson in Augusta Ga. ; one from Esqr Mills & one from Joe Bigham, all of Chester. Had prayers at the Med Col Hos.

Monday, October 26, 1863

Another week has set in – beautiful day. Took clothing to Fair Grd Hos. Bro Lindsay assisted me – To Female Hos. T J Collins is improving; found some needy. Called at Med Col Hos.: met a Tenn Soldier who knew Rev A S Montgomery.[1] Lt R F McCaslan is better.

Tuesday, October 27, 1863

Another day has passed away. Oh that the war would come to an end! Wrote letters to Dr. Grier & J Y Mills, Esqr. Visited Female Col & Med Col Hospitals; friends & Soldiers in general are doing well. Wrote letter for Miss. Sol. Had prayer in Hospital after supper.

Wednesday, October 28, 1863

Health good, God is still gracious and full of mercy. Wrote letter to Sister Sarah. Went to Hospitals. Saw Robt Mills' wound. Called on Collins. He left Hos for home; met him at cars, gave him my over coat & 5 dols. Sent dispatch to his wife. Met J O Lindsay on Street. He & I bought 30 yds of dark calico at 5.25 per yd. Commenced letter to Robt Hemphill. Went to hospital; had prayers with the Soldiers.

Thursday, October 29, 1863

Blessed with health. Finished letter to Robt H.; wrote a note to Belle – went to Fair Ground Hos. Met Bro A Sloan with his brother – met Jim Murphy's brother. Bro Lindsay left for home. Saw V.P. Al Stephens[2] – went to Hos after supper, had prayers.

Friday, October 30, 1863

The month is rapidly drawing to a close. *Hora fugit*! Life is waning like the moon to-night. God is long suffering and kind to me. Oh that I might serve him more devotedly; visited the sick at Female Inst Hos and Medical Col. May God restore the sick and wounded to health. Felt tired at night. Wrote letter to Mrs. Mayo, Richmond, Va. Went to Hos in a heavy rain to night.

Saturday, October 31, 1863

This is the last day of October. How swiftly the months do pass! The year will soon be gone, with all joys and many sorrows! Alas, how many have passed from time to eternity. Visited Fair Ground Hos. Had a long chat with Bro. Sloan. His bro. is doing well.[3] Mr. Price went to Cartersville: I am alone. The month is gone; farewell October '63.

Sunday, November 1, 1863

The holy Sabbath begins another month. Oh that the nation may enjoy a Sabbath, a rest from war and bloodshed. Read Bible. Studied scripture. Text, "Jesus the Same &c". Went to Med Col, distributed papers and tracts to sick and wounded. Went to Fair Ground, Sloan is still improving. Bro. A.S. Sloan is going home to-morrow morn.

Monday, November 2, 1863

Time is ever moving and I should be up and doing for I am drawing near the grave. Price returned from Cartersville. Met D Gills at store room. Wrote letter to Rev Lindsay. Went to Roys Hos'. Then to Med Col. Lt R F McCaslan started home this even. Met Woodson, an old Due West Student of the 41 Ala Co E – glad to see him.[4]

Tuesday, November 3, 1863

Tempus fugit. Yet God is good. Went to P.O., received nothing, then to Ex. Office: returned to my room, wrote letter to a Soldier's wife, Mrs. Isam Padgett.[5] Met S.C. Soldiers [wounded] at the train; gave them some brandy. Began a letter to Miss Maggie Jones of Ala. Met Woodson in even. Capt Bradley left for home.

Wednesday, November 4, 1863

The earth is full of the goodness of God, blessed be the name of the Lord. Finished letter to Miss Maggie Jones. Wrote to Mr. Sloan. Bought a lamp, price $5; 1 qt. lard oil, $7.50. Visited Hospital, distributed tracts. Went to Med College at night through rain; had prayers & returned.

Thursday, November 5, 1863 [6]

I am a daily receiver of great blessings at the hand of God. Read Bible & engaged in secret prayer for Soldiers and my country. Had a litter made to take Mills home on. Went to Med. Col. but the Surgeon would not grant a furlough to Mills until Monday. Rec'd a letter from Moffatt Grier.

Friday, November 6, 1863

This is a world of trial and of disappointment. Expected to start home to-morrow but Mills' wound is not doing well. Sold my silver chain at auction at $27.00. Bought hooks and eyes. Went to Fair Ground Hos to see Sloan, but he was not doing so well. Wrote a letter to his brother. And one to J Y Mills, Esqr. Had prayers at Med. Col.

Saturday, November 7, 1863

Time is still moving. Oh that this cruel war was over. Went to Female Institute; distributed tracts and papers, and conversed with sick and wounded. Then to Fair Ground. Sloan is improving; wrote to his brother, also to Mrs. Brakefield about her husband, very sick. Met a great many sick S.C. Soldiers; gave them some brandy. Went to Hospital &c.

Sunday, November 8, 1863   *Augusta*

The Sabbath is a day of rest to man and beast. But war destroys all rest, peace and happiness. Read Bible to-day, went to 2nd Presby Church, heard a good sermon. Went to Fair Grnd Hos, had prayers in Ward 8 with Sloan; distributed tracts & papers. To Med. Col. at night, had prayers in Hospital.

Monday, November 8, 1863

Health is still good; God is long suffering & kind. Went to Shop for a litter, took it to Hospital. Bought a lamp, price $30.00, a big price. Went to Fair Ground to see Sloan. Returned to Med College, got a furlough for Mills, went to transportation office. Got Mills on cars & started for home. Sent dispatch to J Y Mills. Eat supper at Social Circle $3.00.

Tuesday, November 10, 1863   *Columbia, Chester*

Reached Augusta this morning at 5; called to see Cousin Thos. Simpson, found him asleep but not doing well. Took train for Col S. C., arrived at 6 P M; stopped at Way Side Hos. Called at S.C. Bureau. Saw Mr. Martin, he gave me a flannel shirt. Slept at Hos'. Supper at Hotel.

Wednesday, November 11, 1863

Eat Breakfast [at] Hospital; gave ladies $2.00. Rode in Carriage to Depot. Set out for home; had a safe journey. Put Mills off at Blackstock with Mr. Jos Bigham. Went up home, glad to meet the "loved ones at Home". Talked with Father, Elihu & William about selling out in Chester. Fixed my lamp. Sister put a bosom in a shirt. Had worship and took the cars for Augusta. Rec'd a telegram at Depot from Cousin T. Simpson.

Thursday, November 12, 1863

Reached Columbia at daylight; went on to Junction, took train for Augusta; had a Safe journey. Arrived at 3rd Ga Hospital at 5 PM; found Cousin Thos Simpson, very low. Had prayers in Hospital. Rec'd a letter from Moffatt Grier & answered it.

Friday, November 13, 1863

Rose early; Cousin Thos is much better. Sent a dispatch home. Wrote letter to Moffatt Grier. Took a walk up the River to the Powder mills. Bought some sugar cane. Took train for Atlanta Ga; cars very much crowded.

Saturday, November 14, 1863

Reached Atlanta this morning; went to Boarding house, found Pickle & went to Hospital, found Sloan & McCormick better. Went to Medical Col. Woodall is improving. Wrote letter to his mother. May God preserve his life.

Sunday, November 15, 1863

The blessed Sabbath has come again. Oh that the land might enjoy a rest from war & blood shed. Mr. Beard came with boxes. Went to Hospital Female Ins, saw Clark Wardlaw. Started for army at night.

Monday, November 16, 1863 [7]

Reached Dalton at 4 A M, breakfast at Hotel. Went down to Mr. Thos Turner's. Wrote letter to Belle H at Knoxville Depot. Took my baggage to Rev Turner's, took supper. Had pleasant time, but Mr. T was absent.

Tuesday, November 17, 1863

Rose early this morning. Mrs. T woke me at 3 — went up to Depot, but train did not leave until 8. Reached Loudon[8] at 6 P.M. Sought Lodging. Slept on a mattress with Lt Hard. Thanks to God for his goodness.

Wednesday, November 18, 1863

Rose early. Slept well. Had a good breakfast from S.C. Soldiers. Found quarter Mas[ter] wagons of 6th S C; glad to meet Robt Poag & Wm McLure, had comfortable bed &c. Sent letter to Sister Sarah and telegram to Guardian.

Thursday, November 19, 1863

Oh for Peace. Went to Hospital, found some very sick men, gave them some brandy. Met Cap Cousan wounded, and others. Sent telegram to Guardian Col S.C. Went to Depot. Mr. Beard came with shoes.

Friday, November 20, 1863

Time is flying rapidly, the month will soon be gone. Oh that peace may soon return to our land. We are in the hands of God who doeth all things well. Failed to get off with shoes; called at Telegraph office, sent dispatch to D D Borgle; gave soldiers some brandy.

Saturday, November 21, 1863

Endeavored to get off to Knoxville, but failed.[9] Maj Quincy seems to be very slow for a Q. M. Went to Hos' found one soldier – Young, very sick, I fear will die. Gave him some brandy and coffee. Oh for peace again.

Sunday, November 22, 1863

The Sabbath has come again, Oh that I were at home. Read Bible. Took a walk down to River to see pontoon Bridge, if washed away.[10] Could not get over; delayed one day longer. Went to Hos, got a lock of hair from Young to send to his mother.

Monday, November 23, 1863

Rose late. Set out from Loudon at last for Knoxville. Detained until evening at ferry over the Tenn. Rode in a wagon the most of the way. Past Lenores Station.[11] The people in this region are Union. Slept in wagon in an old camp.

Tuesday, November 24, 1863

Rose before day; eat breakfast and set out from camp for Knoxville. Saw the camps of the Yankees all deserted.[12] Roads are full of shells and Caisons. Reached 6th Regiment. Stopped with Dav Wilson who is sick. Slept with Sergt Scaffe; had prayer in tent.

Wednesday, November 25, 1863

Rose early. David Wilson is better, was sent to Hos. Rode over to Jenkin's Brig' to distribute Shoes. Glad to see my friends "in *arms*". Many are barefooted. Took a view of Knoxville, and forts. May God give us victory.[13]

Thursday, November 26, 1863

Took a walk all along our front lines to-day. Yankees shelled Kershaw's Brig.[14] Met Dr. Hoyt. Called on 6th Reg. & 2nd Rif. Met many friends, delivered Shoes and packages – Serg Brady, an old college mate, let me ride to *ordnance train*; had prayer in tent.

Friday, November 27, 1863

Had a good night's rest, rose late in good health – thanks to God for his goodness. Heard the 6th S.C. band play "maidens prayer". Called at Hospital. Went to Kershaw's Brig; dined with the Gen' – played piano in his Headquarters. Called on Capt Nance;[15] asked about Bro H T Sloan's brother.

Saturday, November 28, 1863

Another month is drawing to a close. My life and health are continued. "God is love"! Heard that Longstreet would storm the enemy's breast works tomorrow. The Sabbath to be a day of bloodshed! Went to Bratton's headquarters.

Sunday, November 29, 1863[16]

Sabbath has dawned upon a field of blood and carnage. Went to camp before day light — the 6th Reg. had gone to attack the enemy's breast works. I saw our brave men charge the fort but they failed to take it — I saw the flash of the guns. Terrific sight! Jenkins Brig. returned to camp. Wagons were ordered to Loudon.

Monday, November 30, 1863

The month is drawing to a close. Hold prayer meeting every night in our tent. Wagons were ordered back to Knoxville. Very cold — returned to our old camp; made some beef foot oil for lamp.

Tuesday, December 1, 1863

God's mercy never fails. Finished my oil; put it in lamp. Went over to Reg. Yankees fired two or three shells into camp. Orders for marching towards Bristol – anxious to know the object of the move.[17] Dined in camp.

Wednesday, December 2, 1863

Remained with wagons which were ordered towards Bristol. Ordnance wagons left at 10 A M. Segt Scaffe was detailed to remain with Brigade; I remained with him. Had prayers and retired expecting to move early tomorrow.

Thursday, December 3, 1863

Left Knoxville this evening at 3 o'clock. Lt Tom Brice & Bob Brice started with us. Had a circuitous road to go round Knoxville.[18] Marched about 8 mi. My lamp did me great good. Had a good bed of hay.

Friday, December 4, 1863

Marched, through rain & mud; very wet day but a soldier has to take it. Roads very muddy. Bought some cabbage and meat — found a large dog, but lost him. God is love. He supplies my wants.

Saturday, December 5, 1863

Marched all day — had but little to eat; bought some meat & a goose. Rain — roads very muddy, but Soldiers have to go through all. Oh that these Scenes of exposure may soon pass away!

Sunday, December 6, 1863

Marched all day — roads very muddy. This is the holy Sabbath! but it is not a day of rest. The land is in trouble and affliction, war is desolating the country. Oh for peace! peace that never ends.

Monday, December 7, 1863

Reached Rulleggville[19], passed on through. Had difficulty in finding camp — went back two miles — camped near Moseburg. Went out foraging; a good lady gave me flour & a pumpkin.

Tuesday, December 8, 1863

Passed Moseburg, did not see the place. Streets very muddy; my lamp did me great good. The Bible is *The Lamp* which shows the way of eternal life. The peace of God passeth all understanding.

Wednesday, December 9, 1863

Marched within 5 miles of Rogersville. Rode to town; dined with a Union Lady Mrs. Caldwell, whose husband was a prisoner in Richmond. She treated me kindly. Sold me flour, butter, and some applebutter. Returned to camp but the Brigade wagons were ordered back to troops. Had trouble in finding wagons; lost a pocket handkerchief. Eat walnuts with Robt Poag.

Thursday, December 10, 1863

Left Jenkins Brig 6 miles west to Rogersville. Lt T. Brice & Robt Brice & I set out for home on foot. I had a great many letters for friends at home. Stopped at Rogersville, dined with my union friend. Found lodging with a S.C. lady Mrs. Miller 2 miles east of Rogersville.

Friday, December 11, 1863[20]

Left one Mr. Miller's near Rogersville. Bought a young iron grey horse, gave my watch & 120 dollars. Met with kind friends on way. Lt Brice & Robt Brice rode my horse by turns, dined without charge, and got apples. Reached Kingsport.

Saturday, December 12, 1863

Left Kingsport, paid $2.50 doll for night's lodging; crossed the Holston River. Met an old friend Little Bob Ferguson who once worked with father in Chester. Walked nearly all day — passed through Bluntville. Stopped 4 miles from town.

Sunday, December 13, 1863

Reached Bristol. Travelled 4 miles on the Sabbath; Oh that I could spend the day aright! Exchanged bottle of oil for 2 hanks of Shoe thread. The holy Sabbath has not been observed as it should have been. Lt Brice & Bob took train for Wytheville; I was left alone. Went to a kind widow's house Mrs Stewart, eat supper — went to depot, saw my friends leave; felt sad — returned to Mrs. Stewart's.

Monday, December 14, 1863

Rose in good health — conducted worship for Mrs. Stewart — felt lonely. Went to Mr. Jno Ryburn's, 5 miles from Bristol, an old acquaintance of father Patrick's; dined. Went to Mr. Lathins who agreed to feed my pony until I returned from home.

Tuesday, December 15, 1863

Conducted worship for Mrs Stewart. Washed my horse's back. Went to Mr. Ryburn's with Mrs Stewart's boys; left one horse with Mr. Carmack to board. Met Dr. Willeby at Mr R's, dined, eat apples. Took my pony to Lathim's; borrowed 50 dollars from him, returned. Sold my lame horse to Dr. Willeby for 100 dols — returned to Bristol. Mr. Ryburn gave me grafts of his apples.

Wednesday, December 16, 1863

Returned to Bristol on train. Yankees stopped me.[21] Train was ordered back to Bristol. I felt very bad. Stopped at Mrs. Stewart's — went to depot — No prospects of getting home by R.R. Mrs. S son took me over to Mr Ryburn's. Went up to Mr. Lathims after my horse.

Thursday, December 17, 1863[22]

Left Mr. Jno Ryburns' on foot for home, leading my horse through rain and mud. Passed through Abington. Warned at Depot, got directions to Col. Wm Ryburns', came to his house at dark, crossed Holston River at dusk. It was very dark, Col Ryburn is an old Seceder & his wife conducted worship — had a long talk about the church.

Friday, December 18, 1863

Left Col Wm Ryburns at 9 A.M. Col R & family were very kind. Mrs R gave me a pair of nice Socks. My horse's back is no better; had it opened. Travelled Blue Spring Road; passed Sinclair Botton Church. Bought some nice cloth at Holston mills — Cap Thomas, price $10 yd. Reached the Allegheny mountains. Stopped at Barnetts.

Saturday, December 19, 1863

Thus far has God brought me on my way, safely through another week. Crossed the mountains on foot — had my horse shod. Reached New River at mouth of the Wilson. Stopped with Mr. Ross, a good Methodist, a friend of Bro Hunter — conducted worship — cold.

Sunday, December 20, 1863

Beautiful day, but very cold — river full of ice. Felt it necessary to travel on the Sabbath. Oh that war would end. Fell in company with one Mr. Maxwell & travelled together — stopped at the same house 6 miles from top of Blue Ridge.

Monday, December 21, 1863

God is blessing me with good health, and yet how I abuse his goodness. Crossed the mountains, Oh the greatness of the Creator's works! The mountains speak His praise. Crossed Yadkin River at Jonesville. Stopped at one Mr. Wells, 10 miles from Jonesville.

Tuesday, December 22, 1863

Rose early, settled my bill $5 for myself & horse — Beautiful day — had no dinner. Rejoiced to hear the Steam whistle at Statesville.[23] Reached depot before sunset — tried to get horse on train. Stopped at College with Rev Miller.

Wednesday, December 23, 1863   *Home Again*

Rose before day; went to depot; took train for Charlotte — left my horse with Bro. M — Left C. at 7 P.M. with Miss Herndon. Reached home at 10, found my mother very sick. Glad to meet the loved ones at home. Sister Mary & Flora were with mother.

Thursday, December 24, 1863

The year is drawing to a close. Oh that the war would come to a close! The Lord reigneth — let the nations fear & tremble. Remained at home all day. Miss Mag Alexander & Mrs. M came over to see me. Bro I[saiah] came home last night.

Friday, December 25, 1863

Another Christmas has come and the war is still raging and no prospect of peace on earth. But there is peace in heaven my home — Mother is improving. Went over to Mr. Hemphill's; happy to meet Joe Moffatt, Lois G. & Lizzie Q. Dined with Mrs. Melton.

Saturday, December 26, 1863

The year is fast drawing to a close. Many have passed from time to eternity. God has preserved my unprofitable life. Bought 50 bushels corn, $5. per bu. Played violin. Elihu came up & returned with uncle John.

Sunday, December 27, 1863

Rose in good health; conducted worship. Mother is still improving. Rain; but went to Hopewell in buggy. Heard Mr. Brice preach. Went home with him. Took Jane in buggy, very wet & muddy.

Monday, December 28, 1863

Rose early, blessed with health. Had a long talk with Mr. B about false reports. Was glad to hear them. Rec'd 300.00 dols; set out for home in rain — sun came out before reached home. Mother is improving; Sister Mary went home. Played violin. Isaiah started to Col[umbia]. Rev Oats called to see me. Aunt Linda Martin took cars for first time. Called on Mr. Harris. Rec'd 300 dolls from Bank.

Tuesday, December 29, 1863

Rose in good health. Mother still improving. Elihu came up from Col[umbia]. Went to P.O. Sister Sarah had 3 teeth extracted. Took train for Charlotte. Stopped with Miss Laura Kerrs; she played for me.

Wednesday, December 30, 1863   *Statesville*

The year is drawing to a close; how rapidly it has passed, how like a dream! Was introduced to Miss Harty; heard her sing and play. Had a fine dinner. Miss Laura & Miss H went to Catholic church to hear Miss H sing & play the Catholic chants. Took cars for Statesville, had a slow ride — fire in engine went out.

Thursday, December 31, 1863

1863 closes to day. My life & health have been preserved; I have great reason to adore God's patience & goodness to me. Many far more obedient and deserving than I have been called to meet their God. I have committed many great sins during the year past. But God has not dealt with me according to the measure of my iniquity. May I fear lest He speedily executes righteous judgments and cuts me off in the midst of my days. May his mercy and goodness go with me at all times. I left Statesville this morning on horse back [Bristol] which I had left with Mr. Miller on my way from Tenn. Rained all day on me. Night overtook me. I got lost in the woods, but found the road, yet it was so dark I could not see. Fortunately I heard a negro and called him who came to me and lead my horse out of danger and took me to Mr. Helper's at Davidson College. 1 was wet and muddy. Mrs. Helper gave me a good supper; I talked with Mrs. McGaw & Miss Carrie. Conducted worship. Played piano before lying down.

So dies 1863. Where will I be the last day of 1864? The past is full of buried hopes. Oh thou future! what hast thou in store for me?

Notes

[1] Rev. Andrew Spence Montgomery, a graduate of the Seminary at Erskine College. Montgomery served a church in Marshall County Tennessee at the beginning of the war, and moved in 1862 to Illinois to take another Church away from the seat of the war.

[2] Confederate Vice President Alexander Stephens, of Georgia.

[3] Thomas Galloway Sloan, 3rd South Carolina Infantry, wounded in action at Chickamaugua.

[4] W. M. Woodson, a member of the senior class of Erskine College in 1861, from Wilcox, Alabama.

[5] Private Isham Padgett, 24th South Carolina Infantry.

[6] Lieutenant General James Longstreet moved from North Georgia into East Tennesse with his two divisions, including the 6th South Carolina. Simpson would follow the regiment in a few days.

[7] Longstreet's divisions entered the outskirts of Knoxville Tennessee on this day, beginning a long siege of the city.

[8] Loundon Tennessee was the railhead for Longstreet's East Tennessee Campaign.

[9] Union forces under Major General Ambrose Burnside still held on to Knoxville. The railroad halted at the bridge over the Holston River, and heavy rain slowed the Confederate supply route east to Knoxville.

[10] The Holston or Tennessee River was running strongly due to recent rains.

[11] Leniors Station, a short distance up the railroad from Loudon Station.

[12] Burnside's men withdrew into Knoxville to defend the city.

[13] At this time, Longstreet and his commaders were planning an assault on Knoxville as quickly as possible.

[14] General Joseph B. Kershaw's brigade of South Carolinians, in Major General Layfayette McLaw's Division.

[15] Colonel James D. Nance, 3rd South Carolina Infantry, Kershaw's Brigade.

[16] In the early morning cold, Longstreet attacked the Union defense line at Fort Sanders. In twenty minutes, the Confederates suffered a bloody repulse, losing 813 men.

[17] General Braxton Bragg's army in North Georgia was badly beaten at Missionary Ridge, leaving Longstreet cut off in Tennessee. The Confederate general determined to withdraw toward Bristol, drawing the Union army away from the Georgia theater of operations.

[18] Burnside still held Knoxville, and forced the Confederates into a wide detour toward Bristol.

[19] Russellville, Tennessee.

[20] Longstreet halted his men at Rogersville, where he still hoped to capture Knoxville with reinforcements from Virginia.

[21] Union forces operating from Cumberland Gap, Kentucky ranged into Southwest Virginia to cut the rail lines.

[22] On this date, Simpson resolved to cross the Smokey Mountains to reach a North Carolina railhead, no easy task in the dead of winter.

[23] Statesville, North Carolina.

Chapter 13

"*MAY GOD GRANT ME GRACE*"

The events of 1864 are now lost to the reader of John H. Simpsons diaries. Although he did continue to keep his diary throughout the year, this volume has been lost to posterity. It is known that he continued his work with the two South Carolina Brigades of McGowan and Jenkins, which are united within Lee's army in Virginia in 1864. These units fought in all the major battles from the Wilderness in May of 1864 to the siege line of Petersburg at the end of the year. More of the slain from the Virginia battlefields were brought home to South Carolina for their final resting place, so Simpson spent much of his time in 1864 concentrated in Virginia as before, making his way back and forth from the soldiers in the field to his home state. The new year would bring one last visit to Virginia.

As the new year began, there was little reason to hope for the success of Southern Confederacy. Defeat after defeat struck the Southern cause, until in January 1865, there was very little of the territory of the new nation left. The Army of Northern Virginia commanded by General Lee still held Richmond and Petersburg, but Sherman was beginning his move through South Carolina, and all but two major Confederate ports had been captured. It seemed to many just a matter of time until the war would end with the inevitable collapse of the South. Until that would happen, those who still believed in the cause of the Confederacy would remain loyal to the new nation, despite the rising tide of defeat.

John H. Simpson began the year recovering the body of a South Carolina soldier from the hospitals of Danville, Virginia. The trip in 1865 was considerably more complex than the previous years, primarily due to the capture of the direct southern railroad lines from Richmond. Simpson now could only travel by the sometimes unreliable Richmond and Danville railroad and then south.

Cornelius M. Sharp, Company G, Orr's Rifles killed in the Battle of North Anna. ARP Cemetery, Due West, South Carolina (grave site).

Sabbath, January 1, 1865

Today a new year begins its round. No one but the all wise Ruler of the universe knows what will take place during the year 1865. May God grant me grace to live in his fear, mindful of my dependence upon Him. Spent this day in Danville; very unpleasant and cold. Endeavored to get off to Greensboro. Oh, that I had the opportunity of attending the house of God.

Monday, January 2, 1865

Very cold today. Still in Richmond & DRR car. Met one Mr. Levy, a very wicked man. Slept with him last night. Longing to get home. Trains very irregular, great detention at Danville. Oh for peace.

Tuesday, January 3, 1865

Still in Danville. Brought up to the Piedmont depot. Supplies transferred for Greensboro. Went to Hotel for supper, $15.00 a meal. Great extortion everywhere. Read Bible but my mind is too much distracted about the war and things of the world. Oh for more grace.

Wednesday, January 4, 1865

Left Danville this morning at one o'clock with my car full of soldiers. Reached Greensboro at 10 A.M.; missed connection for Charlotte. Transferred my supplies and corpse.[1] Supper at Hotel. Retired in my car. God is love.

Thursday, January 5, 1865

Cold today. Troops [Conners Brig.] are going to S.C.[2] Met Mr. Summer who ordered my car to go with the troops.[3] Sent Kelly's body on train. Visited the Manassas R.R. Shops. Had a good supper on honey at Hotel. Met Dr. Jordan, took him in my car with soldiers; left for Charlotte at 8 P.M.

Friday, January 6, 1865

Reached Charlotte this morning. Very heavy rain. No prospects of getting to Col[umbia]. Put my supplies in Depot. Met Hammond en route to Hampton's Cavalry with boxes.[4] Met Thos. Howze & eat dinner with [him]. Enjoyed his Sausages &c. Bought 4 doz. spools thread & 41 1/2 yds. bleached shirting. Sent Sam home [on] night train. Saw Tho. Simpson.

Saturday, January 7, 1865

Aroused this morning by the alarm of fire. The QM, Store, R.R. car Stores and S.C. Depot were all consumed with their contents of corn, sugar and all kinds of government Stores. Soldiers of Conners Brig. stole part of my supplies and Hammond's. It was a sad sight to see so much corn, 60,000 bushels, consumed.

Sabbath, January 8, 1865

Another Sabbath has dawned upon this sinful world. Oh for the return of peace, to be permitted to enjoy its rest. Fixed up my corpse, which very narrowly escaped being burned. Put my trunks & machine case on trains and left for Chester. Met Capt. Aleck Wylie & Jno. McFadden on train. Met Father and Mother, Sisters Mary & Sarah at depot. Sister M. was on her way to Charleston to see Jno. C. sick with measles. She did not go. I went up home. Gave Capt. W. my horse to ride home. Had a long talk about the war.

Monday, January 9, 1865

Happy to get home once more. There is no place like home. Conducted worship this morning. Went to depot after trunks and machine. Put it up and showed Sister how to use it. Went to Depot, met the corpse and went on to Col[umbia]. Met Rev. Kelly at Winnsboro. Reached Col[umbia]. at 5 1/2 P.M. Bro. Kelly took me up to his mother-in-laws, Mrs. Wilburn, to spend the night.

Tuesday, January 10, 1865[5]

Spent the day in Col[umbia] preparing a shipment for Charleston. Very heavy rain today. Stopped out of the rain & ignorantly went into a house of ill fame for shelter but I soon left, preferring the rain to such a place. Met my dear old friend, Robert Hemphill, just from home. Had a long talk with him. Gave him a piece of soap. Bought a coffee pot; had a smoke with Robert. Supper at Nickerson's & lodging with Boseman.

Wednesday, January 11, 1865

Rose very early, left Bro. Bozeman at Nickerson Hotel. Took train for Charleston. Met with Mrs. Neely on train going to see her son sick with measles. Reached Charleston at 5 P.M. Stopped at Wayside, had supper and a good bed. Met Mr. Wiley formerly of Chester. Went to Receiving Hos., saw Jno. C. Burns[6] transferred to Summerville.

Thursday, January 12, 1865

Left Charleston for Summerville to see Jno. C. Burns. Met Maj. Pagan[7] on train. Got in ladies car with Mrs. Neely. Stopped at Summerville. Walked to Hos. N. 2. Found Jno. C. going about. Gave him his box from home, a welcome visitor. Saw a good number of boys of Chester. Left Jno. C. at Hos., transferred to Columbia. I took train for Charleston, train behind time. Met Bozeman on train. Stopped at Mrs. Finney's house.

Friday, January 13, 1865

Wayside full of Refugees from Savannah.[8] Bozeman and I had a bed last night at hotel. We went to S.C. Depot, received boxes, went over to Mt. Pleasant[9] in a row boat. I went to Sul. Isl.,[10] took a view of Ft. Moultrie[11] and the Yankee fleet.[12] Returned to the City at Sunset. Met Mr. McMaster at Wayside; we went to Mr. Cook's Hotel, a very poor house.

Saturday, January 14, 1865

Breakfast at the Wayside. Went to Bu Store with Bozeman, bought two pair cards [or cords?] & some castile soap. Called on Mr. Kerrison, he gave me a check on Charleston Bank for $800 to buy salt. Went to salt works, did not buy. Delivered boxes and went to Ft. Pringle[13] to see Bro. William. Reached fort about 8 P.M. Happy to see Bro. Wm in good health. Gave him his box from home, also one to Stokes and one to Culp. Had supper, talked about home.

Sabbath, January 15, 1865[14]

A quiet Sabbath on the Stone River at Ft. Pringle in sight of the Federal fleet. Had a good breakfast. Went out and studied sermon, preached at 12 M. to a small audience from Mat. 5, "Seek ye first". Oh for more grace to serve my Master better. Met Lewis Wylie & other old friends unexpectedly. Had a splendid dinner in Brother's tent, had a nice turkey sent to Mr. Stokes. Had prayer meeting in his tent. Sung some good old songs. Slept with Brother William.

Monday, January 16, 1865

Rose very early, breakfast on turkey and sausages. Bro. William and Andrew White went with me to Hospital at the McCloud house to see Mr. W's cousin. But we found his grave, having died on last Monday. Parted with them at the bridge. Came to the city. Met McMaster and Mr. Kerrison. Went to S. Col. Depot. A stranger gave me a good mattress. Met Bozeman, agreed to take his shipment to Green Pond. Had an oyster dinner, $7.00 each. Met Ward. We took boxes to Savannah Depot and made our bed on boxes.

Tuesday, January 17, 1865

Had a cold sleep last night. Rose early. Put boxes on train at 9 A.M. for Salketchie, Green Pond etc. Met Jim Brawley and David Hemphill at Rantowles Station. Delivered boxes at Adams Run,

Green Pond and went to Salketchie; found no one there to receive boxes. Made our bed in R.R. car, had coffee and bread for supper. Oh for peace again.

Wednesday, January 18, 1865

Rose early, had a good rest. Thanks to God for his great mercies to me. Made coffee at Salketchie, very cold morning. Left for Charleston, delivered boxes at Green Pond. Reached City at 1 P.M. Went to Col. Depot to see about trains to Col. Hunted some salt. Walked down to the battery[15] and burnt Dis[trict][16]. Bought some oysters for supper at Wayside.

Thursday, January 19, 1865

Rose late. Mr. Bozeman met me on street. We bought some kegs and filled them with coffee and sugar. I bought 4 1/2 lbs. coffee and 15 lbs. sugar at $10. per pound, coffee at 21. Heavy rain all day. Gave $5 for 2 kegs. Bozeman packed up to leave. Good health, thanks to God for mercies.

Friday, January 20, 1865

Bozeman left me today for his home; I wish I was on my way, too. Went to depot; nothing from the S.C.R.R. Bought 17 bushels of salt at $45 per bus. Heavy rains. Watched the flowing tide. Took train for Summerville. Reached Hos. at 8 P.M. Found Jno. C.B. doing well.

Saturday, January 21, 1865

Rose early this morning. Slept in the ward with the Sick. Jno. still in bed. Ben R. Scott was worse and dying[17]. Hospital in confusion; all were to be moved to Col[umbia]. Wrote to Capt. Patterson. Had prayers in Ward H where Mrs. Neely and son were. Returned to Ward C, found Scott dead. Had to dress him myself, made a tub and put my draw's and shirt on the body.

Sabbath, January 22, 1865

All were up early to go to Col. I went to Depot with Jno. C. Burns. Mrs. Neely left on passenger train. I took her trunks. Could not get them and Scott's body on express train — had to wait for next train. Cooked sausages, bought some bread. Read New Tes[tament]. Felt lonely.

Monday, January 23, 1865

Glad when daylight came — tired lying in bed. Train from Charleston arrived at 8 A.M. Put corpse and trunks on train for Col. Glad to start towards home. Uneasy about the R.R. But got over River safely.[18] Reached Col. at 7 1/2 P.M. Stopped at Nickerson's Hotel. Wrote letter to Dr. I. S. Scott about his son's death.

Tuesday, January 24, 1865

Went to College Hos', found John C. and all the boys doing well. Called on Dr. Gibes about furloughs for them. Met Mr. Peay hunting for his nephew, Ben Scott. Dined with him at Hotel. Went to Bureau. Sent Despatch to Mrs. West. Stopped at Janey's.

Wednesday, January 25, 1865[19]

Rose late. Went to Bureau. Wrote 18 letters to all who lost by fire at Charlotte. Met John C. & Mr. Marion on Street. Found graves of Morris and Callahan[20]. Called on Dr. Gibes again and Dr. Thomson about furloughs. Dr. Babcock received furloughs from Dr. G. and gave them to all the Chester boys. We went for transportation. Thence to Depot. I lost my coffee. Sent John C. on - I stopped to hunt it; found it in the Street. Spent night with Cousin Hugh. Had a long hunt for my coffee, but was fortunate. I retired with W. Smith in Cousin Hugh's tent.

Thursday, January 26, 1865

Rose at 5 o'clock. Went to Depot. Met Mr. and Mrs. Neely and Mr. Marion at Depot. We all took train for Chester. Arrived safely at 2 p.m. Glad to get home again. Found Isaiah at home. John C. still improving and anxious to go down home.

Friday, January 27, 1865

Blessed with good health. God is loading me with his benefits. Conducted worship. Flora and Servant Jno. came with horse for Jno. C. They went home this evening. Weather very cold. I worked with sewing machine to make it sew coarse thread but the needles were too small. Bro. Elihu's family came up at dusk. All very cold. Isaiah and I put bees in house.

Saturday, January 28, 1865

Rose early. Worked with machine. Went to P.O. Met Jas [or Jno ?] Hemphill. Called at Bank. Mr. Harris cashed a check. Margaret and family went to Mr. Bigham's. I studied sermon. Oh, for peace again! Oh! God deliver this land from war.

Sabbath, January 29, 1865

The holy Sabbath has returned. Went to Presby. Church, heard Mr. White. Returned in evening and preached for Bro. White from Mat. 6.33. Oh, for grace and strength to serve my Master better. Without divine assistance I can do nothing. Heard that Stephens, Hunter and Campbell had gone to Washington to make peace with the U.S.[21] God grant that they may gain their object.

Monday, January 30, 1865

Rose early, blessed with good health. Put rollers on Sewing machine. Mr. Strong called. Mr. Thos. McDill dined with us. Isaiah left for Col. and the Coast. I put a sight on his pistol. Went up to town. Bought lb. of soda, $10. Had hair trimmed. Called on Mrs. H. Tea with Mrs. Gaston.

Tuesday, January 31, 1865

Rose late but in good health. God is good to me beyond my deserts. Heard good news about peace. God grant it may be true. Made a pair of suspenders, but were too thick. Sister Sarah has a cold. Weather much warmer. Father did not come up. Mrs. Kennedy called. Another month has passed away.

Wednesday, February 1, 1865

Rose early. Conducted worship. Made another pair of suspenders. Went up town, called on Miss Mag Alexander. Stopped at Mrs. Elliots, fixed her sewing machine. Father came up with wagon. Heard Sherman was advancing on Branchville.[22]

Thursday, February 2, 1865

Rose early, blessed with health. Put straps on Bro. Elihu's box; packed up Sister Mary's potatoes for Richmond. Mr. & Mrs. Strong called and dined. Father and I went to Depot. Isaiah came up for Rich', gave him boxes. He gave me $210. for Sister S. Father went down home with wagon. Heard of Jack McDaniel's death[23], another victim on the altar of our country.

Friday, February 3, 1865 [very dim ink]

Rose early. Blessed with good health. Heard that Sherman had been ordered to stop hostilities. Rain and cold. Set out for the Old place. Stopped at Store. Talked with family (?) about the war. He is opposed to the Governor calling out the old men up to 60. Charley Fudge overtook me. He was out making his company ... Stopped to see Mr. McDonald. I came to Sister Mary's. Found Jno. C. down with ?

Saturday, February 4, 1865 [very dim ink]

Another week has ended. Oh that God would remove the scourge of war from this land. Left Sister's early. John came with me to father's. We drank cider. I made some shoe blackener out of China berries. Made essence of coffee. Fixed mother's wheel. Jno. returned home after dinner, conducted worship & retired in my old native home.

Sabbath, February 5, 1865

Permitted to see another Sabbath dawn upon this troubled land. Oh that my native land may soon enjoy a rest from war! Went to Union [Church], heard Mr. M.D., a good sermon from —. Saw my good old friend, Mrs. Moffatt. Great excitement about the old men of 60 going to camp. I came to Sister Mary's. John C. is improving in health. Conducted worship and retired.

Monday, February 6, 1865

Rose early, conducted worship. Waited for Lewis with wagon to go after molasses. Mules ran away with barrels at Steadman's. Borrowed Sister's wagon. Lewis and I set out for Rocky Mount. I called at Uncle Jno. F. He is not going to War. Jno C. B. took

Aunt Betsy J. to Uncle Jno. W's. I called to see him, he did not know me. I went to Robertson's; measured up 30 gals. I left Lewis' wagon at Robertson's and came to Dr. Scotts. Found him and family very kind and thankful for my kindness to their son, Ben S.

Tuesday, February 7, 1865

Cold and raining, trees are covered with ice. A severe day to ride. Returned to Robertson's, bought 4 bu. potatoes (sweet), $10 per bu. Went to Mrs. Pickett's; she gave me 15 gals. Stopped at Dr. Clouds, he gave me 15 or 20. Met horses and wagons of Young's Cavalry going to the Coast.[24] Oh for peace. Came to Mrs. Dr. Gaston's. Called at the door. Was taken for Soldier for some time. But they soon found me out. Found Chalmers at home. Put potatoes in kitchen. Conducted worship and retired.

Wednesday, February 8, 1865

Cold and windy. Conducted worship. Talked with the family and soldiers who spent the night with Mrs. Gaston. Miss Liza played for us. Left Mrs. Gaston's and came to Thomas Howze. Found his family very kind – has some nice little children. Lucius and Issac sang for me. Dined, Handhope Crocket also dined – he is out hunting horses for Butlers Cav.[25] He left but returned. We both spent the night with Mr. H.

Thursday, February 9, 1865

Rose early. Cold morning but clear. Conducted worship. Mr. H. gave me 8 gals. for the S.C. Home, Richmond. Looked at Mrs. H's bees, found all dead but 3 gums. I stopped at Chap H., he gave 7 gals — dined with him. Returned to Father's. Creek deep. Put potatoes in chaff. Heard that our Commissioners to Washington returned without making peace. They were insulted by the Federal Government. Nothing but War.[26]

Friday, February 10, 1865

Clear, frosty morning — conducted worship. Went to Sister Mary's. Found John killing hogs. I went on to Bro. William's, found sister in a new house at her father's. Fixed her clock and cords, dined; made her some coffee out of sorghum. Talked with

Rev. McCoy. Read letter from Harper Millen about Young John M's death. Returned to Chester. Found Sister and children well. But Servant Mother sick in bed. Cut out cloth for harness after worship. Retired at 11.

Saturday, February 11, 1865

Spent this day at the sewing machine making cloth for wagon harness. Succeeded finally. Went to Depot at up-train. Met Dr. Murry. Great excitement – Yankees reported to be at Orangeburg.[27] Lewis came up with wagon. Brought 2 barrels of sorghum and keg of cider and 2 pigs for Grier and Joe. Conducted worship. Retired 11 1/2.
[Grier and Joe Baird, nephews of John H. Simpson.]

Sabbath, February 12, 1865

Spent this day at home in Chester. Did not attend church anywhere. Had to go to Depot. Read Henry's Com[mentary] on Psalms. Oh, for the spirit of wisdom. Blessed with good health, food and raiment. No news from the armies. God grant us peace for thy truth and mercy's sake.

Monday, February 13, 1865

Rose in good health. Thanks to God for his loving kindness to me. Lewis and I went out to Gilmore's & Ed McLure's for molasses. A very cold day. Returned late at night. Sat up late talking. Great excitement about Col[umbia] raiders are near the City.[28] Citizens are leaving. May God deliver this land from war.

Tuesday, February 14, 1865

Weather still cold. No good news. Yankees still approaching Col. Bottled up my cider. Went over to Mrs. Melton's to see Dr. Murry and Mr. Clark. Mrs. Murry is a very nice lady. Oh for peace. I hope that truth and right will prevail, whether Confederate or Federal.

Wednesday, February 15, 1865

Rose late. Trees loaded with ice. Very cold. Sat in house until one o'clock. Loaded wagon with corn, started for father's. Grier and Lewis with wagon. I went to Depot to get news. Federal Army in front of Col. and in possession of Kingsville. Rode down to Lewisville — night came on and we all went to Sister Mary's. Eat roasted potatoes and talked about the War.

Thursday, February 16, 1865

Rose early. Breakfast & had worship. Started to Father's. Found creek too full for wagon to cross; took mules over and left wagon until evening. Father made some nice tar for harness and wagon. I started for Chester. Called at Mrs. Moffatt's — had short conversation with my good Christian friend. Reached Chester about 7 P.M. Heard the federal army were shelling Col[umbia][29].

Friday, February 17, 1865

Great excitement today. Col[umbia] has fallen[30]. It was evacuated this morning. The Federal army took possession at 12. Went up Street, called on Mr. H. & Mrs. Gaston. Gave her 2 gallon of vinegar — bought lb of tea for Mrs. Moffatt, 120 dolls. Oh for peace again; father came up in evening.

Saturday, February 18, 1865

Great rumors about the enemy today. Some say they are 10 or 15 miles from Chester. Went to depot to hear news; father went down to Fishing Creek. Met Dr. LaBrodes' daughter on Street; her par' remained in Col. Oh for peace. Mr. Stevenson of the Carolinia & Dr. Lever of the Med. D'pt came up to get lodging.[31]

Sabbath, February 19, 1865

Great excitement, enemy still advancing on Chester[32]. May God deliver us. Brother Isaiah came home today with Hammond. Met Col. Miller[33], Mr. Price and Pickle at depot, brought them all to spend night. Father came up with wagon.

Monday, February 20, 1865

Rose early, never lay down last night. Writing letters to Dr. Grier and Mrs. Morris by Col. Miller.[34] Loaded wagon for old place. Went to depot, enemy advancing. Father went down in wagon;

Isaiah and I in Sister's buggy. Stopped at Mrs. Moffatt's; Sister Mary's for dinner. Found all very much alarmed. We went over to Father's. Jno. C. brought over his wagon and horses. Everyone much alarmed. Wild rumors afloat.

Tuesday. February 21, 1865[35]

Rose early. Loaded wagons for N.C. with provisions and clothing.[36] Isaiah and Jno. started at daylight. I went over to Mr. Fudge's; found Sister Flora and all there. Left home last night, afraid to stay at home. I took Grier behind me and set out for Chester. Met troops at Mrs. Moffatt's. Reached home at one o'clock; enemy not come yet.

Wednesday, February 22, 1865

Wheeler's Cavalry came in today.[37] Depot was thrown open to all.[38] I got a sack of coffee, a large looking glass and the depot clock. Looking for the enemy. Citizens very much excited. Oh for peace. "Oh that I like a dove had wings &c." Soldiers called to get something to eat. Met some of Rev. Bryson's members. Saw Young Murphy in camp. Gave him jug of cider.

Thursday, February 23, 1865

Expected to see the Stars and Stripes today, but was disappointed.[39] No enemy yet. Rec'd dispatch yesterday from Isaiah at Charlotte, N.C. Went to depot to hear news. Met Joe Orr in the 4th Tenn. C.[40]; glad to see him. Wheelers Cav is not such a lawless band as represented.[41]

Friday, February 24, 1865

The enemy is going by Rocky Mt, not coming through Chester; glad to hear such good news. God has been merciful to us. Oh how thankful we should be. Went to Depot, called on Mrs. Gaston and Mr. Hemphill; they were glad to see me. Heard that Mrs. Jno. Bell lost her Silver. Called on Mrs. Legare. Joe Orr left today.

Saturday, February 25, 1865

Blessed with health and plenty to eat and wear. Oh how thankful I should be. Read Bible, man's only guide and comfort in the day of trouble. Went to depot to hear news. Called on Mrs. Gaston. Oh for peace! peace!!

Sabbath, February 26, 1865

Clear & pleasant day, roads and streets muddy. Conducted worship. Went to depot to hear news. Saw some federal prisoners. Heard Robt Hemphill had suffered heavily.[42] Saw Mr. Brennicke. Said Isaiah was about to start for home. I have not spent the Sabbath as it should be. Read Com[mentary] on 1st Kings. This is a world of sin and sorrow but there remaineth a rest &c. Heard from Brother Wm.

Monday, February 27, 1865

Although I am a sinful and rebellious creature yet God is daily mindful of my wants. Went to depot for news, nothing of importance; trains running as before by day. Walked down to father's. Stopped at Sister Mary's for dinner. H. Moffatt lost 7 mules, Rev. McDonald 1 horse. Crossed creek in flat, reached father's at 2 1/2. Spent night with Bro. Elihu's family. Wrote letter to William by Capt. Patterson.

Tuesday, February 28, 1865

Another month ends today; how rapid is the flight of time! Conducted worship for Margaret; returned to father's. Took up Sister Sarah's box uninjured. Made a box for Green Doors sewing machine. Rode my mule for the first [time] to Aunt Molly Hamilton's; all were frightened by the Army. Returned by John Dickey's to hear news. All the old men left – or hid. The enemy are all crossing at Peay's ferry.[43]

Wednesday, March 1, 1865

Rose late, all blessed with health. Weather very gloomy. Isaiah and Jno. C. have not returned from Charlotte. Anxious to hear from them. Rode down toward Dr. Anderson to hear from the enemy. Met Green Ferguson who said all had crossed the river. Returned to father's for dinner. Oh for peace and rest from War! God is our refuge in trouble.

Thursday, March 2, 1865

Creek too full to cross on horse. Great deal of rain, days are gloomy and dull. Went to Mrs. Culp to get fodder, no positive answer. Heard no news from the armies — anxious to hear. Isaiah and Jno. C. have not returned; getting uneasy about them. Read Scott's Com[mentary] on 1st Kings. This is a world of sin. Oh, for deliverance from sin.

Friday, March 3, 1865

Creek still up. Set out for Chester by Eaves'. Saw Jno. Dickey, heard from Isaiah on his way home. But think he is water bound.[44] Dined at Sister Mary's. Called at Rev. McD. and H. Moffatt's and Mrs. M's. Reached Chester at dusk. Called on Mrs. Gaston after supper; took her some fruit. Heard sad news from Fairfield. Dr. Boyce is burnt out.

Saturday, March 4, 1865[45]

Blessed with health. God is long-suffering to his creatures. Man knows not what is best for him. Chastisements are blessings to prevent us from pride and self-reliance. Rose early this morning, went to depot to hear news. Mrs. Gaston sent me her stray dog "Braddock". Rode mule down to father's. Went to creek but could not cross. Isaiah and John C. came home today, they had a long and muddy trip. They succeeded in saving everything. I went to Aunt Linda Martin's; all had retired but I scared them all and they let me in. Sat and talked.

Sabbath, March 5, 1865

Rose late – conducted worship after breakfast. Aunt is very anxious about Wm Martin at Elmyra prison[46]. I went to Sister Mary's, not knowing there was any preaching at Union. Mr. Millen stopped and told us that Rev. Robt McCoy preached. Heard that Alex' Rosborough, old Col Brown, Legare and others were captured in Lancaster[47]. Isaiah came over and I went to father's.

Monday, March 6, 1865

Up early. Set out for Mrs. Dr. Gaston's and Uncle Jno. Wylie's to hear how the Yankees treated them. All fared badly; Chalmers &

Jno Hemphill were captured with all the[y] had in Lancaster. Uncle John W. lost all his meat &c. Met Dr. Jas Gaston at his mother's. Miss K lost all her clothing. Met Riley Smith at Uncle Jno.'s. Returned to Sister Mary's. Met Thos. Howze returning home with his horses & mules. Mr. McDonald called at night. Flora is over at Father's.

Tuesday, March 7, 1865

Rose early, conducted worship — went over to father's. Isaiah and I packed up for home. Put my mule to the buggy, Isaiah rode in the wagon. Reached home at 2 P.M. Went to depot to hear news. Nothing of importance. Sherman is not marching so rapidly. I hope and pray that an army may never come near my home again.

Wednesday, March 8, 1865

There is no place like home — Yet many are deprived of its joys & delights. Thousands of peaceful homes are desolate by the march of hostile armies. I was pressed by Dr. Jas. Gaston to go out to gatherup supplies for the destitute in Col[umbia][48]. Went to Cousin Thos. Simpson's for dinner. Called on John Knox, was not at home. Went [to] C McFadden's, Jno. Agnew & Thos. Torbit; reached the latter at dusk. Rode all the day in the rain. Conducted worship for Mr. Torbit.

Thursday, March 9, 1865[49]

Set out from Mr. Torbit's for Blackstock's but did not go far. Got Mr. T's mule to pull wagon out of the mud for 1/2 mile. Met Riley Smith and Mag Montgomery. Shot pistol at some squirrels. Heavy rain all evening. Took wagon to Boyd's School house to camp. I went to Robt Hemphill's to spend the night. He did not know me at first. Conducted worship.

Friday, March 10, 1865

Sun came out today — oh! how cheering. Went with Mr. H. to Mr. Brice's — did not tarry long. Set out to find Dr. Gaston. Found him at Col. McDill's all afoot. Wagon broke; I went to Robt. H's to get it fixed. Thence to Blackstock's. But could not find my wagon. It had gone on to Col. I rode until midnight hunting it. Reached Robert H's at midnight. Sorry to wake up a good old bachelor.

Saturday, March 11, 1865[50]

Conducted worship for Mr. H. Set out for Chester. Glad to get home. Went to depot to hear war news. Met Jno. R. Ellis from Due West. He & Joe Moffatt came over on horse. A great many paroled prisoners arrived on the train and among them my dear friend, Jno. L. Hemphill.[51] Went to Mr. Jas H's to see him — he looks badly but better than many others.

Sabbath, March 12, 1865

Another Sabbath has returned to this troubled land. Happy is the nation that has rest from war. May God soon deliver this country from a most desolating war. I went to Hopewell, heard Mr. B. sung for him. Met Thos. Moffatt just from prison[52]. Mr. Brice thanked Sister Mary and myself for his mule. Read Henry's Com[mentary]. Oh for a pure heart!

Monday, March 13, 1865[53]

Rose early. Conducted worship. Fixed up fence round turnip patch. Then went to Maj. Jas Lowry to hunt fodder. Dined with him. Thence to Mi Ervins — and to Mrs. Bratton's — she promised me fodder shucks and oats. Saw Jno. H. this morning on street. He said he wanted to start home. I reached home tonight about half past 8. Somewhat tired. I am a great sinner.

Tuesday, March 14, 1865

Rose late this morning — went up town. Met my good friend Joe Moffatt. Went with him to Mrs. Hemphill's. Got his horse and we went to Mr. Marion's for dinner. I fixed his sewing machine. Stopped at Wm Knox for seed oats. Came to Mrs. M's there met Aunt Liza F. I thought of many happy days I spent near this place in my schoolboy days.

Wednesday, March 15, 1865

Rose early. Fixed Mrs. M's clock. Joe and I had a long talk last night. He gave me his experience in married life. He seems to be very happy. I went over to father's; got sacks for oats. Called at Sister M.B.'s [Mary Burns]. Dined with Joe M. To Wm Knox's and Mr. Marions. Reached home at 8 P.M. Tired, retired early.

Thursday, March 16, 1865

Time is hastening me on to the grave. Oh for grace and strength to resist the evil one. Very heavy rain today — I was drenched. Called on Mr. Melton and Mr. Hemphill. Made 4 backbands. Put locks on the stable doors. Oh for the merry sunshine and rest from war and confusion. The Lord reigns.

Friday, March 17, 1865

Rose early. Blessed with health. Took Martha [Servant] to old Willis'. Went to hear news. Wrote letter to R. E. Guthrie about flour. Met him at depot. Engaged some flour. Examined my bees. Went to the field, helped to build fence. Four soldiers called to spend the night. Oh for peace!

Saturday, March 18, 1865

No one knows the value of mercies and privileges until they are withheld. I should be thankful for good health. Worked hard today building fence. Went to Depot in evening — read paper. Grier [Baird] and I came down to father's this evening. Grier rode Sal all the way. Stopped at Mary's — I came over the Creek after supper. Ralph has the measles.

Sabbath, March 19, 1865[54]

Happy to go to church today to Union where I have often heard the gospel preached. I drove Elihu's carriage. Heard my dear friend Josiah Moffatt from Colossians 3.4, "When Christ who is our life appears..." I think Joe is improving. I came to spend the night with Bro. William's family. Johnny is better.

Monday, March 20, 1865

Left Margaret's this morning — came to Chester. Saw Mr. Guthrie. Bought 1000 lbs. of flour from him, $2.50 per lb. Called on Joe M. at Mr. Hemphill's. Joe expects to start for Due West tomorrow — horseback. Called on Mrs. Gaston. Heard that Chalmers

had recovered some of his lost clothing. I built fence in evening.
Ross McCain called to see Sister — he has lost his leg in the war.
Isaiah called on the ladies.

Tuesday, March 21, 1865

Blessed with health. Heavy rain all day and I was out with wagon.
Went to Wm Knox's for oats and to J. Agnew's for peas. Dined
with Mr. Marion — 13 1/2 bu. Irish potatoes from him. Reached
Sister Mary's after dark — Creek up — I was very wet and tired.
Lewis and Henry with me.

Wednesday, March 22, 1865

Rose early — conducted worship for Sister. Took Lewis and Henry
to Jno. Millen's for Irish potatoes. Dined with him. I walked over
to Father's by the mill. Crossed creek in bottom. Always happy
to get to my old native home. Conducted worship and retired to
rest. Oh for peace!

Thursday, March 23, 1865

Rose early — conducted worship — tied the dog, Braddock. Went
over to Sister Mary's — took Lewis with wagon for Guthrie's flour
at Jas. Ervins — had to go to Blake's mill for it — 1000 pounds —
roads bad; had to unload once. Returned to Sister's late at night.
Got wet in creek.

Friday, March 24, 1865

Blessed with health — should be very thankful. Father is planting Irish potatoes today. I walked over to Sister Mary's and on to
Chester. Left Sister's at 2 P.M., reached Chester at 6 P.M. Met
Rev. Wm. Martin at our gate — he returned and spent the night
with us. He is on his way to Lincolnton for his daughters. Mr. Bell
of Due West came here today — very sick.

Saturday, March 25, 1865

Somewhat tired today on account of my walk. Conducted worship. Went to depot with Bro. Martin. Saw Mr. Wolfe, depot agent
at Col[umbia]. Rented a room to him. Saw Col. Bigns Mobley
— got 8 bu. peas from him. Thankful for health of body and

mind. Took my watch out of ground whurt[?]. Joe Forsyth, Sister's cousin came here this evening. Uncle Hugh here for dinner and will spend the night. He told us that Brother Wm was home very badly hurt.

Sabbath, March 26, 1865

The holy Sabbath has returned again. Spent the day at home with Mr. Bell. Read Henry's [commentary] on Kings and Psalms. Found text for a sermon, last verse of Ezekiel, "The Lord is there". Oh for an opportunity to study and preach the gospel every Sabbath! Joe F., Sister and Isaiah went to church.

Monday, March 27, 1865[55]

Rose early this morning — did nothing of any importance today. Joe Forsyth and Sarah walked down to Uncle J. Smith's. Fixed the well bucket; made a honey box for my bees. Went to depot to hear news from the armies.

Tuesday, March 28, 1865

Conducted worship night and morning. Made another honey box — went to depot. Heard that there was a fight at Petersburg — heavy loss on both sides.[56] Isaiah came home this evening with sore feet. Nothing new from Sherman. Stoneman reported marching on Charlotte. Wagon came up late, Father and Grier with it. Robert Fennell came home today from Johnson's Isle. Hemphill Smith called on his way home. Mrs. Roddy called to spend the night but we were too much crowded.

Wednesday, March 29, 1865

Rain today — very heavy. I went to Mr. Bigns Mobley's for 8 bu. peas, and to Mrs. Gooch's for oats — talked with the Misses Gibson about their trip from the Yankees — Father commenced sowing oats. Went to depot — no news. Bro. William came up to report to hospital — he is recovering from his wound.

Thursday, March 30, 1865

Blessed with good health. Very fine weather. Time is more than lost in war. Joe Forsyth came up with Leroy Smith – Leroy was arrested going and brought him back to Chester [heavy rain]. Went to depot — read newspaper. Great reports about the raiders.

Friday, March 31, 1865

This day closes another month and yet the war is still going on desolating our land. Joe Forsyth left for his Regt. Sorry to see him leave. Sent advertisement to Carolinian by him. Got Mr. Bell set in a wagon for Newberry.

Notes

[1] Probably Private M. B. Kelly, Company C, Orr's Rifles, who died of disease in Danville, Virginia.

[2] These men were actually Kershaw's old South Carolina brigade, commanded now by Brigadier General John D. Kennedy. Brigadier General James Conner commanded the unit in September-October 1864 and was wounded at the Battle of Cedar Creek. The unit left Richmond on January 4.

[3] The Brigade was being transferred from Lee's army to defend South Carolina.

[4] Major General Wade Hampton commanded the cavalry of the Army of Northern Virginia. On January 19, the South Carolinian with one division of cavalry would be sent to hold back Sherman's advance into South Carolina.

[5] At this point of time, Sherman's army occupied Beaufort South Carolina, and was preparing to move inland.

[6] Possibly Private John C. Burns, Company D, 5th South Carolina Infantry.

[7] Major James Pagan, Brigade Quartermaster, Evans South Carolina Brigade.

[8] Sherman's occupation of Savannah Georgia, in December 1864, created thousands of refugees who took shelter in South Carolina.

[9] Mount Pleasant is across the Cooper River and harbor from Charleston.

[10] Sullivan's Island, one of the islands which controlled the entrance to Charleston Harbor. The Confederate defenders of the city heavily fortified the island.

[11] One of the most famous forts in South Carolina, Fort Moultrie, at this time was a vital link in the chain of Confederate fortifications protecting Charleston.

[12] The Union fleet at this time stood off Charleston, blockading the port.

[13] Fort Pringle protected Charleston by holding the Stone River on James Island.

[14] Fort Fisher, North Carolina, fell to Union forces, thereby closing the port of Wilmington. Charleston alone remained as the last major Confederate port.

[15] The "battery" is the famed section of Charleston fronting the harbor.

[16] The "Burnt district" of Charleston resulted from a fire December 11, 1861, which left this section of the city in ruins until after the war.

[17] Ben R. Scott, Marion South Carolina Artillery.

[18] The recent rains created the possibility of the railroad bridge becoming flooded out.

[19] Slowed by the rains, Sherman's entire army moved over the border into South Carolina by the end of January, prompting a state of alarm over the state. Simpson's removal of the wounded and sick of Chester from the Confederate hospitals wounded prove to be providential as the Union army advanced.

[20] Possibly Private Andrew H. Callahan, 19th South Carolina, died in Columbia of typhoid fever, July 14, 1862.

[21] On January 29, A peace commission composed of Vice President Alexander Stephens, Senator R. M. T. Hunter, and Judge James A. Campell, a former Supreme Court Justice, entered Union lines outside Richmond to attempt to negotiate a peaceful end to the war.

[22] Sherman's men were pushing forward to the Columbia and Augusta railroad, to further cut South Carolina from the western Confederacy.

[23] Private E. Jackson McDaniel, Company F, 6th South Carolina, died in Chester on February 1, 1865, age 30 years old.

[24] BGen Pierce M. B. Young's commanded a brigade of cavalry in Hampton's division, which left Richmond on January 19.

[25] Major General Matthew C. Butler commanded Hampton's division, which was in desperate need of horses to fully mount the command, one of the reasons to transfer the unit to South Carolina.

[26] The peace commissioners returned without settlement, as the Union government demanded surrender as a condition of peace.

[27] Orangeburg was occupied by Federal Soldiers on January 12. Almost one half of the town was burned, and the remainder severely looted.

[28] Sherman's men moved on Columbia after the destruction of Orangeburg, nearing the state capitol on January 15.

[29] Sherman's army was now massed across the Congeree River from Columbia. Union artillery did shell the city, leaving scars that can be seen today on the capitol building.

[30] On February 16, Mayor T. J. Goodwyn surrendered Columbia to Sherman.

[31] The approach of the Union army to Columbia prompted a mass exodus of civilians to the safety of outlying areas of North and South Carolina.

[32] Sherman's main army resumed their march north on January 20th.

[33] Colonel George McDuffie Miller, was granted leave on February 10 by General Lee for "indulgence," to return to South Carolina to marry Miss Virginia Griffin, of Ninety-Six.

[34] Colonel Miller would deliver the letters to Due West on his way to Ninety-Six.

[35] Sherman's army entered Winnsboro on this day, approximately 25 miles from Chester. Over 30 buildings in the town were burned by Sherman's men. Union cavalry were in the advance of the army, approaching to within 10 miles of Chester.

[36] With Chester in the direct path of the Union advance, many of the residents fled to safety in North Carolina.

[37] Confederate cavalry under the command of Lieutenant General Joseph Wheeler screened the Union advance, providing the Confederate army with intelligence of Sherman's movements.

[38] Rather than lose the supplies stored in the Chester Depot to Sherman's men, Wheeler opened the depot to the citizens of Chester to take what they could carry home.

[39] Sherman turned east from Winnsboro, toward Fayetteville, North Carolina, having threatened Charlotte, North Carolina and forced the Confederate army to concentrate to defend that city. Chester was thus spared the direct Union advance, although the railroad and telegraph wires were destroyed close to the town.

[40] The 4th Tennessee Cavalry served in Wheeler's cavalry command, having a long attachment to the Confederate Army of Tennessee.

[41] Wheeler's command had a somewhat deserved reputation for a lack of discipline, and for liberal foraging among civilians.

[42] Robert Hemphill owned a large plantation within reach of the Union advance. Hemphill fled his home, leaving behind Burrel Hemphill, one of his slaves to defend the plantation. Burrel was killed by the Union soldiers when he would not reveal where the valuables of the estate were hidden.

[43] Sherman's right wing crossed the Wateree River at Peay's Ferry on February 23.

[44] The tremendous rains of late February rendered much of South Carolina impassible for travel, slowing even Sherman's army.

[45] On this day, Abraham Lincoln was inaugurated for his second term as President of the United States.

[46] The prison camp at Elmira New York proved to be one of the worst of many such camps in the Civil War. Almost 3,000 Confederate soldiers died while in captivity there, averaging sixteen a day in March 1865.

[47] Union calvary raided Lancaster in a feint towards Charlotte, as the Union army occupied Cheraw on March 3.

[48] When Sherman's men left Columbia, the city and supply network lay in ruins, with little food to subsist the remaining population.

[49] The Confederate Congress approved the use of slaves as soldiers in the field, demonstrating the desperation of the Confederate cause.

[50] Sherman's army occupied Fayetteville, North Carolina on this day, leaving a wide swath of destruction behind in South Carolina.

[51] As the war drew near a conclusion, many Confederate prisoners of war were paroled and sent south, unable to take up arms again until properly exchanged for Union soldiers. John L. Hemphill had been in prison camp since the Gettysburg campaign of July 1863, Company G, Orr's Rifles.

[52] Thomas H. Moffatt, 10th Battalion, South Carolina Cavalry.

[53] President Davis signed into law the measure to enlist Black soldiers in the Confederate cause.

[54] The Confederate army under General Joe Johnston attacked Sherman's army at Bentonville, North Carolina in an attempt to halt the Federal advance. In two days of heavy fighting, the Confederate army was forced to withdraw.

[55] Lincoln, Grant and Sherman and Admiral David D. Porter meet at City Point Virginia to plan the final campaigns to put an end to the war.

[56] Lee's army attacked the Union lines at Fort Stedman in a final attempt to break the siege of Petersburg. The assault was bloodily repulsed with heavy loss.

Chapter 14

"THERE IS A BETTER COUNTRY FOR THE RIGHTEOUS"

John H. Simpson no longer needed to go to the war to support his friends and country. The war was now on his doorstep, with Chester threatened from every side, first by Sherman and then by Union cavalry from the North. Simpson experienced the last days of the Confederacy in a unique way, hosting one of the highest ranking Confederate generals as well as welcoming the returning soldiers of Lee and Johnston's armies. The area from Chester to Charlotte became one of the last refuges of President Davis and the Confederate government, bringing the final moments of a nation under the direct gaze of Simpson. The uncertainty of what was to happen to South Carolina became a heavy strain on Simpson and the rest of the town of Chester, a strain that only the passage of time could relieve.

Saturday, April 1, 1865[1]

Another month gone of this life of toil and tumult. My days are swiftly gliding by. Went up to Bennett's to mend my watch and father's. Succeeded in fixing both. Eyes very sore and tired. Saved $100. today — "A penny saved is a penny earned — a willing mind makes ready hands."

Sabbath, April 2, 1865[2]

The quiet Sabbath has once more returned. Spent the day at home — read the Bible. Read a little in Armageddon. Oh, for the dawn of the millenium. "God is our refuge and strength...".

Monday, April 3, 1865

Great excitement about the raiders on Salisbury.[3] Town full of people. Went to Bennett's to mend the chain of my watch again. Met Mrs. McMaster and little girl at depot just from Richmond.

Brought them up for dinner. Fixed Hinton's watch. Great many boxes came in to go to Richmond. Father finished sowing oats. Soldiers called to spend the night.

Tuesday, April 4, 1865[4]

Rose early in good health. God is daily loading me with his benefits. Planted some irish potatoes. Father put manure on orchard and planted it in corn. Heard that Richmond was evacuated. Oh for peace. Saw General Hood at depot.[5] Went up to P.O. Mr. R. W. Brice called.

Wednesday, April 5, 1865

Great excitement about the FALL of RICHMOND, VA on the 2nd of Apr 1865. The Yankees have accomplished their long sought object. Went up town — talked with Mr. Hemphill. To Printing Office for "Extra Carolinian". Wm Hood of Newberry came. We made a box for his books. I rode his horse to Rev. Brice's — there spent the night.

Thursday, April 6, 1865

Rose early. Mr. Brice conducted worship. I fixed Mrs B's piano. Mr. B. went with me to Mr. Thos. McDill's — fixed his clock. Misses McDill gave me some seeds. Went to Robt Caldwell's to tune piano but did not do it. Dined. Called on Miss Kate C. Returned home by Torbit's Mill.

Friday, April 7, 1865

Rose early. Worked hard all day in the garden — planted corn and beans. Mr. W. Caldwell called to barter candles for thread. I gave 10 spools for 6 lbs. candles. Slight rain all day. No news of importance. Looked at my bees — doing well. Wm Hood called — dined with us.

Saturday, April 8, 1865

Blessed with good health. Worked some in garden. Went up town — bought 12 lbs nails, $4 per lb and 10 lbs at $6. Hood got off to Newberry; looked at bees. Worked at a music box. Mrs. Elim finished my hat. Took bread out of McDill's Box.

Sabbath, April 9, 1865[6]

Blessed with good health. Rose early — conducted worship this morning. Set out to Union on foot — reached church an hour before time for preaching. Mr. McD preached. I rode in Sister Mary's carriage to Boyds — then in Elihu's to father's. Felt very tired and sleepy all evening — rained a little at dusk.

Monday, April 10, 1865

God is daily loading me with his benefits. Some rain fell last night — ground a little wet. Went up to Margaret's — plowed some for Brown. I sold Elihu's young mule for 50 bus. corn to Irvin White. Dick & I went to Mrs. N. Millen's for fodder and hay. Late getting home — dam gave out and fell down in the road.

Tuesday, April 11, 1865

Rose at my usual time. After worship and breakfast Dick & I burnt out Beck's mouth for Brown. Saddled up my mule for Chester. Called at Sister Mary's. Emeline has the measles. Called at Mrs. Moffatt's — reached home at 3 P.M. Heard Yankees at Sumter & near Col[umbia].[7] Wm got a 10-day furlough.

Wednesday, April 12, 1865[8]

Very warm today — worked hard in putting manure on patch by shop. Went up town. Called on Miss Anna E. Wylie — looked at her bees. Miss Maggie Caldwell called to see Isaiah's coat. I sold her a piece of Confed' grey. Yankees have taken Salisbury today.[9] Cousin Joe Martin came home today with sad news. Cousin Sam died at Danville; was buried at Greensboro.

Thursday, April 13, 1865

The day bid fair to be rainy in the morning — but the sun came out. Fixed up the fence round the Shop patch. Went to mill for corn I bought from Jas McCochran, $35. per bus'. Went up to Dr. Wylie's to work with Miss Anna's bees — they stung everyone on the place. Called on Miss Virgie & the ladies. Heard that Davidson College was burned by the enemy.

Friday, April 14, 1865[10]

Blessed with good health and abundance to eat and wear. I should be a grateful and happy man. Took Mrs. Bell to depot but no train to York. Took some supplies to the "Wayside". Great excitement about the "Raiders" near Charlotte, N.C.[11] Worked hard in putting on potato patch. Covered Irish potatoes. Cut bottles. Saw Maj. Lowry at depot. Introduced me to Dr. Bratton's wife.

Saturday, April 15, 1865

April is half gone — Time waits for no man. Rose at 5, took Mrs. Bell to the York train. Had worship — set out cabbage — planted sweet potatoes above Wm's house — made a ditch across the yard. Nothing from the Raiders today. Looked at my bees. Blessed with good health.

Sabbath, April 16, 1865

A beautiful day — heard sad reports today — that <u>Gen. R. E. Lee had surrendered</u>! Went to Union alone in buggy. Heard Rev. R. A. Ross and Mr. Oats preach; Ross, Brice, Oats and McD. addressed tables. Mr. McD. announced that the First Presbytery would not meet tomorrow. I took Grier and Joe to father's. Called on Elihu's family.

Monday, April 17, 1865

Rose early — blessed with health. Set out for Chester in buggy with Grier and Joe. Went by Sister Mary's — did not see Flora or John C. — brought up a bushel of apples for Bennett. Plowed some in patch by Shop. Scattered manure — Col Lewis paid for keeping his horses. News still bad from Gen. Lee.

Tuesday, April 18, 1865[12]

Another day of great excitement — heard that my friend R. R. Hemphill was slightly wounded[13]. Gen Lee's surrender was confirmed — a part, of his men arrived on parole. Went to Soldiers Home at 9 A. M. Bees swarmed and hived — planted part of patch in corn — fine rain. Oh for peace.

Wednesday, April 19, 1865

Day of intense excitement. Yankees expected — the Catawba R.R. Bridge [14] was burned this morning by Gen Stoneman. I took Sister's buggy down to father's. Called at Sister M's. Dined at father's — received note from Bro. Isaiah that the enemy were at Rock Hill — I set out for Chester — Commissaries abandoned. I got salt (5 sacks) and rice. Hurt my back.

Thursday, April 20, 1865

Rose early — felt weak in the back on account of my hurt last night. Gen. Chestnut[15] stopped the taking of Com. stores. Went to depot — heard that an armistice was declared by Gen. Sherman to J. E. Johnston. Some say the war is over — hope it is — heard the enemy had returned to N. C.

Friday, April 21, 1865

The "reign of terror" is almost over — enemy not expected in Chester at this time. Thanks to a kind Providence for another Signal deliverance from a cruel foe. May Chester always be thankful. Heard that Abe Lincoln was assassinated in a theatre at Washington. Great excitement. C. D. Melton returned home from refugeeing.

Saturday, April 22, 1865

Not able to do much today. Made a hive for my bees. Cousin Hugh S[impson] took away his salt. News still exciting — oh! for peace with liberty and independence. Gen. Bragg[16] and wife came to Chester today; we had to give them a room. The first General ever in this house!

Sabbath, April 23, 1865

Health improving — glad to see another Sabbath. Spent the day at home — read Bible and religious books. A number of General Bragg's staff called to see him. Some ladies called on Mrs. Bragg. She is a pleasant lady — converses freely. Gen. B. does not talk much — his looks are determined and resolute[17]. Had worship tonight — Mrs. B. asked us to sing for her.

Monday, April 24, 1865

My health is improving; back not so sore. In great suspense about the effort to make peace — may God interfere and stop the War! Received despatch from Rev. W. Martin. Father came up with wagon and negro to work on farm.

Tuesday, April 25, 1865

Gen. Bragg still with us. Wish he would leave; not able to keep such big men. Isaiah went up to Charlotte. Went up town to see about my shoes. Waited at depot to see the paroled soldiers of Lee's army[18] — Sam McDill and Nixon, Jim Fennell, Thos. Wylie, Robt. Hemphill, Jim Latimer, M. Galloway, and Jno. Dixon all arrived. I went with Robt. to his Uncle James'. Called on Jim Fennell at Mr. Elim's.

Wednesday, April 26, 1865[19]

Rose early — had the pleasure of meeting my friends of Co. G, Orr's Regiment at home[20]. Robt. H. amused us all — I treated them. Gave Robt. his shoes. They all left for Robt N. H. I rec'd letter from Jno. L. H., Joe M. Glad to hear from Due West. Happy to see a few of my dear friends return. But alas, how many will [not] return. Sad, Sad to think of it.

Thursday, April 27, 1865[21]

Excitement very great. Heard that the President had gone by Union C.H. Mr. Stubs, Gen. B's orderly — left for home this evening and carried away our stable keys. Went to depot — heard that Gen. Johnson had surrendered to Sherman. Was introduced to Pres. Davis' aid, Col. Johnson[22], who came in for tea with Gen. Bragg and spent the night.

Friday, April 28, 1865

Rose at 3 o'clock to give General B. an early start. He and wife and Maj. Ellis and Col. Johnson all left for the Trans Miss. at 7 A.M. Sorry to see them leave.[23] Mrs. B. took one of my photographs for a keepsake. They left Union to meet the President. General B. left us a good grey mare, a Con. Flag, maps and swords and trunks. I went out to get some harness from the abandoned artillery.[24] Claud Hicklin did not want me to get any but I took as much as I needed.

Saturday, April 29, 1865

Still blessed with health. Great excitement, a world of rumors. Went to field in the morning to guard the mule. Went to depot to hear news. Got some caps for a musket, powder abundant. Isaiah got some last night. Oh for peace and security of life and property! Retired early.

Sabbath, April 30, 1865

Spent the Sabbath at home to guard the house. Bees swarmed, hived them successfully. Flora, Sister, Isaiah, and children went to Church. One more month of suspense and anxiety gone! Went up to draw leather from the abandoned train, got a side and a half.

Monday, May 1, 1865

Lovely May has returned. Finished planting corn. Went up to powder train. Found a great crowd there. Any quantity of powder — got two boxes of cartridges. Jno. Douglas got a load, brought some boxes of brass fuses. Maj. Melton got some powder.

Tuesday, May 2, 1865

Rose before day to go up to the powder train to get powder and brass and copper. Got 4 loads of powder and metal. Train moved and engine set powder on fire — three heavy explosions. Maj. Melton was near to the place — his horses ran away — fired sky rockets and fuses.

Wednesday, May 3, 1865

Rose early. Went to field to watch the mule — horse thieves are numerous and daring. Our country is in a dreadful condition — there is neither civil nor military law. Father went home this morning; took some powder. I went up town — had my hair trimmed; met Rev. M. Anderson. Called on Mrs. Gaston — rec'd letter from Joe Moffatt; Sister one from Calvin Moffatt. Rode the grey mare up to Maj. McLure's. Burnt some fuses at night — retired to rest in the barn.

Thursday, May 4, 1865[25]

Went to the field — used powder as manure for experiment — a strange manure. Went up town to hear news — tired of so much excitement and confusion! There is a better country for the righteous. Thanks to God.

Friday, May 5, 1865

Blessed with usual good health — went to field to guard the mule. Blocked out some axe handles. Isaiah goes to the field every evening. Worked on my copper kettle — hung it up. Went to depot for Johnson McCain's salt. Sam McDill came up to spend night. Maj. Walcott of U.S. Army came this evening to give paroles to Soldiers of the C.S.A.[26]

Saturday, May 6, 1865

Went to field this morning. Cleaned out the shot gun — tried it with Enfield cartridges. Grier made two shots. Isaiah went to field in evening. Middleton finished plowing. I cut off Isaiah's pistol. He tried Nelly with the buggy. Heard that Billy McLure died this evening — poisoned by whiskey — he and others.

Sabbath, May 7, 1865

The best of all the week has returned — but a sad day for Chester — the town is filled with gloom on account of so many deaths from poison: Billy McLure, Col. Secrest, Billy Coleman — all died from poisoned wine. They all broke into the Medical Dept. Friday night — a sad end. Frank McNinch is also very low with poison. Laura Brawley died this morning from "maningitis"[sic]. Sister Sarah took sick with rheumatism. I went for Dr. Wylie. Mr. Harris called. Isaiah and I reported for a guard [duty] at the Commissary.

Monday, May 8, 1865

Great excitement in consequence of the poisoned Raiders. Secrest, Coleman and McClure were buried today. A fine rain.

Set out plants and tomatoes. Cleaned out the bee room — put a hive in. Rev. Brice and Rob. Hemphill called. Cousin John Simpson came down. Isaiah has a headache. Traded nails to Sam McDill for corn at old prices.

Tuesday, May 9, 1865

Blessed with health — many have been cut off but I am spared. Great excitement about the Country Raiders on the R.R. and depot[27]. Mr. Wolfe, R.R. con[ductor], had his train stopped. Commenced a bee hive. Sister Sarah is better. Worked in garden — cleaned out the walks — fixed gate. Cleaned out a can for powder. Retired in the barn.

Wednesday, May 10, 1865[28]

Rose early from my bed in the barn. Felt dull all day; took a nap. Worked on a bee hive. Shot birds eating cherries. Bro. Elihu came up today. Isaiah stood guard at Com'. Finished plowing the Shop patch — buried powder — gave Rev Say and Legt Patterson of Liberty Hill some powder. Wm Cherry and Bob Slick called to spend night.

Thursday, May 11, 1865

Oh, how happy a healthy man should be. I pray for a new heart. Finished burying the powder. Elihu went home — J. C. Burns came up. Riley Smith and Brown Wylie came up and dined. Worked on my beehive. Read Charlotte Bulletin, printed under the U.S. Government. Read Louisville Journal. Went up town. Very heavy wind from the west — a little rain. Mr. Wolfe gave me some Sweet Spirits of Ammonia.

Friday, May 12, 1865

Rose early — in good health. Family all well except Sister Sarah. She is sick with dysentery; hope and pray God will soon restore her to health. Worked on beehive and in the garden. Went up town — rec'd letter from Harrison about his tobacco. Worked on the well house. Dr. Wylie called to see Sister. Isaiah on guard today at Com[missary].

Saturday, May 13, 1865

Another [week] gone forever; what have I done for the glory of God and my eternal welfare? Rose at 4 A.M. Sister was worse in the morning but better at night. Went for Dr. Wylie. He gave me some medicine. Had fresh irish potatoes and cherry pie for dinner. Met Major Waudlow on street. Beef sold today at 3¢ per lb. in gold. Put lead pipes to the milk house and horse trough. Finished bee hive. Isaiah got some sugar. Sleep in barn every night. No news. Mr. Austone left his trunk here today.

Sunday, May 14, 1865

Blessed with good health. Spent the day at home. No preaching at any church in town. Rev. Lam's brother was buried this evening. Isaiah on guard today. I read Bible — and "Rise and Progress" by Doddridge. Oh for more grace to serve God better.

Monday, May 15, 1865

Rose early — went to work in garden — planted cabbage by the gate. Sister is improving in health. Isaiah drew candles &c. I went up town to hire a Servant. Rev. Hixe called — just from Richmond — took dinner and spent the night. Read Leslies Dictora with Pres. Lincoln funeral procession and killing of Booth.[29]

Tuesday, May 16, 1865

Rose late — breakfast. Mr. Hixe left for Mrs. Flenniken's. I went up town to see about a Servant — got meal from Kees Mill. Drew salt for Aunt Mollie Hamilton. Met Dr. Walter Brice of Troy, Tenn. Played bass violin.

Wednesday, May 17, 1865

Highly favored from day to day. In good health and [not] afflicted in special manner. Rose early and conducted worship. Flora and I started for Fishing Creek. Called at Mrs. Moffatt's. Reached Sister's at 12 — dined — took a sleep. Jno. and Flora and I went to strawberry patch. Found as much as we could eat. I went over to father's — killed a squirrel. Found all well. Conducted worship.

Thursday, May 18, 1865

Rose early — conducted worship — talked a while with Bro. Elihu. Took gun to kill crows — found none. Dick shod my mule — Father went up to Eaves Mill. I set out for Chester. Called at Mary's and Mrs. Moffatt's. Went by Jno. Agnew's for peas — he was absent. His son Wm gave me dinner. Shot rifle — put peas (4 bu) in buggy. I walked — rain caused me to leave peas at Tom Adams. Reached home at 5. A light rain.

Friday, May 19, 1865

Did nothing of importance today. Conducted worship. Worked in garden, planted beets and onions. Went to depot. Johnson McCain went up to Charlotte. Gave Jno Dickey some cartridges. Sent letter to Josiah M[offatt] for his Mother. A raid on Commissary about 9 P.M. — the guard captured the party wounding two and killing a negro.[30]

Saturday, May 20, 1865

Great excitement about the capture of raiders. Two white were severely wounded, a negro killed; one horse killed and two wounded. Went to depot to see the Yankees come to Chester but they stopped at Rock Hill to take the Raiders to Charlotte. Read newspaper, Schoffield order about the negro in N. C.[31]

Sunday, May 21, 1865

The holy day of rest returns — thanks to God for such a blessing. Sister Sarah in bed all day — medicine from Nancy Elam. I spent the day at home; but my heart and mind are too much on the world. Isaiah went to Presbyterian Church. He heard Rev. Witherspoon. I read the Bible. Oh for the spirit of wisdom to be poured out upon my darkened understanding! Sister better at night. A heavy wind and rain about 5 P.M.

Monday, May 22, 1865

Rose early — conducted worship. Fixed entrance of one beehive. Took Henry and went to Jno. Millen's for potato plants. Rode Nelly — did not see Bro. Wm. Saw his family. Got 400 sweet potato plants. Reached home at 2 p.m. I planted out plants. Went down to depot. Mr. Wolfe came down on a visit. We talked about the Yankee and negro. Called on the ladies at Mr. Melton's. Had some good music from Miss Mag Alexander. Examined hive nearest the door, found some young bees.

Tuesday, May 23, 1865

In good health — conducted worship morning and night. Opened box of tobacco for Mr. Wolfe. Worked on sewing machine. Mrs. Melton called to get the use of it for Mrs. Dr. Murry. Jno. Bigham and Col. McDill called for evidence from Isaiah and myself against John Flenniken on drinking and swearing. Gave them a bottle of wine for Comm. Took a nap. Fixed a honeybox for a bee hive — watered potatoes. Young Mills, Esqr. & Son Robert called to spend night and Messrs. Wolfe.

Wednesday, May 24, 1865

Life and health continued, I am greatly blessed — therefore I should love and serve God the more. Went to field to guard my mule. Took shot gun and old Enfield. Grier shot twice — found a partridge's nest — read beebook. Father and Sister Mary with Lewis came up in wagon — brought flour and shucks.

Thursday, May 25, 1865

Rose early. Slept in barn last night. Did not go to the field. Conducted worship night and morning. Father brought up lumber from the shop — he and Sister went home after dinner. I fixed sewing machine — fed bees in hive nearest door. Took out some things from concealment — worked on Mr. Reenan's magnetic machine; failed to work it. A fine rain after dark. Forrest captured Vicksburg.

Friday, May 26, 1865 [32]

Blessed with health. Conducted worship. Went to the garden to work — ground too wet to plow. God has sent a plentiful rain. Dr Boyce called and spent the day. He called on Mr. Hemphill and took tea; returned to spend the night. Happy to meet him.

Saturday, May 27, 1865

The month is drawing to a close. Thankful for life and health. The War is over, but very little signs of peace. Heard that Stephens & Cobb of Ga. had gone to Washington with Jeff Davis. Mrs. Dr. Murry spent the day with us stitching shirt bossoms on machine. Dr. Boyce went to Hopewell to assist Mr. Brice with a Communion. Assisted Mrs. Murry. Tried to make shot. Planted out pepper. A very cool day. No news from Yankees.

Sabbath, May 28, 1865

Another Sabbath day of rest. Went to Hopewell; Sister and I took the children in Mr. Melton's old carriage. Enjoyed a communion with the good people of Hopewell. Very late to Church. Mr. Boyce preached a good sermon from Mat.24:4, "Take heed that no man deceive you". Lunch with Mrs. McMaster. I assisted in Singing.

Monday, May 29, 1865

Rose early — conducted worship, night and morn. Worked in garden; planted beans. Fixed an old gun. Fixed sewing machine — made a new foot for it — made it do well. Called on Mrs. Murry. Gave Joe Nunnary some cartridges. Yankees came at last — one Co. of Kilpatrick's cavalry[33] — Negroes very much disappointed. Isaiah went to work at Jno. Smith's & returned. I bid Mr. Clark and Miss Sallie Clark goodbye.

Tuesday, May 30, 1865

Conducted worship night and morn. Went up to Bennetts, talked with Brandt — fixed foot for sewing machine. Rec'd letters from Mr. Scott and Rev. Martin about the flour. Showed letters to Mr. Harris. Assisted Mrs. Murry to sew. She dined with us. Planted beans. Took a ride with Miss Lillie Clark and Miss F. Legare. Rained on us. Yankees making the negroes clean the streets good!

Wednesday, May 31, 1865

Today is the last of May. The year is nearly half gone. Rose in good health — heavy rain early this morning. Set out pepper and potato plants. Sent Mrs. Legare some irish potatoes. Gathered peas for dinner. Mrs. Murry finished sewing. Sister tried the machine. No news. Called on Mr. Melton. Went up town to see Mr. Beasly.

Thursday, June 1, 1865

Crowned with another day's mercies. Conducted worship. Isaiah fixed Sister's buggy which McCormick broke. I went to Jas. Fenney's for potato plants — got a few. Returned by dinner. H. Smith dined. I worked on machine. Showed my bees to H.S. Heard that Jeff Davis had escaped — from the Yankees[34]. Worked garden — planted cabbage. Isaiah has had headache. Yankees are gathering up all arms &c.

Friday, June 2, 1865

Rose early. Isaiah is better with the headache. He finished the buggy. Sister called on Mrs. Melton. I went to Rev. R. W. Brice's for dinner — met T— Brice; then looked at garden and bees. Called at Billy Caldwell's — Saw Miss Maggie, Miss K not at home. To Robt Caldwell's — heard Miss Carrie play. Got bushel of black peas. Called Thos. McDill, saw Sam. Home....

Saturday, June 3, 1865

Another week gone. I have committed many sins, but pray for grace to go and sin no more. Isaiah went visiting in buggy on Fishing Creek, to singing at Union. I planted cucumbers and cantalopes. Tried to make shot but failed. Grier and I went to plantation — gathered some dew berries. Sent Miss Maggie Legare irish potatoes. I watched the patch.

Sabbath, June 4, 1865

Spent the day at home. Sister and the children went to Presbyterian Church — heard Rev. White — I [read] the Bible and religious reading — my heart is too much on worldly things. Oh for more grace to preserve me of all iniquity. I hope to spend the next Sabbath. Warm weather.

Monday, June 5, 1865

Slept in garden last night. Watched potatoes until 1 o'clock. No thief came. Took a nap before breakfast. Conducted worship. Worked garden. Cleaned up smoke house. Sister scoured the house — put up shelf in dining room. Played violin — fed chickens. No news from any quarter.

Tuesday, June 6, 1865

The days seem like moments. Rose early — began and ended the day with prayer. But my heart is cold — my devotions dead. Took a nap before dinner — worked in garden. Read Barnes Notes. Played violin — out of practice. Young Mills and Uncle Hugh Simpson called to spend night. Showed Mills my bees. Mrs. Howell and a daughter Jennison Cherrys called today.

Wednesday, June 7, 1865

Rose late, in good health. Thanks to a kind Providence. Worked garden. Middleton plowed shop patch, planted black peas there. Took some very nice honey. Brought little puppies to house. Mrs. Murry came to sew. I broke a fine needle. Yankees passed down today — I put away some things. A light [rain] this afternoon. Robert Banks called.

Thursday, June 8, 1865

A kind and merciful Providence is still watching over all my goings. Oh that I were more grateful and obedient to His will. Worked in garden. Commenced a beehive for Rev. Brice. Killed a rabbit, gave it to puppies. Went to shop. Saw card making for the first time in my life.

Friday, June 9, 1865

Rose in excellent health — began and ended the day with prayer. Bro. Isaiah came home this morning. John Millen came up — brought potato plants. Mrs. Murry came over to sew. Sister, the children and Henry went in buggy down to father's. Mr. Wolfe came down today. Read Chester Standard. Yankees and the Negroes had a ball and Supper last night!! Went out with Grier and Joe and killed 4 jay birds for puppies.

Saturday, June 10, 1865

Rose at sunup — conducted worship. Went up town. Saw Mr. Harris — gave me a Singing book — fixed the melodeon in Pr' Church. Saw Mr. Hemphill. Set out for Union — dinner at Joe Wylie's. Sung several tunes and made up a class for me to teach. Heavy rain — I got wet — went to creek — could not cross — went to Sister Mary's.

Sabbath, June 11, 1865

Went to Union Church; Mr. McD. preached. Creek very full. Father could not get to Church. Called at Aunt Linda's. I sung at church. Singing announced for Friday and Saturday week. I went to Brother William's to spend night. John Millen came up and talked awhile — all well.

Monday, June 12, 1865

Rose early. Set out for Chester. Called at Finney's for potato plants — got none; called at Mr. Atkinson's, got a good many. Saw a splendid garden. Came to Chester. Found Sister S. and children at home. Commenced cutting wheat. Dick came up to help. Planted out potatoes — worked on bee-hive.

Tuesday, June 13, 1865

Very warm weather — conducted worship night and morning. Finished Mr. Brice's bee hive. Went up to Lipford's for my shoes. Met Mrs. Hemphill and Bell. Heard President Davis died in prison[35]. Played violin, conducted worship.

Wednesday, June 14, 1865

Blessed with usual good health — I should be a very grateful and humble creature after worship. Set out for Rev. Brice's with his bee hive — he was not at home. Went on to Young Mills — talked — ate apples — drove his bees. Miss Lizzie gave me some nice flowers. Came to Mr. Brice's — drove his bees before he came home. Concluded to spend night with him.

Thursday, June 15, 1865

Rose late this morning. Mr. Brice conducted worship — looked at bees. Set out for home with a promise of two bushel of corn — home at 9 1/2 A.M. Played violin — took a sleep. Went to Dr. Wylie's — took some honey for Miss Anna. Gill assisted me. Appearance of rain. Stopped at Depot. W. W. Boyce arrived from Washington.

Friday, June 16, 1865

Brought to the close of another day in safety. God is dealing kindly with me. Conducted worship morning and night. Worked on bee hive — felt dull — took a sleep. Went to Mrs. Elliott's to fix her machine. Talked with Dr. Ready about the times — no news of interest.

Saturday, June 17, 1865

Fine rain today. Grier and I went gathering blackberries with Henry. Took bath in branch. Very warm before rain. Mrs. Murry came over to sew; fixed needle for her. Worked on key of Melodeon of Pres[byterian] Church. Hog eat some lard in closet. God has brought me safely through another week.

Sabbath, June 18, 1865

Spent day at home reading the Bible and other books — read 65 lectures of Dick. Very pleasant day. Sent horse and mule to graze in wheat pasture. Sister and Isaiah and children went to Presby' Church. Dr. Wylie called to tell me of a memorial to [be] sent to Washington.

Monday, June 19, 1865

Rose early and in good health — all the family are well. Worked on Sister Mary's bee hive. Went to Pres' Church — fixed melodeon. Called on Dr. Wylie; signed a memorial to Andrew Johnson. Called on Mrs. Melton to tell Mrs. Murry goodbye. Miss Maggie played for all. Mr. C. D. M. played the flute. Miss Ella Wright is on a visit to Mrs. Melton's.

Tuesday, June 20, 1865

Felt dull and sleepy all day. Finished bee hive. Had Nelly shod by Pervus. Had backs put on Mrs. Flennikins cards. Isaiah and Grier went blackberry hunting. Mrs. Martin is very low with Consumption. Took some birds to Mrs. Elam.

Wednesday, June 21, 1865

Rose early — mouth very sore — fixed sewing machine. Sister cut out my flannel suit. Rode down to Mr. Thos. McDill's - talked with Sam and the girls. Called at Mr. Brice's — his bees doing well — urges me to get a Singing School at Hopewell. Returned home by sunset. Put nitrate of Silver on my mouth.

Thursday, June 22, 1865

In usual health — tongue and mouth a little sore. Went up town — called on Mr. Hemphill — dined with him. Brandt fixed my gold watch. Mr. H. gave me $5 gold piece for Mrs. Moffatt — bought her 5 lbs. coffees 50 cts per lb. John Bigham and Rev. Brice dined with Sister. Jimy Bigham got home from prison to-day. Grier and I came down to Sister Mary's. Called at Mrs. M's — played violin.

Friday, June 23, 1865

Rose late — drove Sister's bees into a palace I made — took Flora and Emaline to Union — commenced Singing School. Called at Mrs. M's and fixed her clock — came over to father's to spend night.

Saturday, June 24, 1865

Conducted worship for father — looked at mother's garden. Went up to Bro. Elihu's for musical manual. Started to church, took Grier and Joe to Sister's. Called at Mr. McD's — had a very good class; offended some ladies who were talking in school. Rain in evening. Came to Uncle Jno. Smith's — had some good music. Thos. Wylie was here. Had the pleasure of meeting Hemphill, Leroy and Riley all at home.

Sabbath, June 25, 1865

Rose late, conducted worship for Uncle Jno. — walked into his garden. Set out for home — appearance of rain. Found all well at home. Went to Pres[byterian] Church. Mr. Douglas gave a good sermon on "All things shall work & ". Wore my new flannel suit for the first time.

Monday, June 26, 1865

June is nearly gone. Time waits for no man. Rose early. Conducted worship night and morning. Sister cut out my blue everyday suit — played piano — called on Mrs. Melton. Rev. Gaston is on his [way?] by wagon to Miss. Took a long nap; felt dull.

Tuesday, June 27, 1865

Still enjoying good health. Warm day. Went up to Brandt's - had Sister's watch fixed — got vermifuge for Joe. Miss Virgie and Miss Wright came over to learn to make pants. Yankees came to get a U.S. flag from us but were mistaken. We commenced a pair of spoon moulds. Called on Capt. Brown about Sister Mary's Harriet.

Wednesday, June 28, 1865

Rose late. Conducted worship night and morning. Went to depot to see Canon about Singing books. Fixed Mrs. Buckhannon's sewing machine. Charged one dollar in greenbacks — paid Daviga for "vermifuge", bought N.Y. Herald, 15 cts. Called at bank. H. Smith was here for dinner. I fixed electric machine. Electrified horses and negroes. Mr. Melton borrowed gun to watch garden.

Thursday, June 29, 1865

Very warm weather. Had a warm ride today from Chester — reached Sister M's at noon. Took a nap, dined, and gave Harriet a lecture about her impudence. Came over to father's; began a pair of spoon moulds. Went up to Elihu's and spent the night.

Friday, June 30, 1865

Conducted worship for Bro. Elihu. Came to Shop and worked on spoon moulds until 8 1/2. Went to Union — had a good Singing School. All behaved well. Returned to Father's; worked on spoon mould with some success. Conducted worship and retired.

Saturday, July 1, 1865

Another month begins its round — health good. Rose early, finished moulds. Went to church; had a large class with good order. Mr. McDonald made some remarks. I returned to Father's; saw some new spoons. Walked up to Aunt Mollie Hamilton's; felt sad to revisit the scenes of my childhood where so many are gone no more to return. Where are the friends of my youth?

Sabbath, July 2, 1865

Bid my good old aunt farewell; returned to father's and went on to Union. Heard Mr. McDonald preach two good sermons. Sung "Woodlands" for the first time at Union — a large turnout. Called at Joe Wylie's for dinner — started home at 6 P.M. Very warm. Reached home at 9. Went to the garden to watch potatoes.

Monday, July 3, 1865

Lay in garden all night but caught no thief. Felt very dull — took a sleep. Worked on sewing machine. Sister sewed some for Miss Virgie. Drove Miss Anna Wylie's bees — called on Mrs. Alexander to get her to put up a hat for me. Father came with wagon.

Tuesday, July 4, 1865

Fourth of July has returned but not as in years past. The Yankees [were] firing salutes all day [to] the U.S. which exists only in name. No [one] celebrated the day but the Negroes — great crowds came to town, some of them made speeches at a picknick. I went up to Maj. Jas. Lowry's to spend the day — had a fine dinner and a very pleasant visit. We made arrangements about going to Due West.

[As was his custom, John Hemphill Simpson made plans to attend Commencement Exercises in Due West — a place dear to his heart.]

316

Notes

[1] Union forces defeat the Confederate detachment at Five Forks, Virginia, which doomed the Confederate defense of Richmond and Petersburg.

[2] Richmond and Petersburg are evacuated, while the Union army captures the siege works around Petersburg.

[3] A Union cavalry force under the command of Major General George Stoneman was raiding Western North Carolina, threatening Salisbury and Charlotte. The refugees now fled south to avoid Stoneman.

[4] President Davis sets up a new Confederate capitol in Danville, Virginia, while Lee's army withdraws toward Lynchburg in an effort to escape capture from Grant's army.

[5] Lieutenant General John B. Hood was one of the highest ranking Confederate generals of the war. He was relieved of command of the Army of Tennessee following the disastrous battle of Nashville, and now without a command was trying to escape the approaching Union columns. He would eventually surrender in Natchez, Mississippi.

[6] On this day, General Lee surrendered his Army of Northern Virginia to General Grant at Appomattox Courthouse, Virginia, thus signalling an end to Confederate resistance.

[7] Union forces under the command of Brigadier General Edward E. Potter moved from Georgetown South Carolina to further destroy the railroads in Sumter and Camden.

[8] Surrender of Mobile, Alabama, the last Confederate port City to fall.

[9] Stoneman's cavalry captured the town on this day, destroying the large Confederate supply base there.

[10] The United States flag was raised over the ruins of Fort Sumter in Charleston Harbor, and on this day President Lincoln was assassinated in Washington, DC.

[11] Stoneman again threatened Charlotte, but turned west to capture Asheville, North Carolina.

[12] General Joe Johnston surrendered the last major army east of the Mississippi River at Durham Station, North Carolina.

[13] Hemphill was wounded on March 31 during an action at Hatchers Run, just prior to the battle at Five Forks.

[14] Stoneman's cavalry rearguard crossed into South Carolina and destroyed the bridge over the Catawba. There was no real intent to proceed further. "...the magnificent railway bridge, eleven hundred feet long, of the S. C. Railway....", p. 400, *Mathew Brady's Illustrated History of the Civil War* by Benson J. Lossing.

[15] Brigadier General James Chesnut served on the staff of Jefferson Davis, who reached Charlotte on April 19. Chesnut arranged for his family to stay in Chester to escape the union advances.

[16] General Braxton Bragg, served as an army commander and chief of Staff to Jefferson Davis, and under Joe Johnston in North Carolina. He was now on his way to rejoin Davis as a military advisor.

[17] Bragg was one of the most controversial generals in the Confederacy, and one of the most disliked by his contemporaries.

[18] Instead of going to prison camp, the soldiers of Lee's army were released from Appomattox on parole, as Grant recognized the end of the war was near.

[19] Joe Johnston again surrenders his army at Durham Station, North Carolina, after the initial terms of surrender are rejected. The new terms were fashioned after those of Appomattox.

[20] Orr's Rifles surrendered at Appomattox with Lee's army.

[21] President Davis left Charlotte for South Carolina on April 26.

[22] Colonel William Preston Johnston, aide to Jefferson Davis.

[23] Bragg would join Davis on the road to Abbeville, South Carolina, where the Confederate government would hold it's last cabinet meeting.

[24] With the withdrawal of Confederate forces, the supplies left behind on trains and at the railroad depot were opened to the citizens of Chester.

[25] Lieutenant General Richard Taylor surrendered his forces in Mississippi and Alabama, based on the Appomattox agreements.

[26] Any soldiers not included in the major surrenders still had to be accounted for by the United States Army. Soldiers on leave and detached duty still could bear arms until properly paroled.

[27] In the absence of government authority, small groups of men took the opportunity to raid and pillage across the South, and were loosely termed "raiders".

[28] Jefferson Davis is captured in Irwinville, Georgia, and President Andrew Johnson declares an end to armed resistance to the United States.

[29] John Wilkes Booth, who assassinated President Lincoln was himself captured and killed on April 26 at the Garrett Farm, Virginia.

[30] The local band of "raiders" were eliminated in this raid on the local area food bank.

[31] General John M. Schofield commanded the Department of North Carolina.

[32] Surrender of the Confederate forces in the Trans-Mississippi, ending the last large organized Confederate force in the field.

[33] The arrival of Union cavalry filled the gap between the last Confederate government and movement of Chester back into the Union.

[34] This rumor was not true. Davis remained a prisoner of the Federal government.

[35] Another rumor not true, Davis was still alive in captivity.

John H. Simpson family, o/a 1910. L to R - 1st Row: Eunice Torbit, Rev. John H. Simpson, Sarah Baird. 2nd Row: Elizabeth Moffatt, David Moffatt, Mary Lois. Mary E. Moffatt Simpson and oldest daughter Nancy Law (Nannie Lawlie) not pictured.

Epilogue

With the demise of the Confederacy, John Hemphill Simpson tried to resume some semblance of his prewar life. In doing so, he relied on the pillar of his Christian Faith as well as his love of knowledge and music. Commenced Hebrew and violin music at the same time, Simpson later wrote, "have kept up the study of them since, but I do not expect to make a finish of either till I get to heaven." After the war the town of Chester again became his home, with family and friends around him. On May 8th 1866, Simpson married Miss Elizabeth Moffatt of Chester County. This union provided much happiness for both husband and wife. In the first years after the war, Simpson resumed his life in the pulpit and supplied vacancies in the various churches in and around Chester.

Life again changed for the Simpson's on June 2, 1867, when John received the call to the ministry at New Lebanon, West Virginia church and was ordained only months later on October 24, 1867. The Simpson's turned to their work in the mountains of West Virginia with great vigor and John was installed as pastor on August 28, 1869. The quiet of the mountains and the spiritual needs of the mountain people seemed to grow on the family and John and Lizze (Mary Elizabeth) remained in the New Lebanon church area for the next twenty-three years.

On October 3, 1891, due to Lizzie's poor health, the Simpson family left the church in West Virginia for Huntersville, North Carolina, where John performed mission work for the First Presbytery. John later served as principal of Hickory Grove Academy, South Carolina. Some years later, an orphanage opened in Hickory Grove, North Carolina and John and Lizzie agreed to return and run the institution. After Lizzie died, John accompanied 15 children from the orphanage with daughter Eunice to West Tennessee and served two years there.

John Hemphill Simpson died July 12, 1914 and was buried in Old Purity Cemetery, Chester County, South Carolina. He had for twenty years out-lived his wife, Mary Elizabeth Moffatt Simpson who died August 27, 1894. Mary Elizabeth is also buried at Old Purity Cemetery.

Today John Simpson lives on through the reading of his diaries, including both the common every day entries and those describing the horror of the battlefield. Through his own words, written over 100 years ago, John H. Simpson is revealed today as he lived then as "remarkably cool, calm and patient, his habits were plain, his information minute. He was never guilty of copying any man, ...(his writings) all sparkled with originality, ...a chaste Christian speech, a devotion and love for his church, a pure life and a personal piety."

ONE MORE WORD ABOUT GRANDFATHER

Maybe he was a bit eccentric...
Maybe he was hepped on religion—
A zealot, or hepped on "singing only the Psalms"
But he must have had a "heart of gold" to take so many bodies
"Stiff and cold" back to home and family

M.L.M

Nannie Lawlie Simpson, oldest daughter of J. H. Simpson and Mary Elizabeth Moffatt Simpson. Nannie married J. Marion Knox.

321

Family Data

John Hemphill Simpson
Birthdate: August 3, 1834
Birthplace: Fishing Creek Community, Chester County, S.C.

Married to: Mary Elizabeth Moffatt on May 8, 1866 at Hazelwood,
             the bride's home, near Blackstock, S.C. – b. 12-19-1839;
             d. 8-27-1894; buried: Old Purity Cemetery

             Wife's parents:
             Father: David Moffatt – b. 6-19-1814; d. 6-16-1886
             Mother: Nancy Law Torbit – b. 12-3-1821; d. 2-19-1903;
             buried: Old Purity Cemetery

Death: July 12, 1914; Buried: Old Purity, Chester County, S.C.
Father: John Simpson, Jr. – b. 2-9-1803; d. 7-12-1884
Mother: Sarah Wylie Simpson – b. 1803; d. 5-15-1866; Buried at
            Union A.R.P. Church in Chester County, S.C.

Sisters and Brothers

   Thomas Elihu (CSA) – b. 3-2-1824; m. 3-2-1853; d. 9-21-1874(m.
      Margaret Jane Bigham; b. 1-12-1831; d. 6-28-1913; seven
      children[1]):
            (1) John Brown Simpson – b. 1-30-1854; d. 1-13-1934;
            m. Martha Ann Eugenia Bigham b. 1-25-1860[2]; d. 8-30-1927
            (2) Francis McDonald Simpson – b. 5-31-1855; d. 11-2-1937;
            m. Harriette Isabella Wylie b. 10-22-1855; d. 04-5-1915;
            Children: Albert McDonald Simpson; Grandchildren:
            Frances Wylie Simpson d. ?; Great grandchildren:
            George Harry Stewart, Jr. 12-28-1922
            (3) Lois Isabella Simpson – b. 11-9-1856; d. 8-21-1902;
            m. Theodore Stewart Furguson; three Children
            (4) Robert Brice Simpson – b. 3-9-1858; d. 6-4-1859
            (5) James Hemphill Simpson – b. 5-20-1859; d. 3-12-1860
            (6) Henry Calvin Simpson – b. 10-1-1860; d. 5-22-1927
            (7) Sarah Agnes Simpson – b. 6-1-1862; d. 10-23-1942

Martha Simpson – b. 3-20-1826; d. 5-15-1827

Mary Jane Simpson – b. 6-6-1827; d. 11-1-1901
(m. William A. Burns; b. 2-12-1822; d. 4-12-1860)

Margaret – b. 9-14-1829; d. 10-1-1862
(m. John Calvin Moffatt; (four children)

William Blackstock (CSA) – b. 7-9-1831; d. 1-5-1901
(m. Margarette Millen; b. 7-7-1837; d. 10-13-1901; (eight children)

* John Hemphill's place in the family – b. 8-3-1834

Sarah – b. 12-25-1836; d. 4-15-1913
(m. J. W. Baird (CSA); d. 10-5-1862; two children: (1) Grier; (2) Joe b. 3-16-1862; d. 1870

Isaiah (CSA) – b. 10-14-1838; d. 12-14-1911
(m. Sallie Patton of York, S.C.; d. 6-6-1867; (seven children)

Henry Calvin – b. 1841; d. 11-15-1846

Children
Nancy Law – b. 3-24-1867; d. 5-22-1893
(m. James Marion Knox on 10-15-1890)

Sarah Baird – b. 9-4-1869; d. 4-25-1964
(m. Robert Preston Hawkins on 9-7-1893; (five children: Preston, Susie, Mary, John, James)

Mary Lois – b. 10-17-1871; d. 11-8-1949
(m. Rev. John Robert Millen on 12-26-1901; (four children: Elizabeth Moffatt, John S., Mary Isabella, Lawlie)

Elizabeth (Lizzie) Moffatt – b. 12-9-1873; d. 12-12-1964
(m. Dr. Harvey E. McConnell on 12-26-1901; (five children: Harvey Russell (step), John Wallace, Elizabeth Moffatt, David Moffatt, Harvey Edward)

Eunice Torbit – b. 5-6-1876, d. 4-26-1953
  (m. Rev. Charles Davis McCormick on 12-31-1913; (three children: Anna Moffatt b. 7-25-1915, Sarah Elizabeth b. 1-18-1918, d. 11-28-2000, Mary Law b. 4-10-1922)

David Moffatt – b. 5-16-1879, d. 10-1951
  (m. Norma (Nancy) Courts in 1917; (two children: Nancy Rose, John)

Research on descendents of John Hemphill Simpson other than John Hemphill and Thomas Elihu has not been accomplished by M. L. McCormick in this volume.
[1] per August 11, 1992 letter from Jean Todd, Gastonia, N.C.
[2] Information copied from material received from George Stewart (b. 12-28-1922), a descendant of Francis McDonald Simpson. His address is 1799 John Gray Road, Cincinnati, OH 45240).

Index of 1861 Diary

Index of 1862 Diary

Index of 1863 Diary

338

Index of 1865 Diary

Jan - July 4